Fifty Lectures
American Mathematics Competitions

Problems Book 1

Guiling Chen

Yongcheng Chen

http://www.mymathcounts.com/index.php

ACKNOWLEDGEMENTS

We would like to thank many students and parents who participated in the 50 AMC Lectures 2012 Summer Program. Without their support and trust, this program would not be possible. These parents and students reviewed the draft of the lectures, made corrections to some errors, and provided excellent insights to some solutions.

We would like to thank the following math contests for their problems used in this book:

The AMC 10/12. An examination in secondary school mathematics containing problems which can be understood and solved with precalculus concepts.

The AIME (American Invitational Mathematics Examination). An intermediate examination between the AMC 10 or AMC 12 and the USAMO. It is a 15 question, 3 hour examination in which each answer is an integer number from 0 to 999. As with the AMC 10 and AMC 12, all problems can be solved by pre-calculus methods.

The ARML (American Regions Mathematics League). An annual high school mathematics competition held simultaneously at five locations in the United States.

The China Middle School Math Competition.
The China High School Math Competition.

Copyright © 2013 by Guiling Chen, and Yongcheng Chen

All rights reserved. Printed in the United States of America

Reproduction of any portion of this book without the written permission of the authors is strictly prohibited, except as may be expressly permitted by the U.S. Copyright Act.

ISBN-13: 978-1477600160
ISBN-10: 1477600167

Table of Contents

Chapter 1 Algebra Manipulations	1
Chapter 2 Radicals	7
Chapter 3 Solving Radical Equations	26
Chapter 4 Absolute Values	36
Chapter 5 Solving Absolute Value Equations	48
Chapter 6 Vieta Theorem and Applications	53
Chapter 7 Square Numbers	62
Chapter 8 Divisibility	70
Chapter 9 Geometry Congruent Triangles	83
Chapter 10 Geometry Area and Area Method	95
Chapter 11 Geometry Eight Methods To Draw Auxiliary Lines	109
Chapter 12 Trigonometry Six Functions	122
Chapter 13 Cubic Identities	133
Chapter 14 Arithmetic Sequence	139
Chapter 15 How to Use the Discriminant	155
Chapter 16 Completing the Square	162
Chapter 17 Analytic Geometry Distance and Lines	170
Chapter 18 Functional Equations	177
Chapter 19 Squeezing Method	185
Chapter 20 Nonnegative Numbers	191
Chapter 21 Geometry Similar Triangles	198

Chapter 22 Geometry Angle Bisector And Median   210

Chapter 23 Geometry Eight More Methods To Draw Auxiliary Lines   223

Chapter 24 Trigonometry Identities   231

Chapter 25 AM-GM Inequality   238

Index   249

50 AMC Lectures Problems Book 1   (1) Algebraic Manipulation

PROBLEMS

Problem 1: Find $m^2 + \dfrac{1}{m^2}$ if $m - \dfrac{1}{m} = 1$.

Problem 2: Find $m^4 + \dfrac{1}{m^4}$ if $m - \dfrac{1}{m} = 1$.

Problem 3: (1966 AMC) If the sum of two numbers is 1 and their product is 1, find the sum of their cubes.

Problem 4: (1953 AMC) If $y = x + \dfrac{1}{x}$, then $x^4 + x^3 - 4x^2 + x + 1 = 0$ becomes:

(A) $x^2(y^2 + y - 2) = 0$ (B) $x^2(y^2 + y - 3) = 0$ (C) $x^2(y^2 + y - 4) = 0$
(D) $x^2(y^2 + y - 6) = 0$ (E) none of these.

Problem 5: If $x + \dfrac{1}{x} = 3$, find the value of $\dfrac{x^2}{x^4 + x^2 + 1}$.

Problem 6: Find $\dfrac{2x^2 + 3xy - 2y^2}{x^2 - 2xy - y^2}$ if $\dfrac{x}{y} - \dfrac{y}{x} = 3$.

Problem 7: Find $\dfrac{2x^2 + 3y^2 + 6z^2}{x^2 + 5y^2 + 7z^2}$ if $4x - 3y - 6z = 0$ and $2x + 4y - 14z = 0$.

Problem 8. (1978 AMC) If $1 - \dfrac{4}{x} + \dfrac{4}{x^2} = 0$, then $\dfrac{2}{x}$ equals
(A) -1 (B) 1   (C) 2   (D) -1 or 2   (E) -1 or -2

Problem 9. (1958 AMC) If $xy = b$ and $\dfrac{1}{x^2} + \dfrac{1}{y^2} = a$, then $(x + y)^2$ equals:

1

(A) $(a+2b)^2$ (B) a^2+b^2 (C) $b(ab+2)$ (D) $ab(b+2)$ (E) $\frac{1}{a}+2b$

Problem 10: Find all real numbers x for which $\frac{8^x+27^x}{12^x+18^x}=\frac{7}{6}$.

Problem 11: (1979 AMC 29) For each positive number x, let

$$f(x)=\frac{\left(x+\frac{1}{x}\right)^6-\left(x^6+\frac{1}{x^6}\right)-2}{\left(x+\frac{1}{x}\right)^3+\left(x^3+\frac{1}{x^3}\right)}.$$

The minimum value of $f(x)$ is
(A) 1 (B) 2 (C) 3 (D) 4 (E) 6

Problem 12. (1960 AMC) The fraction $\frac{a^2+b^2-c^2+2ab}{a^2+c^2-b^2+2ac}$ is (with suitable restrictions on the values of a, b, and c):

(A) irreducible (B) reducible to -1 (C) reducible to a polynomial of three terms
(D) reducible to $\frac{a-b+c}{a+b-c}$ (E) reducible to $\frac{a+b-c}{a-b+c}$

Problem 13. Find x^6+y^6 if $x=\sqrt{3+\sqrt{3}}$ and $y=\sqrt{3-\sqrt{3}}$.

Problem 14. (1975 AMC #29) What is the smallest integer larger than $(\sqrt{3}+\sqrt{2})^6$?

(A) 972 (B) 971 (C) 970 (D) 969 (E) 968.

Problem 15. (2010 NC Math Contest) Let x, y, and z be positive real numbers such that $x+y+z=1$ and $xy+yz+xz=1/3$. The number of possible values of the expression $\frac{x}{y}+\frac{y}{z}+\frac{z}{x}$ is

a) 1   b) 2   c) 3   d) more than 3 but infinitely many   e) infinitely many

SOLUTIONS TO PROBLEMS

Problem 1: Solution: 3.

$$m^2 + \frac{1}{m^2} = \left(m - \frac{1}{m}\right)^2 + 2 = 1 + 2 = 3.$$

Problem 2: Solution: 7.

$$m^4 + \frac{1}{m^4} = \left(m^2 + \frac{1}{m^2}\right)^2 - 2 = \left[\left(m - \frac{1}{m}\right)^2 + 2\right]^2 - 2 = 9 - 2 = 7$$

Problem 3: Solution: -2.

Let the numbers be x and y. Then since
$$x + y = xy = 1,$$
$$1 = (x+y)^3 = x^3 + y^3 + 3xy(x+y) = x^3 + y^3 + 3(1)(1) = x^3 + y^3 + 3.$$
$$\therefore x^3 + y^3 = -2.$$

Problem 4: Solution: D.

$$x^4 + x^3 - 4x^2 + x + 1 = x^2\left[\left(x^2 + \frac{1}{x^2}\right) + \left(x + \frac{1}{x}\right) - 4\right] = 0.$$

Since $x^2 + \frac{1}{x^2} = \left(x + \frac{1}{2}\right)^2 - 2$, we have

$$x^2(y^2 - 2 + y - 4) = x^2(y^2 + y - 6) = 0.$$

Problem 5: Solution: $\frac{1}{8}$.

$$x^2 + \frac{1}{x^2} = (x + \frac{1}{x})^2 - 2 = 3^2 - 2 = 7.$$

$$\frac{x^2}{x^4 + x^2 + 1} = \frac{1}{x^2 + 1 + \frac{1}{x^2}} = \frac{1}{8}.$$

Problem 6: Solution: 9.

$$\frac{2x^2+3xy-2y^2}{x^2-2xy-y^2} = \frac{\frac{2x}{y}+3-\frac{2y}{x}}{\frac{x}{y}-2-\frac{y}{x}} = \frac{2\times 3+3}{3-2} = 9.$$

Problem 7: Solution: 1.

Solving the system of equations:

$$\begin{cases} 4x-3y-6z=0 & (1) \\ 2x+4y-14z=0 & (2) \end{cases}$$

We get $\begin{cases} x=3z \\ y=2z \end{cases}$.

Hence $\dfrac{2x^2+3y^2+6z^2}{x^2+5y^2+7z^2} = \dfrac{18z^2+12z^2+6z^2}{9z^2+20z^2+7z^2} = 1$.

Problem 8. Solution: 1.

(B) $1 - \dfrac{4}{x} + \dfrac{4}{x^2} = \left(1-\dfrac{2}{x}\right)^2 = 0$; $\dfrac{2}{x}=1$.

Problem 9. Solution: C.

$\dfrac{1}{x^2}+\dfrac{1}{y^2} = \dfrac{y^2+x^2}{x^2y^2} = a$; $\therefore a = \dfrac{x^2+y^2}{b^2}$ or $x^2+y^2 = ab^2$;

$(x+y)^2 = x^2+2xy+y^2 = ab^2+2b = b(ab+2)$.

Problem 10: Solution: 1 and −1.

By setting $2^x = a$ and $3^x = b$, the equation becomes

$\dfrac{a^3+b^3}{a^2b+b^2a} = \dfrac{7}{6} \Rightarrow \dfrac{a^2-ab+b^2}{ab} = \dfrac{7}{6} \Rightarrow 6a^2-13ab+6b^2=0 \Rightarrow (2a-3b)(3a-2b)=0$

We have $2a-3b=0$ or $3a-2b=0$.
Therefore $2^{x+1} = 3^{x+1}$ or $2^{x-1} = 3^{x-1}$, which implies that $x=-1$ and $x=1$. It is easy to check that both $x=-1$ and $x=1$ satisfy the given equation.

Problem 11: Solution: 6.

(E) By observing that $\left[x^3 + \dfrac{1}{x^3}\right]^2 = x^6 + 2 + \dfrac{1}{x^6}$, one sees that

$$f(x) = \dfrac{\left[\left(x+\dfrac{1}{x}\right)^3\right]^2 - \left[x^3 + \dfrac{1}{x^3}\right]^2}{\left(x+\dfrac{1}{x}\right)^3 + \left(x^3 + \dfrac{1}{x^3}\right)}$$

$$= \left(x+\dfrac{1}{x}\right)^3 - \left(x^3 + \dfrac{1}{x^3}\right) = x^3 + 3x^2 \times \dfrac{1}{x} + 3x \times \dfrac{1}{x^2} + \dfrac{1}{x^3} - x^3 - \dfrac{1}{x^3} = 3\left(x+\dfrac{1}{x}\right).$$

Since $x + \dfrac{1}{x} \geq 2$, $f(x) = 3\left(x+\dfrac{1}{x}\right) \geq 3 \times 2 = 6$.

The minimum value of $f(x)$ is 6 and it can be obtained at $x = 1$.

Problem 12. Solution: E.

$$\dfrac{a^2 + b^2 - c^2 + 2ab}{a^2 + c^2 - b^2 + 2ac} = \dfrac{(a+b)^2 - c^2}{(a+c)^2 - b^2} = \dfrac{(a+b+c)(a+b-c)}{(a+c+b)(a+c-b)} = \dfrac{a+b-c}{a+c-b} \text{ with } (a+c)^2 \neq b^2.$$

Problem 13. Solution: 108.

Since $x = \sqrt{3+\sqrt{3}}$ and $y = \sqrt{3-\sqrt{3}}$, $x^2 \cdot y^2 = (3+\sqrt{3})(3-\sqrt{3}) = 9 - 3 = 6$.
$x^2 + y^2 = (3+\sqrt{3}) + (3-\sqrt{3}) = 6$
$x^6 + y^6 = (x^2 + y^2)^3 - 3(x^2 + y^2) \cdot x^2 \cdot y^2 = 6^3 - 3 \times 6 \times 6 = 36(6-3) = 108$

Problem 14. Solution: 970.

Let $x = \sqrt{3} + \sqrt{2}$ and $y = \sqrt{3} - \sqrt{2}$.

$x + y = (\sqrt{3} + \sqrt{2}) + (\sqrt{3} - \sqrt{2}) = 2\sqrt{3}$.
$xy = (\sqrt{3} + \sqrt{2})(\sqrt{3} - \sqrt{2}) = 3 - 2 = 1$.
$x^2 + y^2 = (x+y)^2 - 2xy = 12 - 2 = 10$
$x^6 + y^6 = (x^2 + y^2)^3 - 3(x^2 + y^2) \cdot x^2 \cdot y^2 = 1000 - 3 \times 10 = 970$.
$x^6 = 970 - y^6 \quad \Rightarrow \quad \left(\sqrt{3} + \sqrt{2}\right)^6 = 970 - \left(\sqrt{3} - \sqrt{2}\right)^6$.

We know that $0 < \sqrt{3} - \sqrt{2} < 1$. So $0 < (\sqrt{3} - \sqrt{2})^6 < 1$.
$(\sqrt{3} + \sqrt{2})^6 < 970$
The smallest positive integer greater than $(\sqrt{3} + \sqrt{2})^6$ is 970.

Problem 15. Solution: (a).

Since $1 = (x + y + z)^2 = x^2 + y^2 + z^2 + 2(xy + yz + xz) = x^2 + y^2 + z^2 + 2/3$, we get $x^2 + y^2 + z^2 = 1/3$. Then $x^2 + y^2 + z^2 - xy - yz - xz = 0$.

We know that $x^2 + y^2 + z^2 - xy - yz - zx = \frac{1}{2}[(x-y)^2 + (y-z)^2 + (z-x)^2]$.

Therefore $\frac{1}{2}[(x-y)^2 + (y-z)^2 + (z-x)^2] = 0$.

Since x, y, and z be positive real numbers, we have $x = y = z$, which implies that $\frac{x}{y} + \frac{y}{z} + \frac{z}{x} = 3$.

3 is the only value for $\frac{x}{y} + \frac{y}{z} + \frac{z}{x}$. So the answer is (a).

PROBLEMS

Problem 1: (1989 AMC) $\sqrt{\dfrac{1}{9} + \dfrac{1}{16}} =$

(A) $\dfrac{1}{5}$ (B) $\dfrac{1}{4}$ (C) $\dfrac{2}{7}$ (D) $\dfrac{5}{12}$ (E) $\dfrac{7}{12}$

Problem 2: (1956 AMC) Simplify $[\sqrt[3]{\sqrt[6]{a^9}}]^4 [\sqrt[6]{\sqrt[3]{a^9}}]^4$; the result is:
(A) a^{16} (B) a^{12} (C) a^8 (D) a^4 (E) a^2

Problem 3: (1952 AMC) With a rational denominator, the expression $\dfrac{\sqrt{2}}{\sqrt{2}+\sqrt{3}-\sqrt{5}}$ is equivalent to:

(A) $\dfrac{3+\sqrt{6}+\sqrt{15}}{6}$ (B) $\dfrac{\sqrt{6}-2+\sqrt{10}}{6}$ (C) $\dfrac{2+\sqrt{6}+\sqrt{10}}{10}$

(B) $\dfrac{2+\sqrt{6}-\sqrt{10}}{10}$ (E) none of these

Problem 4: Simplifying $\sqrt{11+2(1+\sqrt{5})(1+\sqrt{7})}$.

Problem 5: Comparing $\sqrt{2}$, $\sqrt[3]{3}$, and $\sqrt[5]{5}$.

Problem 6: Comparing $\sqrt{19}$ and $6-\sqrt{3}$.

Problem 7: Comparing $\sqrt[3]{\dfrac{9-5\sqrt{3}}{9+5\sqrt{3}}}$ and $\dfrac{\sqrt{3}-1}{\sqrt{3}+1}$.

Problem 8: Comparing $\dfrac{3}{2}\sqrt{48}$ and $\dfrac{5}{7}\sqrt{147}$.

Problem 9: Show that $\sqrt{a}+\sqrt{b} > \sqrt{a+b}$ is true for all positive numbers a and b.

Problem 10: Find the value of $6x + (\dfrac{x}{x-2} - \dfrac{x}{x+2}) \div \dfrac{4x}{x^4 - 2x^3 + 8x - 16}$ if $x = -\dfrac{1}{2+\sqrt{3}}$.

Problem 11: Find the value of $\dfrac{80}{x^2 - y^2}$ if $x = \dfrac{1}{\sqrt{5}-2}$ and $y = \dfrac{1}{\sqrt{5}+2}$.

Problem 12: (1995 AMC) If $\sqrt{2+\sqrt{x}} = 3$, then $x = $
(A) 1   (B) $\sqrt{7}$ (C) 7   (D) 49   (E) 121

Problem 13: Simplifying $\sqrt{3+\sqrt{5}} + \sqrt{3-\sqrt{5}}$.

Problem 14: Simplifying $\sqrt{x+2\sqrt{x-1}} + \sqrt{x-2\sqrt{x-1}}$, $(x \geq 1)$.

Problem 15: Find the rational numbers x and y if $\sqrt{x-\sqrt{50}} = y - \sqrt{2}$.

Problem 16: Find the positive integers of P, M, and N if $\sqrt{P-2\sqrt{10}} = \sqrt{M} - \sqrt{N}$.

Problem 17: Simplifying $\sqrt{4-\sqrt{10+2\sqrt{5}}} + \sqrt{4+\sqrt{10+2\sqrt{5}}}$.

Problem 18: Find the value of $\sqrt{4x^2+12x+9} + \sqrt{4x^2-20x+25}$ if $4x^2 - 4x - 15 \leq 0$.

Problem 19: (2006 AMC 12 A) For how many real values of x is $\sqrt{120-\sqrt{x}}$ an integer?
(A) 3   (B) 6   (C) 9   (D) 10   (E) 11

Problem 20: Show that $\dfrac{\sqrt{a}+\sqrt{b}}{\sqrt{a+b}} = \dfrac{\sqrt{c}+\sqrt{d}}{\sqrt{c+d}}$ if $\dfrac{a}{c} = \dfrac{b}{d}$.

Problem 21: (1974 AMC) Let $T = \dfrac{1}{3-\sqrt{8}} - \dfrac{1}{\sqrt{8}-\sqrt{7}} + \dfrac{1}{\sqrt{7}-\sqrt{6}} - \dfrac{1}{\sqrt{6}-\sqrt{5}} + \dfrac{1}{\sqrt{5}-2}$; Then
(A) $T < 1$ (B) $T = 1$ (C) $1 < T < 2$ (D) $T > 2$

Problem 22: Compute $\dfrac{1}{1+\sqrt{2}}+\dfrac{1}{\sqrt{2}+\sqrt{3}}+\cdots+\dfrac{1}{\sqrt{8}+\sqrt{9}}$.

Problem 23: Prove that $\dfrac{1}{\sqrt{2}+1}+\dfrac{1}{\sqrt{3}+\sqrt{2}}+\cdots+\dfrac{1}{\sqrt{n+1}+\sqrt{n}}=\dfrac{n}{\sqrt{n+1}+1}$.

Problem 24: Simplifying $\dfrac{1}{1+\sqrt{3}}-\dfrac{1}{\sqrt{3}+\sqrt{5}}+\cdots+\dfrac{1}{\sqrt{1997}+\sqrt{1999}}$.

Problem 25: Find $\dfrac{1}{\sqrt{a}+\sqrt{a+1}}+\dfrac{1}{\sqrt{a+1}+\sqrt{a+2}}+\dfrac{1}{\sqrt{a+2}+\sqrt{a+3}}+\cdots+\dfrac{1}{\sqrt{a+1999}+\sqrt{a+2000}}$ if a is a positive solution to $x^2-19x-150=0$.

Problem 26: Simplifying $\sqrt{6-\sqrt{17-12\sqrt{2}}}$.

Problem 27: Simplifying $\sqrt{4+\sqrt{15}}$.

Problem 28: (1954 AMC) When simplified $\sqrt{1+\left(\dfrac{x^4-1}{2x^2}\right)^2}$ equals:

(A) $\dfrac{x^4+2x^2-1}{2x^2}$ (B) $\dfrac{x^4-1}{2x^2}$ (C) $\dfrac{\sqrt{x^2+1}}{2}$ (D) $\dfrac{x^2}{\sqrt{2}}$ (E) $\dfrac{x^2}{2}+\dfrac{1}{2x^2}$.

Problem 29: (1954 AMC) The roots of the equation $2\sqrt{x}+2x^{-\frac{1}{2}}=5$ can be found by solving:
(A) $16x^2-92x+1=0$ (B) $4x^2-25x+4=0$ (C) $4x^2-17x+4=0$
(D) $2x^2-21x+2=0$ (E) $4x^2-25x-4=0$.

Problem 30: (1956 AMC) The expression $1-\dfrac{1}{1+\sqrt{3}}+\dfrac{1}{1-\sqrt{3}}$ equals:
(A) $1-\sqrt{3}$ (B) 1 (C) $-\sqrt{3}$ (D) $\sqrt{3}$ (E) $1+\sqrt{3}$

Problem 31: (1958 AMC) The expression $2 + \sqrt{2} + \dfrac{1}{2+\sqrt{2}} + \dfrac{1}{2-\sqrt{2}}$ equals:

(A) 2 (B) $2 - \sqrt{2}$ (C) $2 + \sqrt{2}$ (D) $2\sqrt{2}$ (E) $\dfrac{\sqrt{2}}{2}$

Problem 32: Simplifying $\sqrt{9 - 4\sqrt{5}}$.

Problem 33: Simplifying $\sqrt{\sqrt{48} - \sqrt{45}}$.

Problem 34: Compute: $\dfrac{\sqrt{2} + \sqrt{3}}{\sqrt{10} + \sqrt{14} + \sqrt{15} + \sqrt{21}}$.

Problem 35: Find $\dfrac{1}{a+1} + \dfrac{1}{b+1}$ if $a = \dfrac{1}{2+\sqrt{3}}$ and $b = \dfrac{1}{2-\sqrt{3}}$.

Problem 36: Find value for $2x^2 - 3xy + 2y^2$ if $x = \dfrac{2+\sqrt{3}}{2-\sqrt{3}}$ and $y = \dfrac{2-\sqrt{3}}{2+\sqrt{3}}$.

Problem 37: Find $x^6 + y^6$ if $x = \sqrt{5 + \sqrt{5}}$ and $y = \sqrt{5 - \sqrt{5}}$.

Problem 38: Find $\dfrac{1}{2}x^3 - x^2 - x + 3$ if $x = \dfrac{2}{\sqrt{3}-1}$.

Problem 39: Find $x^3 + 12$ if $x = \sqrt[3]{4(\sqrt{5}+1)} - \sqrt[3]{4(\sqrt{5}-1)}$.

Problem 40: Find $x^6 + 2\sqrt{2}x^5 - x^4 + x^3 - 2\sqrt{3}x^2 + 2x + \sqrt{2}$ if $x = \sqrt{3} - \sqrt{2}$.

Problem 41: Simplifying $\sqrt{11 - \sqrt{120}}$

Problem 42: Simplifying $\sqrt{11 + 6\sqrt{3}}$.

Problem 43: Simplifying $\sqrt{2 + \sqrt{3}}$.

Problem 44: Simplifying $\sqrt{14 + 5\sqrt{3}}$.

Problem 45: (1954 AMC) The square of $5 - \sqrt{y^2 - 25}$ is:
(A) $y^2 - 5\sqrt{y^2 - 25}$ (B) $-y^2$ (C) y^2 (D) $(5-y)^2$
(E) $y^2 - 10\sqrt{y^2 - 25}$

Problem 46: (1955 AMC) The expression $\sqrt{25 - t^2} + 5$ equals zero for:
(A) no real or imaginary values of t
(B) no real values of t, but for some imaginary values
(C) no imaginary values of t, but for some real values
(D) $t = 0$ (E) $t = \pm 5$

Problem 47: (1955 AMC) If a, b, and c are positive integers, the radicals $\sqrt{a + \dfrac{b}{c}}$ and $a\sqrt{\dfrac{b}{c}}$ are equal when and only when:

(A) $a = b = c = 1$ (B) $a = b$ and $c = a = 1$ (C) $\dfrac{b(a^2 - 1)}{a}$
(D) $a = b$ and c is any value (E) $a = b$ and $c = a - 1$

Problem 48: (1970 AMC) The fourth power of $\sqrt{1 + \sqrt{1 + \sqrt{1}}}$ is
(A) $\sqrt{2} + \sqrt{3}$ (B) $\dfrac{1}{2}(7 + 3\sqrt{5})$ (C) $1 + 2\sqrt{3}$ (D) 3 (E) $3 + 2\sqrt{2}$

Problem 49: (1986 AMC) Simplify $(\sqrt[6]{27} - \sqrt{6\dfrac{3}{4}})^2$.

(A) $\dfrac{3}{4}$ (B) $\dfrac{\sqrt{3}}{2}$ (C) $\dfrac{3\sqrt{3}}{4}$ (D) $\dfrac{3}{2}$ (E) $\dfrac{3\sqrt{3}}{2}$

Problem 50: (2005 AIME 2) Let $x = \dfrac{4}{(\sqrt{5}+1)(\sqrt[4]{5}+1)(\sqrt[8]{5}+1)(\sqrt[16]{5}+1)}$. Find $(x + 1)^{48}$.

11

Problem 51: Find $a^2 + \frac{1}{2}ab + b^2$ if the integer part is a and the fraction part is b of $\frac{\sqrt{5}+1}{\sqrt{5}-1}$.

Problem 52: Find the numerical value of $\frac{2x+\sqrt{xy}+3y}{x+\sqrt{xy}-y}$ if $\sqrt{x}(\sqrt{x}+\sqrt{y}) = 3\sqrt{y}(\sqrt{x}+5\sqrt{y})$, and $x > 0, y > 0$.

Problem 53: (1961 AMC) The symbol $|a|$ means a if a is a positive number or zero, and $-a$ if a is a negative number. For all real values of t the expression $\sqrt{t^4+t^2}$ is equal to:
(A) t^3 (B) t^2+t (C) $|t^2+t|$ (D) $t\sqrt{t^2+1}$ (E) $|t|\sqrt{1+t^2}$

Problem 54: (1987 ARML) If $y = x+1$ and $\sqrt{y}-\sqrt{x} = \frac{1}{3}$, compute $\sqrt{y}+\sqrt{x}$.

Problem 55: Find the value of xy if $x+y = \sqrt{7\sqrt{3}-5\sqrt{2}}$ and $x-y = \sqrt{7\sqrt{2}-5\sqrt{3}}$.
(A) $3\sqrt{3}+3\sqrt{2}$. (B) $3\sqrt{3}-3\sqrt{2}$. (C) $7\sqrt{3}-5\sqrt{2}$. (D) $7\sqrt{2}-5\sqrt{3}$.

Problem 56: Find the value of $\frac{10x+2\sqrt{5}}{10x-5\sqrt{2}}$ if $x = \frac{\sqrt{5}-\sqrt{2}}{2\sqrt{3+\sqrt{5}}-\sqrt{2}}$.

Problem 57: If the square of a positive number is $5-2\sqrt{6}$, what is its cube?

Problem 58: The decimal parts are a and b of $9+\sqrt{13}$ and $9-\sqrt{13}$, respectively. Find the numerical value of $ab - 4a + 3b + 8$.

Problem 59: If $\sqrt{5} = a$ and the decimal part of a is b, find the value of or $\frac{1}{b}-a$.

Problem 60: If the decimal part of $5+\sqrt{7}$ is a and the decimal part of $5-\sqrt{7}$ is b, find the value of $ab - 2a + 3b + 12$.

SOLUTIONS

Problem 1: Solution: (D).
$\sqrt{\dfrac{1}{9}+\dfrac{1}{16}} = \sqrt{\dfrac{16+9}{144}} = \sqrt{\dfrac{25}{144}} = \dfrac{5}{12}$.

Problem 2: Solution:
$a^{9(\frac{1}{6})(\frac{1}{3})4} \cdot a^{9(\frac{1}{3})(\frac{1}{6})4} = a^2 \cdot a^2 = a^4$.

Problem 3: Solution: (A).
The conjugate of $\sqrt{2}+\sqrt{3}-\sqrt{5}$ is $\sqrt{2}+\sqrt{3}+\sqrt{5}$.

$\dfrac{\sqrt{2}}{(\sqrt{2}+\sqrt{3})-\sqrt{5}} \cdot \dfrac{(\sqrt{2}+\sqrt{3})+\sqrt{5}}{(\sqrt{2}+\sqrt{3})+\sqrt{5}} = \dfrac{2+\sqrt{6}+\sqrt{10}}{2\sqrt{6}}$;

$\dfrac{2+\sqrt{6}+\sqrt{10}}{2\sqrt{6}} \cdot \dfrac{\sqrt{6}}{\sqrt{6}} = \dfrac{2\sqrt{6}+6+2\sqrt{15}}{2 \cdot 6} = \dfrac{3+\sqrt{6}+\sqrt{15}}{6}$.

Problem 4: Solution:
We can use the formula to solve the problem:
$(\sqrt{x}+\sqrt{y}+\sqrt{z})^2 = x+y+z+2(\sqrt{xy}+\sqrt{yz}+\sqrt{zx})$.
First we write the original expression as $\sqrt{13+2\sqrt{5}+2\sqrt{7}+2\sqrt{35}}$.
Then we let $\sqrt{13+2\sqrt{5}+2\sqrt{7}+2\sqrt{35}} = \sqrt{x}+\sqrt{y}+\sqrt{z}$.
Squaring both sides: $13+2\sqrt{5}+2\sqrt{7}+2\sqrt{35} = x+y+z+2\sqrt{xy}+2\sqrt{yz}+2\sqrt{zx}$.
Therefore we have:
$x+y+z=13$ (1)
$xy=5$ (2)
$yz=7$ (3)
$zx=35$.   (4)

Solving (2), (3), and (4), we get: $x=5$, $y=1$, $z=7$. It is seen that they also satisfy (1).
$\therefore \sqrt{11+2\sqrt{5}+2\sqrt{7}+2\sqrt{35}} = 1+\sqrt{5}+\sqrt{7}$.

Problem 5: Solution:
We make the radicals with the same exponent:

$\sqrt{2} = \sqrt[6]{8}$
$\sqrt[3]{3} = \sqrt[6]{9}$.
Therefore $\sqrt[3]{3} > \sqrt{2}$.
$\sqrt{2} = \sqrt[10]{2^{10}} = \sqrt[10]{1024}$
$\sqrt[5]{5} = \sqrt[10]{25}$
Therefore $\sqrt{2} > \sqrt[5]{5}$.
Finally $\sqrt[5]{5} < \sqrt{2} < \sqrt[3]{3}$.

Problem 6: Solution:
We know that both $\sqrt{19}$ and $6 - \sqrt{3}$ is greater than 0.
$(\sqrt{19})^2 = 19 = 39 - 20 = 39 - \sqrt{400}$
$(6 - \sqrt{3})^2 = 39 - 12\sqrt{3} = 39 - \sqrt{432}$.
$39 - \sqrt{400} > 39 - \sqrt{432} \Rightarrow \sqrt{19} > 6 - \sqrt{3}$.

Problem 7: Solution:

$\left(\sqrt[3]{\dfrac{9-5\sqrt{3}}{9+5\sqrt{3}}}\right)^3 = \dfrac{9-5\sqrt{3}}{9+5\sqrt{3}} = \dfrac{(9-5\sqrt{3})^2}{6} = 26 - 15\sqrt{13}$

$(\dfrac{\sqrt{3}-1}{\sqrt{3}+1})^3 = [\dfrac{(\sqrt{3}-1)^2}{2}]^3 = (2-\sqrt{3})^3 = 26 - 15\sqrt{15}$

Therefore $\sqrt[3]{\dfrac{9-5\sqrt{3}}{9+5\sqrt{3}}} > \dfrac{\sqrt{3}-1}{\sqrt{3}+1}$.

Problem 8: Solution:
$\dfrac{3}{2}\sqrt{48} = 6\sqrt{3}$.
$\dfrac{5}{7}\sqrt{147} = 5\sqrt{3}$
Since $6\sqrt{3} > 5\sqrt{3}$, $\dfrac{3}{2}\sqrt{48} > \dfrac{5}{7}\sqrt{147}$.

Problem 9: Solution:

Let $a_1 = 0$, $a_2 = b$, $a_3 = a$, $a_4 = a + b$. We get the conclusion.

Problem 10: Solution:

The original expression $= = 6x + [\dfrac{x(x+2) - x(x-2)}{(x-2)(x+2)}] \times \dfrac{(x-2)(x^3+8)}{4x}$

$= 6x + \dfrac{4x}{(x-2)(x+2)} \times \dfrac{(x-2)(x+2)(x^2-2x+4)}{4x}$

$= 6x + x^2 - 2x + 4 = (x+2)^2$.

Since $x = \dfrac{1}{2+\sqrt{3}} = \sqrt{3} - 2$, $x + 2 = \sqrt{3}$.

Therefore The original expression $= (\sqrt{3})^2 = 3$.

Problem 11: Solution:

$x = \dfrac{1}{\sqrt{5}-2} = \sqrt{5} + 2$.

$y = \dfrac{1}{\sqrt{5}+2} = \sqrt{5} - 2$

$\dfrac{80}{x^2-y^2} = \dfrac{80}{(x+y)(x-y)} = \dfrac{80}{2\sqrt{5} \cdot 4} = 2\sqrt{5}$.

Problem 12: Solution: (D).

Square both sides of the given equation to obtain $2 + \sqrt{x} = 9$. Thus $\sqrt{x} = 7$, and $x = 49$, which satisfies the given equation.

Problem 13: Solution:

Let $A = \sqrt{3+\sqrt{5}} + \sqrt{3-\sqrt{5}}$.

Squaring both sides: $A^2 = (3 + \sqrt{5}) + (3 - \sqrt{5}) + 2\sqrt{3^2 - (\sqrt{5})^2} = 6 + 2\sqrt{4} = 10$.

Since $A > 0$, $A = \sqrt{10}$.

Therefore $\sqrt{3+\sqrt{5}} + \sqrt{3-\sqrt{5}} = \sqrt{10}$.

Problem 14: Solution:

Let $S = \sqrt{x+2\sqrt{x-1}} + \sqrt{x-2\sqrt{x-1}}$.

Squaring both sides:

$S^2 = 2x + 2\sqrt{x^2 - 4(x-1)} = 2x + 2\sqrt{(x-2)^2} = 2x + 2|x-2|$

When $x \geq 2$, $S^2 = 4(x-1)$, $S = 2\sqrt{x-1}$.
When $1 \leq x < 2$, $S^2 = 4$, $S = 2$.
Therefore $\sqrt{x+2\sqrt{x-1}} + \sqrt{x-2\sqrt{x-1}} = \begin{cases} 2\sqrt{x-1}, & x \geq 2 \\ 2, & 1 \leq x < 2 \end{cases}$.

Problem 15: Solution:
Squaring both sides of the given equation: $x - \sqrt{50} = y^2 - 2\sqrt{2}\,y + 2$.
That is $x - y^2 - 2 - (5 - 2y)\sqrt{2} = 0$.
So we have $\begin{cases} x - y^2 - 2 = 0 \\ 5 - 2y = 0. \end{cases}$
Solving we get $x = \dfrac{33}{4}$, $y = \dfrac{5}{2}$.

Problem 16: Solution:
Squaring both sides we get:
$P - 2\sqrt{10} = M + N - 2\sqrt{MN}$ (1)
Or $M + N - P = 2(\sqrt{MN} - \sqrt{10})$.
Since P, M, and N are all positive integers, we must have $\sqrt{MN} - \sqrt{10} = 0$ and $M + N - P = 0$.
Therefore we can have $\begin{cases} M + N = P, & (2) \\ MN = 10. & (3) \end{cases}$
The integer solutions are $M = 10$, $N = 1$, $P = 11$ or $M = 5$, $N = 2$, $P = 7$.

Problem 17: Solution:
Let $x = \sqrt{4 - \sqrt{10 + 2\sqrt{5}}} + \sqrt{4 + \sqrt{10 + 2\sqrt{5}}}$.
$x^2 = (4 - \sqrt{10 + 2\sqrt{5}}) + (4 + \sqrt{10 + 2\sqrt{5}}) + 2\sqrt{(4 - \sqrt{10 + 2\sqrt{5}})(4 + \sqrt{10 + 2\sqrt{5}})}$
$= 8 + 2(\sqrt{5} - 1) = 6 + 2\sqrt{5} = (\sqrt{5} + 1)^2$.
Since $x > 0$, $x = \sqrt{5} + 1$.

Problem 18: Solution:
Since $4x^2 - 4x - 15 \leq 0$, $-\dfrac{3}{2} \leq x \leq \dfrac{5}{2}$.
$\sqrt{4x^2 + 12x + 9} + \sqrt{4x^2 - 20x + 25} = \sqrt{(2x+3)^2} + \sqrt{(2x-5)^2} = |2x+3| + |2x-5|$.

We know that $-\frac{3}{2} \le x \le \frac{5}{2}$.

$|2x+3| = 2x + 3$, $|2x-5| = 5 - 2x$

Therefore $\sqrt{4x^2 + 12x + 9} + \sqrt{4x^2 - 20x + 25} = 2x + 3 + 5 - 2x = 8$.

Problem 19: Solution: (E).

Suppose that $k = \sqrt{120 - \sqrt{x}}$ is an integer. Then $0 \le k \le \sqrt{120}$, and because k is an integer, we have $0 \le k \le 10$. Thus there are 11 possible integer values of k. For each such k, the corresponding value of x is $(120 - k^2)^2$. Because $(120 - k^2)^2$ is positive and decreasing for $0 \le k \le 10$, the 11 values of x are distinct.

Problem 20: Solution:

Let $\frac{a}{c} = \frac{b}{d} = k$.

$a = ck$, $b = dk$ and $a + b = k(c + d)$.

$$\frac{\sqrt{a} + \sqrt{b}}{\sqrt{a+b}} = \frac{\sqrt{ck} + \sqrt{dk}}{\sqrt{k(c+d)}} = \frac{\sqrt{k}(\sqrt{c} + \sqrt{d})}{\sqrt{k} \cdot \sqrt{c+d}} = \frac{\sqrt{c} + \sqrt{d}}{\sqrt{c+d}}.$$

Problem 21: Solution: (D).

By rationalizing the denominator of each fraction, we see
$$T = (3 + \sqrt{8}) - (\sqrt{8} + \sqrt{7}) + (\sqrt{7} + \sqrt{6}) - (\sqrt{6} + \sqrt{5}) + (\sqrt{5} + 2)$$
$$= 3 + 2 = 5.$$

Problem 22: Solution:

The original expression $= (\sqrt{2} - 1) + (\sqrt{3} - \sqrt{2}) + \ldots + (\sqrt{9} - \sqrt{8}) = 2$.

Problem 23: Solution:

Left hand side $= \dfrac{\sqrt{2} - 1}{(\sqrt{2})^2 - 1} + \dfrac{\sqrt{3} - \sqrt{2}}{(\sqrt{3})^2 - (\sqrt{2})^2} + \cdots + \dfrac{\sqrt{n+1} - \sqrt{n}}{(\sqrt{n+1})^2 - (\sqrt{n})^2}$

$= (\sqrt{2} - 1) + (\sqrt{3} - \sqrt{2}) + (\sqrt{4} - \sqrt{3}) + \ldots + (\sqrt{n+1} - \sqrt{n}) = \sqrt{n+1} - 1 = \dfrac{n}{\sqrt{n+1} + 1}$.

Problem 24: Solution:

$$\frac{1}{1+\sqrt{3}} - \frac{1}{\sqrt{3}+\sqrt{5}} + \cdots + \frac{1}{\sqrt{1997}+\sqrt{1999}} = \frac{1}{2}[(\sqrt{3}-1)+(\sqrt{5}-\sqrt{3})+\ldots+(\sqrt{1999}-\sqrt{1997})] = \frac{1}{2}(\sqrt{1999}-1)$$

Problem 25: Solution:

$$\frac{1}{\sqrt{a}+\sqrt{a+1}} - \frac{\sqrt{a+1}-\sqrt{a}}{(\sqrt{a}+\sqrt{a+1})(\sqrt{a+1}-\sqrt{a})} = \sqrt{a+1}-\sqrt{a},$$

$$\frac{1}{\sqrt{a+1}+\sqrt{a+2}} = \sqrt{a+2}-\sqrt{a+1},$$

$$\frac{1}{\sqrt{a+2}+\sqrt{a+3}} = \sqrt{a+3}-\sqrt{a+2},$$

...

$$\frac{1}{\sqrt{a+1999}+\sqrt{a+2000}} = \sqrt{a+2000}-\sqrt{a+1999}.$$

Adding them all we get:

$$\frac{1}{\sqrt{a}+\sqrt{a+1}} + \frac{1}{\sqrt{a+1}+\sqrt{a+2}} + \cdots + \frac{1}{\sqrt{a+1999}+\sqrt{a+2000}} = \sqrt{a+2000}-\sqrt{a}.$$

From $x^2 - 19x - 150 = 0$, we have $(x-25)(x+6) = 0$.
The positive solution is $x = 25$.
Therefore $\sqrt{a+2000} - \sqrt{a} = \sqrt{2025} - \sqrt{25} = 45 - 5 = 40$.

Problem 26: Solution:

$$\sqrt{6-\sqrt{17-12\sqrt{2}}} = \sqrt{6-\sqrt{(\sqrt{9}-\sqrt{8})^2}} = \sqrt{3+2\sqrt{2}} = \sqrt{(\sqrt{2}+1)^2} - \sqrt{2} + 1$$

Problem 27: Solution:
Let $\sqrt{4+\sqrt{15}} = \sqrt{x}+\sqrt{y}$.
Squaring both sides: $4+\sqrt{15} = x+y+2\sqrt{xy}$, or $4+\sqrt{15} = (x+y)+\sqrt{4xy}$

$$\begin{cases} x+y = 4 \\ 4xy = 15 \end{cases}$$

$$\begin{cases} x = \dfrac{3}{2} \\ y = \dfrac{5}{2} \end{cases}$$

Therefore $\sqrt{4+\sqrt{15}} = \sqrt{\dfrac{3}{2}} + \sqrt{\dfrac{5}{2}} = \dfrac{1}{2}(\sqrt{6} + \sqrt{10})$.

Problem 28: Solution: (E).

$$\sqrt{1+\left(\dfrac{x^4-1}{2x^2}\right)^2} = \sqrt{\dfrac{4x^4+x^8-2x^4+1}{4x^4}} = \sqrt{\left(\dfrac{x^4-1}{2x^2}\right)^2} = \dfrac{x^4+1}{2x^2} = \dfrac{x^2}{2} + \dfrac{1}{2x^2}.$$

Problem 29: Solution: (C).

$2\sqrt{x} + \dfrac{2}{\sqrt{x}} = 5$. Squaring, we obtain $4x + 8 + \dfrac{4}{x} = 25$. Multiply both sides of the equation by x and obtain $4x^2 - 17x + 4 = 0$.

Problem 30: Solution: (A).

$$\dfrac{1\cdot(1+\sqrt{3})(1-\sqrt{3})-1\cdot(1-\sqrt{3})+1\cdot(1+\sqrt{3})}{(1+\sqrt{3})(1-\sqrt{3})} = 1-\sqrt{3}.$$

Problem 31: Solution:

$$\dfrac{(2+\sqrt{2})^2(\sqrt{2}-2)+\sqrt{2}-2+2+\sqrt{2}}{(2+\sqrt{2})(\sqrt{3}-2)} = \dfrac{-4}{-2} = 2.$$

Problem 32: Solution:
Method 1 (Completing the squares):

$$\sqrt{9-4\sqrt{5}} = 5+4-4\sqrt{5} = (\sqrt{5})^2 - 2\cdot 2\sqrt{5} + 2^2 = (\sqrt{5}-2)^2$$

Therefore $\sqrt{9-4\sqrt{5}} = \sqrt{5} - 2$.

Note: $\sqrt{9-4\sqrt{5}} = 4 - 4\sqrt{5} + 5 = 2^2 - 2\cdot 2\sqrt{5} + (\sqrt{5})^2 = (2-\sqrt{5})^2$ (Correct).

Therefore $\sqrt{9-4\sqrt{5}} = 2-\sqrt{5}$ (Not correct since $2 - \sqrt{5} < 0$).

Method 2 (Undetermined coefficients):
Let $\sqrt{9-4\sqrt{5}} = \sqrt{x} - \sqrt{y}$, $(x > y > 0)$.
Squaring both sides: $9-4\sqrt{5} = (x+y) - 2\sqrt{xy}$.

Hence $\begin{cases} x+y = 9 \\ xy = 20 \end{cases}$.

Solving we have $x = 5, y = 4$ $\Rightarrow$ $\sqrt{9-4\sqrt{5}} = \sqrt{5} - \sqrt{4} = \sqrt{5} - 2$.

Method 3 (Using the formula):
$\sqrt{9-4\sqrt{5}} = \dfrac{\sqrt{2}}{2} (\sqrt{9+\sqrt{9^2-(4\sqrt{5})^2}}) - (\sqrt{9-\sqrt{9^2-(4\sqrt{5})^2}})$

$= \dfrac{\sqrt{2}}{2} (\sqrt{10} - 2\sqrt{2}) = \sqrt{5} - 2$.

Problem 33: Solution:

$\sqrt{\sqrt{48}-\sqrt{45}} = \sqrt{\sqrt{3}(4-\sqrt{15})} = \sqrt[4]{3}\sqrt{4-\sqrt{15}}$

$4-\sqrt{15} = \dfrac{1}{2}(8 - 2\sqrt{5}) = \dfrac{1}{2}(\sqrt{5}-\sqrt{3})^2$

$\therefore \sqrt{4-\sqrt{15}} = \dfrac{1}{\sqrt{2}}(\sqrt{5}-\sqrt{3})$

$\therefore \sqrt{\sqrt{48}-\sqrt{45}} = \sqrt[4]{3} \cdot \dfrac{1}{\sqrt{2}}(\sqrt{5}-\sqrt{3}) = \dfrac{1}{2}\sqrt[4]{3}(\sqrt{10}-\sqrt{6})$.

Problem 34: Solution:
$\dfrac{\sqrt{2}+\sqrt{3}}{\sqrt{10}+\sqrt{14}+\sqrt{15}+\sqrt{21}} = \dfrac{\sqrt{2}+\sqrt{3}}{\sqrt{2}(\sqrt{5}+\sqrt{7})+\sqrt{3}(\sqrt{5}+\sqrt{7})} = \dfrac{\sqrt{2}+\sqrt{3}}{(\sqrt{2}+\sqrt{3})(\sqrt{5}+\sqrt{7})}$

$= \dfrac{1}{\sqrt{7}+\sqrt{5}} = \dfrac{\sqrt{7}-\sqrt{5}}{2}$.

Problem 35: Solution:
Method 1:

We have $a = 2 - \sqrt{3}$ and $b = 2 + \sqrt{3}$.
Therefore $a + b = 4$ and $ab = 1$.
$$\frac{1}{a+1} + \frac{1}{b+1} = \frac{a+b+2}{1+ab+a+b} = \frac{4+2}{1+1+4} = 1.$$

Method 2:
Rationalizing the denominators: $a = 2 - \sqrt{3}$, $b = 2 + \sqrt{3}$.
$a + 1 = 3 - \sqrt{3}$.
$b + 1 = 3 + \sqrt{3}$.
$$\frac{1}{a+1} + \frac{1}{b+1} = \frac{1}{3-\sqrt{3}} + \frac{1}{3+\sqrt{3}} = \frac{3+\sqrt{3}+3-\sqrt{3}}{(3-\sqrt{3})(3+\sqrt{3})} = 1.$$

Problem 36: Solution:
$$x + y = \frac{2+\sqrt{3}}{2-\sqrt{3}} + \frac{2-\sqrt{3}}{2+\sqrt{3}} = (2+\sqrt{3})^2 + (2-\sqrt{3})^2 = 14$$
$$xy = \frac{2+\sqrt{3}}{2-\sqrt{3}} \cdot \frac{2-\sqrt{3}}{2+\sqrt{3}} = 1.$$
Therefore $2x^2 - 3xy + 2y^2 = 2(x+y)^2 - 7xy = 2 \times 14^2 - 7 = 385$.

Problem 37: Solution:

$x^2 + y^2 = 5 + \sqrt{5} + 5 - \sqrt{5} = 10$.
$x^2 \cdot y^2 = (5 + \sqrt{5})(5 - \sqrt{5}) = 20$
$\therefore x^6 + y^6 = (x^2 + y^2)(x^4 - x^2y^2 + y^4) = (x^2 + y^2)[(x^2 + y^2)^2 - 3x^2y^2]$
$= 10 \cdot (10^2 - 3 \times 20) = 400$.

Problem 38: Solution:
$$x = \frac{2}{\sqrt{3}-1} = \sqrt{3} + 1.$$
$(x-1)^2 = 3 \Rightarrow x^2 - 2x + 2 = 0$.
$\frac{1}{2}x^3 - x^2 - x + 3 = \frac{1}{2}x(x^2 - 2x - 2) + 3 = 3$.

Problem 39: Solution:
We know that $(a - b)^3 = a^3 - b^3 - 3ab(a - b)$.

21

50 AMC Lectures Problems Book 1   (2) Radicals

$$x^3 = 4(\sqrt{5}+1) - 4(\sqrt{5}-1) - 3\sqrt[3]{4(\sqrt{5}+1)} \cdot \sqrt[3]{4(\sqrt{5}-1)} \cdot [\sqrt[3]{4(\sqrt{5}+1)} - \sqrt[3]{4(\sqrt{5}-1)}]$$
$$= 8 - 3 \cdot \sqrt[3]{4^3} \cdot x = 8 - 12x$$
$$\therefore x^3 + 12x = 8.$$

Problem 40: Solution:
Since $x = \sqrt{3} - \sqrt{2}$, $x + \sqrt{2} = \sqrt{3}$.
Squaring both sides: $x^2 + 2\sqrt{2}x + 2 = 3 \quad \Rightarrow \quad x^2 + 2\sqrt{2}x - 1 = 0$.
Similarly we have $x^2 - 2\sqrt{3}x + 1 = 0$.
Therefore $x^6 + 2\sqrt{2}x^5 - x^4 + x^3 - 2\sqrt{3}x^2 + 2x + \sqrt{2}$
$= x^4(x^2 + 2\sqrt{2}x - 1) + x(x^2 - 2\sqrt{3}x + 1) + x + \sqrt{2} = \sqrt{3}$.

Problem 41: Solution:

$$11 - \sqrt{120} = (\sqrt{6})^2 - 2 \cdot \sqrt{6} \cdot \sqrt{5} + (\sqrt{5})^2 = (\sqrt{6} - \sqrt{5})^2$$
Therefore $\sqrt{11 - \sqrt{120}} = \sqrt{(\sqrt{6}-\sqrt{5})^2} = |\sqrt{6}-\sqrt{5}| = \sqrt{6} - \sqrt{5}$.

Problem 42: Solution:

$$11 + 6\sqrt{2} = 3^2 + 2 \times 3 \times \sqrt{2} + (\sqrt{2})^2 = (3+\sqrt{2})^2$$
$$\sqrt{11+6\sqrt{3}} = \sqrt{(3+\sqrt{2})^2} = 3 + \sqrt{2}$$

Problem 43: Solution:
We have $4 + 2\sqrt{3} = (\sqrt{3})^2 + 2 \times \sqrt{3} \times 1 + 1 = (\sqrt{3}+1)^2$

$$\sqrt{2+\sqrt{3}} = \sqrt{\frac{4+2\sqrt{3}}{2}} = \sqrt{\frac{(\sqrt{3}+1)^2}{2}} = \frac{\sqrt{3}+1}{\sqrt{2}} = \frac{1}{2}(\sqrt{6}+\sqrt{2})$$

Problem 44: Solution:

$$28 + 10\sqrt{3} = 5^2 + 2 \times 5 \times \sqrt{3} + (\sqrt{3})^2 = (5+\sqrt{3})^2$$
$$\sqrt{14+5\sqrt{3}} = \sqrt{\frac{28+10\sqrt{3}}{2}} = \sqrt{\frac{(5+\sqrt{3})^2}{2}} = \frac{5+\sqrt{3}}{\sqrt{2}} = \frac{1}{2}(5\sqrt{2}+\sqrt{6}).$$

Problem 45: (Solution: (E).

$(5-\sqrt{y^2-25})^2 = 25 - 10\sqrt{y^2-25} + y^2 - 25 = y^2 - 10\sqrt{y^2-25}$.

Problem 46: Solution: (A)

The expression $\sqrt{25-t^2} + 5$ can never equal zero, since it is the sum of 5 and a non-negative number. (By $\sqrt{25-t^2}$ we mean the positive square root.)
∴ (A) is the correct choice.

Problem 47: Solution: (C).

If $\sqrt{a+\frac{b}{c}} = a\sqrt{\frac{b}{c}}$ then $a + \frac{b}{c} = a^2 \frac{b}{c}$.

∴ $ac = b(a^2-1)$;   ∴ $c = \frac{b(a^2-1)}{a}$.

Problem 48: Solution: (E).

(E) Set $x = \sqrt{1+\sqrt{1+\sqrt{1}}}$. Since $\sqrt{1} = 1$, $x = \sqrt{1+\sqrt{2}}$, $x^2 = 1 + \sqrt{2}$ and $x^4 = (x^2)^2 = 1 + 2\sqrt{2} + 2 = 3 + 2\sqrt{2}$.

Problem 49: (Solution: (A).

$(\sqrt[6]{27} - \sqrt{6\frac{3}{4}})^2 = [(3^3)^{\frac{1}{6}} - (\frac{27}{4})^{\frac{1}{2}}]^2 = [\sqrt{3} - \frac{3\sqrt{3}}{2}]^2 = [\frac{-\sqrt{3}}{2}]^2 = \frac{3}{4}$.

Problem 50: Solution: 125.

Let $y = \sqrt[16]{5}$. Then
$$x = \frac{4}{(y^8+1)(y^4+1)(y^2+1)(y+1)} = \frac{4(y-1)}{(y^8+1)(y^4+1)(y^2+1)(y+1)(y-1)}$$
$$= \frac{4(y-1)}{y^{16}-1} = \frac{4(y-1)}{5-1} = y - 1.$$

Thus $(x+1)^{48} = y^{48} = 5^3 = 125$.

Problem 51: Solution:

$$\frac{\sqrt{5}+1}{\sqrt{5}-1} = \frac{(\sqrt{5}+1)^2}{4} = \frac{3+\sqrt{5}}{2} = 2 + \frac{\sqrt{5}-1}{2}.$$

We know that $0 < \frac{\sqrt{5}-1}{2} < \frac{\sqrt{9}-1}{2} = 1$.

Therefore $a = 2$, $b = \frac{\sqrt{5}-1}{2}$.

$$\therefore a^2 + \frac{1}{2}ab + b^2 = 4 + \frac{1}{2}(\sqrt{5}-1) + \frac{1}{4}(\sqrt{5}-1)^2$$
$$= 4 + \frac{1}{2}(\sqrt{5}-1) + \frac{1}{4}(6-2\sqrt{5}) = 4 + \frac{1}{2}(\sqrt{5}-1+3-\sqrt{5}) = 5.$$

Problem 52: Solution:
Since $\sqrt{x} + 3(\sqrt{x} + \sqrt{y}) = 3\sqrt{y}(\sqrt{x} + 5\sqrt{y})$, $x + \sqrt{xy} = 3\sqrt{xy} + 15y \Rightarrow$
$x - 2\sqrt{xy} - 15y = 0 \Rightarrow (\sqrt{x} - 5\sqrt{y})(\sqrt{x} + 3\sqrt{y}) = 0$.
We know that $\sqrt{x} + 3\sqrt{y} > 0$. Therefore $\sqrt{x} - 5\sqrt{y} = 0 \Rightarrow \sqrt{x} = 5\sqrt{y}$.
Therefore, $\frac{2x + \sqrt{xy} + 3y}{x + \sqrt{xy} - y} = \frac{50y + 5y + 3y}{25y + 5y - y} = \frac{58y}{29y} = 2$.

Problem 53: Solution: (E).
$(t^4 + t^2)^{\frac{1}{2}} = [t^2(t^2+1)]^{\frac{1}{2}} = (t^2)^{\frac{1}{2}}(t^2+1)^{\frac{1}{2}} = |t|(1+t^2)^{\frac{1}{2}}$.

Problem 54: Solution:
$$\sqrt{y} + \sqrt{x} = \frac{y-x}{\sqrt{y}-\sqrt{x}} = \frac{1}{\frac{1}{3}} = 3.$$

Problem 55: Solution: (B).
It is very convenient to use the following relationship:
$xy = \frac{1}{4}[(x+y)^2 - (x-y)^2]$.
$xy = \frac{1}{4}[(x+y)^2 - (x-y)^2] = \frac{1}{4}[(7\sqrt{3} - 5\sqrt{2}) - (7\sqrt{2} - 5\sqrt{3})] = 3\sqrt{3} - 3\sqrt{2}$.

Problem 56: Solution:

$$x = \frac{\sqrt{5}-\sqrt{2}}{2\sqrt{3+\sqrt{5}}-\sqrt{2}} = \frac{\sqrt{5}-\sqrt{2}}{\sqrt{2}\times\sqrt{6+2\sqrt{5}}-\sqrt{2}}$$

$$= \frac{\sqrt{5}-\sqrt{2}}{\sqrt{2}\times\sqrt{(\sqrt{5}+1)^2}-\sqrt{2}} = \frac{\sqrt{5}-\sqrt{2}}{\sqrt{2}(\sqrt{5}+1)-\sqrt{2}} = \frac{\sqrt{5}-\sqrt{2}}{\sqrt{10}}$$

$$10x = \sqrt{10}(\sqrt{5}-\sqrt{2}) = 5\sqrt{2} - 2\sqrt{5}$$

$$\frac{10x+2\sqrt{5}}{10x-5\sqrt{2}} = \frac{5\sqrt{2}}{-2\sqrt{5}} = -\frac{\sqrt{10}}{2}.$$

Problem 57: Solution:
Let the number be x. We have $x^2 = 5 - 2\sqrt{6}$.
We know that $x^2 = (\sqrt{3} - \sqrt{2})^2$. Therefore for positive x: $x = (\sqrt{3} - \sqrt{2})$.
$x^3 = x \cdot x^2 = (\sqrt{3} - \sqrt{2})(5 - 2\sqrt{6}) = (9\sqrt{3} - 11\sqrt{2})$

Problem 58: Solution:
We know that $3 < \sqrt{13} < 4$. So $12 < 9 + \sqrt{13} < 13$.
$a = (9 + \sqrt{13}) - 12 = \sqrt{13} - 3$.
We know that $5 < 9 - \sqrt{13} < 6$. So $b = (9 - \sqrt{13}) - 5 = 4 - \sqrt{13}$.
Therefore $ab - 4a + 3b + 8 = (ab - 4a + 3b - 12) + 20 = (a+3)(b-4) + 20$
$= \sqrt{13} \cdot (-\sqrt{13}) + 20 = 7$.

Problem 59: Solution: 2.
The integer part of $\sqrt{5}$ is 2 and the decimal part $b = \sqrt{5} - 2$.
$\frac{1}{b} - a = \frac{1}{\sqrt{5}-2} - \sqrt{5} = \sqrt{5} + 2 - \sqrt{5} = 2$.

Problem 60: Solution: 12.
Since $2 < \sqrt{7} < 3$, so $7 < 5 + \sqrt{7} < 8$ and $2 < 5 - \sqrt{7} < 3$.
$a = (5 + \sqrt{7}) - 7 = \sqrt{7} - 2$, $b = (5 - \sqrt{7}) - 2 = 3 - \sqrt{7}$.
$ab - 2a + 3b = (\sqrt{7}-2)(3-\sqrt{7}) - 2(\sqrt{7}-2) + 3(3-\sqrt{7}) + 12 = 12$.

50 AMC Lectures Problems Book 1   (3) Solving Radicals Equations

PROBLEMS

Problem 1: Solving $\sqrt{x-4} = \sqrt{x-1}$.

Problem 2: Solving $\sqrt{\dfrac{3x-2}{x-1}} + \sqrt{\dfrac{x-1}{3x-2}} = \dfrac{10}{3}$.

Problem 3: Solving $(\sqrt[4]{5x+1}+1)^2 + (\sqrt[4]{5x+1}-3)^2 = 10$.

Problem 4: Solving $\sqrt{x^2-2x+9} - \sqrt{x^2-2x+4} = 1$.

Problem 5: Solving $\sqrt[3]{x} + \sqrt[3]{2-x} = 2$.

Problem 6: Solving $x^2 + x + 2x\sqrt{x+2} = 14$.

Problem 7: Solving $\sqrt{x^2-5x+1} - \sqrt{x^2-6x+6} = 2$.

Problem 8: Solve $\dfrac{\sqrt{x+1}+\sqrt{x-1}}{\sqrt{x+1}-\sqrt{x-1}} = \dfrac{4x-1}{2}$.

Problem 9: Solve $\dfrac{\sqrt{x+2a}-\sqrt{x-2a}}{\sqrt{x-2a}+\sqrt{x+2a}} = \dfrac{x}{2a}$.

Problem 10: Solving $\sqrt{3}x\sqrt{1+x^2} + x\sqrt{1-x^2} = 2x^2 + 1$.

Problem 11: (AMC 12) The number of distinct pairs of integers (x, y) such that $0 < x < y$ and $\sqrt{1984} = \sqrt{x} + \sqrt{y}$.

Problem 12: (AMC 12) The roots of the equation $2\sqrt{x} + 2x^{-\frac{1}{2}} = 5$ can be found by solving:
(A) $16x^2 - 92x + 1 = 0$ (B) $4x^2 - 25x + 4 = 0$
(C) $4x^2 - 17x + 4 = 0$ (D) $2x^2 - 21x + 2 = 0$ (E) $4x^2 - 25x - 4 = 0$

Problem 13: (AMC 12) The equation $\sqrt{x+10} - \dfrac{6}{\sqrt{x+10}} = 5$ has:

(A) an extraneous root between -5 and -1
(B) an extraneous root between -10 and -6
(C) a true root between 20 and 25   (D) two true roots   (E) two extraneous roots

Problem 14: (AMC 12) The solution of $\sqrt{5x-1} + \sqrt{x-1} = 2$ is:

(A) $x = 2, x = 1$ (B) $x = \dfrac{2}{3}$ (C) $x = 2$ (D) $x = 1$ (E) $x = 0$

Problem 15: (AMC 12) Each of the equations $3x^2 - 2 = 25$, $(2x-1)^2 = (x-1)^2$, $\sqrt{x^2 - 7} = \sqrt{x-1}$ has:

(A) two integral roots   (B) no root greater than 3
(C) no root zero   (D) only one root   (E) one negative root and one positive root

Problem 16: (AMC 12) If $\sqrt{x-1} - \sqrt{x+1} + 1 = 0$, then $4x$ equals:

(A) 5   (B) $4\sqrt{-1}$ (C) 0   (D) $1\dfrac{1}{4}$ (E) no real value

Problem 17: (AMC 12) The number of roots satisfying the equation $\sqrt{5-x} = x\sqrt{5-x}$:
(A) unlimited   (B) 3   (C) 2   (D) 1   (E) 0

Problem 18: (AMC 12) If x is a number satisfying the equation $\sqrt[3]{x+9} - \sqrt[3]{x-9} = 3$, then x^2 is between:
   (A) 55 and 65   (B) 65 and 75   (C) 75 and 85
   (D) 85 and 95   (E) 95 and 105

Problem 19: Solve $x^2 - 6x - 6 + x\sqrt{x^2 - 2x - 2} = 0$.

Problem 20: Solve $2x^2 - 5x - 2x\sqrt{x^2 - 5x - 3} = 19$.

Problem 21: Solve $\sqrt{x + \sqrt{x}} - \sqrt{x - \sqrt{x}} = \dfrac{3}{2}\sqrt{\dfrac{x}{x+\sqrt{x}}}$.

Problem 22: Solve $\sqrt{3x^2 + 5x + 8} - \sqrt{3x^2 + 5x + 1} = 1$.

Problem 23: Solve $\sqrt{x^2 + 3x + 12} - \sqrt{x^2 - x + 4} = 2$.

Problem 24: Solve $\sqrt[3]{2+x} = 1 - \sqrt{x+1}$.

Problem 25: Solve $x^2 + 4x + 4 = 2\sqrt{x^3 + 5x^2 + 8x + 4}$.

SOLUTIONS

Problem 1: Solution:
We know that $\sqrt{x-4} < \sqrt{x-1}$.
No such value for x that would satisfy the given equation.
Therefore there is no solution to the given equation.

Problem 2: Solution:
Let $u = \sqrt{\dfrac{3x-2}{x-1}}$.
$u + \dfrac{1}{u} = \dfrac{10}{3} \Rightarrow 3u^2 - 10u + 3 = 0$.
Solving: $u_1 = 3$, $u_2 = \dfrac{1}{3}$.
$\sqrt{\dfrac{3x-2}{x-1}} = 3 \Rightarrow x_1 = 1\dfrac{1}{6}$.
$\sqrt{\dfrac{3x-2}{x-1}} = \dfrac{1}{3} \Rightarrow x_2 = \dfrac{17}{26}$.
We checked that all are the solutions.

Problem 3: Solution:
Let $(\sqrt[4]{5x+1}+1 + \sqrt[4]{5x+1}-3)/2 = \sqrt[4]{5x+1}-1 = y$.
We have $\sqrt[4]{5x+1}+1 = y+2$ and $\sqrt[4]{5x+1}-3 = y-2$.
Substituting into the given equation we have $(y+2)^2 + (y-2)^2 = 10$.
Simplifying we get: $y^2 = 1 \Rightarrow y_1 = 1$ or $y_2 = -1$.
Therefore we have:
Case I: $\sqrt[4]{5x+1} - 1 = 1 \Rightarrow x = 3$.
Case II: $\sqrt[4]{5x+1} - 1 = -1 \Rightarrow x = -\dfrac{1}{5}$.
We checked that both $x = 3$ and $x = -\dfrac{1}{5}$ are the solutions.

Problem 4: Solution:
We see that the average value of $\sqrt{x^2-2x+9}$ and $-\sqrt{x^2-2x+4}$ is 1/2.
Therefore we let $\sqrt{x^2-2x+9} = \dfrac{1}{2} + t$ and $-\sqrt{x^2-2x+4} = \dfrac{1}{2} - t$, $(t \geq \dfrac{1}{2})$.

Hence
$$x^2 - 2x + 9 = \frac{1}{4} + t + t^2 \qquad (1)$$
$$x^2 - 2x + 4 = \frac{1}{4} - t + t^2 \qquad (2)$$

(1) – (2): $5 = 2t \implies t = \frac{5}{2}$.

Therefore $\sqrt{x^2 - 2x + 9} = 3$.
Solving for x: $x_1 = 0$, $x_2 = 2$.

We checked that all are the solutions.

Problem 5: Solution:
We see that the average value of $\sqrt[3]{x}$ and $\sqrt[3]{2-x}$ is 1.
Therefore we let $\sqrt[3]{x} = 1 + t$ and $\sqrt[3]{2-x} = 1 - t$.
$x = 1 + 3t + 3t^2 + t^3 \qquad (1)$
$2 - x = 1 - 3t + 3t^2 - t^3 \qquad (2)$
(1) + (2): $2 = 2 + 6t^2$.
$t = 0$.
Hence $\sqrt[3]{x} = 1 \implies x = 1$.
We checked that $x = 1$ is the only solution.

Problem 6: Solution:
We add 2 to both sides of the equation: $x^2 + x + 2 + 2x\sqrt{x+2} = 16$.
We get: $x^2 + (x + \sqrt{x+2})^2 = 4^2$.

Therefore we have:
Case I: $x + \sqrt{x+2} = 4 \implies x = 2$ or $x = 7$.
Case II: $x + \sqrt{x+2} = -4$ (no solutions).
We checked that only $x = 2$ is the solution.

Problem 7: Solution:
We see that
$\sqrt{x^2 - 5x + 1} - \sqrt{x^2 - 6x + 6} = 2 \qquad (1)$
$(x^2 - 5x + 1) - (x^2 - 6x + 6) = x - 5 \qquad (2)$
(2) ÷ (1): $\sqrt{x^2 - 5x + 1} + \sqrt{x^2 - 6x + 6} = \frac{x+5}{2}$

Or $2\sqrt{x^2 - 5x + 1} + 2\sqrt{x^2 - 6x + 6} = x - 5$ \hfill (3)

(1) × 2 + (3): $4\sqrt{x^2 - 5x + 1} = x - 1$.

Squaring both sides of the above equation and factor:
$(x - 5)(5x - 1) = 0$ \hfill (4)

Solving we get $x = 5$, $x = \dfrac{1}{5}$.

We checked that only $x = 5$ is the solution.

Problem 8: Solution:

By the property of proportion, we have

$\dfrac{2\sqrt{x+1}}{2\sqrt{x-1}} = \dfrac{4x+1}{4x-3}$.

$\therefore \dfrac{x+1}{x-1} = \dfrac{16x^2 + 8x^2 + 1}{16x^2 - 24x + 9}$.

Using the property of proportion again: $x = \dfrac{32x^2 - 16x + 10}{32x - 8}$.

Solving for x: $x = \dfrac{5}{4}$.

$x = \dfrac{5}{4}$ is indeed the solutions to the original equation.

Problem 9: Solution:

By the property of proportion, we have $\dfrac{\sqrt{x+2a}}{-\sqrt{x-2a}} = \dfrac{x+2a}{x-2a}$.

Squaring both sides: $\dfrac{x+2a}{x-2a} = \dfrac{x^2 + 4ax + 4a^2}{x^2 - 4ax + 4a^2}$.

Using the property of proportion again: $\dfrac{x}{2a} = \dfrac{x^2 + 4a^2}{4ax}$.

Simplifying to get: $x^2 = 4a^2$

Solving for x: $x = \pm 2a$.

$x = \pm 2a$ are indeed the solutions to the original equation.

Problem 10: Solution:

The original equation can be rewritten as $\sqrt{3}x\sqrt{(2x^2+1)-x^2} + x\sqrt{(2x^2+1)-3x^2} = 2x^2+1$.

Let $f(x) = \sqrt{3}x$, $g(x) = x$, $h(x) = 2x^2 + 1$.

The original equation has the same solution as $3x^2 + x^2 = 2x^2 + 1$, $(x \geq 0)$.

Solving: $x = \dfrac{\sqrt{2}}{2}$.

Problem 11: Solution: (C).

Note that the prime factorization of 1984 is $2^6 \cdot 31$, that $x < 1984$ and that
$$y = (\sqrt{1984} - \sqrt{x})^2 = 1984 + x - 2\sqrt{1984x}.$$
It follows that y is an integer if and only if $1984x$ is a perfect square, that is, if and only if x is of the form $31t^2$.

Since x is less than 1984, we have $1 \leq t \leq 7$, yielding the pairs (31, 1519), (124, 1116), and (279, 775) for (x, y), corresponding to $t = 1, 2, 3$.

Since $y \leq x$ for $t > 3$, these are the only solutions.

Problem 12: Solution:

$2\sqrt{x} + \dfrac{2}{\sqrt{x}} = 5$. Squaring, we obtain $4x + 8 + \dfrac{4}{x} = 25$. Multiply both sides of the equation by x and obtain $4x^2 - 17x + 4 = 0$.

Problem 13: Solution: (B).

Multiply both sides of the equation by $\sqrt{x+10}$. $x + 10 - 6 = 5\sqrt{x+10}$, $x^2 - 17x - 234 = 0$, $x = 26$ or -9. -9 fails to check, i.e., it is an extraneous root.

Problem 14: Solution: (D).

$\sqrt{5x-1} = 2 - \sqrt{x-1}$, and $5x - 1 = 4 - 4\sqrt{x-1} + x - 1$. $\therefore 4x - 4 = -4\sqrt{x-1}$, $x - 1 = -\sqrt{x-1}$. Squaring again, we get $x^2 - 2x + 1 = x - 1$, $x^2 - 3x + 2 = 0$, $x = 1$ or 2. Since 2 does not satisfy the original equation, we have one root, $x = 1$.

Problem 15: Solution: (B).

The real roots are, respectively: ± 3; 0 and $\dfrac{2}{3}$; and 3. $\therefore$ (B) is the correct choice.

Problem 16: Solution: (D).

$\sqrt{x-1} + 1 = \sqrt{x+1}$; $\therefore$ x – 1 + $2\sqrt{x-1}$ + 1 = x + 1 $\therefore 2\sqrt{x-1} = 1$; $\therefore$ 4x – 4 = 1;
$\therefore$ 4x = 5. (This value of x satisfies the original equation.)

Problem 17: Solution: (C).
Method 1:
Replace $\sqrt{5-x} = x\sqrt{5-x}$ by $5 - x = x^2(5-x)$. The solution set for this equation is {5, 1, – 1} but the solution set for the original equation is {5, 1}.

Method 2:
$\sqrt{5-x} = x\sqrt{5-x}$. If $5 - x \neq 0$, divide by $\sqrt{5-x}$ and obtain $x = 1$; if $5 - x = 0$, then $x = 5$.

Problem 18: Solution: (C).
Method 1:
$(x+9)^{\frac{1}{3}} - (x-9)^{\frac{1}{3}} = 3$. Cube both sides and obtain
$x + 9 - 3(x+9)^{\frac{2}{3}}(x-9)^{\frac{1}{3}} + 3(x+9)^{\frac{1}{3}}(x-9)^{\frac{2}{3}} - x + 9 = 27$
 Which, when simplified, becomes
$9 = -3(x+9)^{\frac{1}{3}}(x-9)^{\frac{1}{3}}[(x+9)^{\frac{1}{3}} - (x-9)^{\frac{1}{3}}] = -3(x^2-81)^{\frac{1}{3}} (3)$.
$\therefore (x^2-81)^{\frac{1}{3}} = -1$, $x^2 = 80$.

Method 2:
Let $u = (x+9)^{\frac{1}{3}}$, $v = (x-9)^{\frac{1}{3}}$. then $u - v = 3$, $(u-v)^2 = u^2 - 2uv + v^2 = 9$, and
$u^3 - v^3 = x + 9 - (x - 9) = 18 = (u-v)(u^2 + uv + v^2) = 3(u^2 + uv + v^2)$, $\therefore u^2 + uv + v^2 = 6$.
But $u^2 - 2uv + v^2 = 9$, $\therefore 3 uv = -3$, $uv = -1$. Also, $(u + v)^2 = u^2 + 2uv + v^2 = (u-v)^2 + 4uv = 9 - 4 = 5$, $u + v = 5^{\frac{1}{2}}$, $u - v = 3$, so $2u = 3 + 5^{\frac{1}{2}}$.
Hence $(2u)^3 = 8u^3 = 72 + 32(5)^{\frac{1}{2}} = 8(x+9) = 8x + 72$ $\therefore x = 4(5)^{\frac{1}{2}}$, $x^2 = 80$.

Problem 19: Solution (Adding terms):
We add $2x^2$ to both sides of equation and re-write it as
$(3x^2 - 6x - 6) + x \cdot \sqrt{x^2 - 2x - 2} - 2x^2 = 0$
Or $3(\sqrt{x^2 - 2x - 2})^2 + x \cdot \sqrt{x^2 - 2x - 2} - 2x^2 = 0$
The above equation can be factored as:

$(3\sqrt{x^2 - 2x - 2} - 2x)(\sqrt{x^2 - 2x - 2} + x) = 0$.

For $3\sqrt{x^2 - 2x - 2} - 2x = 0$, the solutions are $x_{1,2} = \dfrac{9 \pm \sqrt{171}}{5}$.

For $\sqrt{x^2 - 2x - 2} + x = 0$, the solution is $x_3 = -1$.

We checked and know that all are the solutions: $\{-1, \dfrac{9 \pm \sqrt{171}}{5}\}$.

Problem 20: Solution (substitution):
Let $\sqrt{x^2 - 5x - 3} = y$. The original equation can be written as $y^2 - 2xy + x^2 = 16$ $\Rightarrow$ $(x - y)^2 = 16$. $\therefore x - y = \pm 4$.

Eliminating y we get: $x - \sqrt{x^2 - 5x - 3} = \pm 4$.

From $x - \sqrt{x^2 - 5x - 3} = 4$, we have $x_1 = \dfrac{19}{3}$.

From $x - \sqrt{x^2 - 5x - 3} = -4$, we have $x_2 = -\dfrac{19}{3}$.

We checked and know that both are the solutions. $\{-\dfrac{19}{3}, \dfrac{19}{3}\}$.

Problem 21: Solution:
The domain is $x \geq 1$. So the equation is equivalent to the equations below:

$\sqrt{x + \sqrt{x}} - \sqrt{x - \sqrt{x}} = \dfrac{3}{2}\sqrt{\dfrac{x}{x + \sqrt{x}}}$ $\Leftrightarrow$ $2x + 2\sqrt{x} - 2\sqrt{x^2 - x} = 3\sqrt{x}$ $\Leftrightarrow$

$2x - \sqrt{x} - 2\sqrt{x} \cdot \sqrt{x - 1} = 0$ $\Leftrightarrow$ $\sqrt{x}(2\sqrt{x} - 1 - 2\sqrt{x - 1}) = 0$ (note that $x \geq 1$)

$\Leftrightarrow 2\sqrt{x} - 1 - 2\sqrt{x - 1} = 0 \Leftrightarrow$ $\sqrt{x} = \dfrac{1}{2} + \sqrt{x - 1}$ $\Leftrightarrow$ $x = \dfrac{1}{4} + \sqrt{x - 1} + x - 1$ $\Leftrightarrow$

$\sqrt{x - 1} = \dfrac{3}{4}$ $\Leftrightarrow$ $x = \dfrac{25}{16}$ (≥ 1).

Therefore the solution to the original equation is $x = \dfrac{25}{16}$.

Problem 22: Solution:
Let $u = \sqrt{3x^2 + 5x + 8}$, $v = \sqrt{3x^2 + 5x + 1}$

So $u, v \geq 0$ and $\begin{cases} u - v = 1, \\ u^2 - v^2 = 7 \end{cases} \Leftrightarrow \begin{cases} u - v = 1, \\ u + v = 7 \end{cases} \Leftrightarrow \begin{cases} u = 4 \\ v = 3 \end{cases}$.

So the equation is equivalent to the equation $\sqrt{3x^2 + 5x + 8} = 4$.
Solving we get $x_1 = 1$, $x_2 = -\dfrac{8}{3}$.
These are indeed the solutions to the original equation.

Problem 23: Solution:
Let $u = \sqrt{x^2 + 3x + 12}$, $v = \sqrt{x^2 - x + 4}$

So $u, v \geq 0$ and $\begin{cases} u - v = 2, \\ u^2 - v^2 = 4x + 8 \end{cases} \Leftrightarrow \begin{cases} u - v = 2, \\ u + v = 2x + 4 \end{cases}$.

Adding together we get: $u = x + 3$.
So the equation is equivalent to the equation $\sqrt{x^2 + 3x + 12} = x + 3$.
Squaring both sides we have $\begin{cases} x^2 + 3x + 12 = x^2 + 6x + 9 \\ x + 3 \geq 0. \end{cases}$.

Solving we get $x = 1$.
These are indeed the solutions to the original equation.

Problem 24: Solution:
Let $\sqrt[3]{2 + x} = y$. We get: $x = y^3 - 3$.
The original equation is then $y = 1 - \sqrt{y^3 - 1}$;.
$\therefore y^3 - 1 = (1 - y)^2$ $\therefore (y - 1)(y^2 + 2) = 0$, $\therefore y = 1$.
Therefore $x = -1$.
We checked and $x = -1$ is indeed the solutions to the original equation.

Problem 25: Solution:
Since $x^3 + 5x^2 + 8x + 4 = (x^2 + 3x + 2)(x + 2) \geq 0$, $x + 2 \geq 0$.
Using the inequality $a^2 + b^2 \geq 2ab$ ($a, b \in R$), we have
$x^2 + 4x + 4 = (\sqrt{x^2 + 3x + 2})^2 + (\sqrt{x + 2})^2 \geq 2\sqrt{x^2 + 3x + 2} \cdot \sqrt{x + 2}$.

The original equation is equivalent to $\sqrt{x^2 + 3x + 2} = \sqrt{x + 2}$.
Solving for x: $x = 0$ or $x = -2$.
We checked and they are the solutions of the original equation.

PROBLEMS

Problem 1: (2000 AMC) If $|x - 2| = p$, where $x < 2$, then $x - p =$
(A) -2 (B) 2 (C) $2 - 2p$ (D) $2p - 2$ (E) $|2p - 2|$

Problem 2: Find all values of $a + b$ if $|a| = 1$ and $|b| = 2$.

Problem 3: Simplify $|a| + |b| + |a + b| + |b - c|$. The coordinates of a, b, and c are shown on the number line below.

Problem 4: Evaluate $a^2 - 2ab$ if $|a - 2| + |3 + b| = 0$.

Problem 5: Simplifying $|x + 3| - |2x - 5|$.

Problem 6: Simplifying $a + \left| \dfrac{1 - 2a + a^2}{a - 1} \right|$, ($a < 1$).

Problem 7: (1987 China Middle School Math Contest) What is the range of a if $|x| = ax + 1$ has one negative root and no positive root?
(A) $a > -1$. (B) $a = 1$. (C) $a \geq 1$. (D) None of them.

Problem 8: Which of the following figures in solid line represents the graph of $|y| = x^2 - 1$?

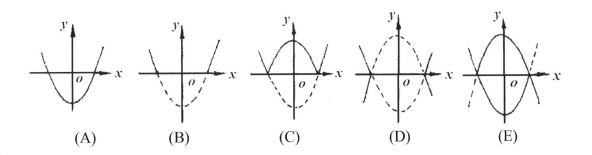

(A)　　　(B)　　　(C)　　　(D)　　　(E)

Problem 9: Find the expression of $f(m)$, where $f(m)$ is the number of real solutions to $|x^2 - 6x + 8| = m$.

Problem 10: Find the expression of $f(m)$, where $f(m)$ is the number of real solutions to $x^2 - 4|x| + 5 = m$.

Problem 11: Find the greatest and the smallest values of u if $|u+5| + |u-2| = 7$.

Problem 12: Find the greatest and the smallest values of x if the following expression is constant. $|x-1| + |x-2| + \ldots + |x-2002|$.

Problem 13: (1999 AMC) The graphs of $y = -|x-a| + b$ and $y = |x-c| + d$ intersect at points (2, 5) and (8, 3). Find $a + c$
(A) 7　　(B) 8　　(C) 10　　(D) 13　　(E) 18

Problem 14: Find $\dfrac{x_1 + x_2 - 1}{x_1 x_2}$ if x_1, x_2 are two roots to the equation $3x^2 - |x| - 4 = 0$.
(A) $\dfrac{1}{2}$　　(B) $\dfrac{9}{16}$　　(C) 1　　(D) $-\dfrac{1}{2}$

Problem 15: Find $a - 2001^2$ if $|2001 - a| + \sqrt{a - 2002} = a$.
(A) 2000.　　(B) 2001.　　(C) 2002.　　(D) 2003.

Problem 16: Find $|a+b+c| - |a-b-c| - |a-b+c| - |a+b-c|$ if a, b, and c are sides of a triangle.
(A) 0. (B) $2a + 2b + 2c$. (C) $4a$. (D) $2b - 2c$.

Problem 17: Find the sum of the two roots of $|1002x - 1002^2| = 1002^3$.

Problem 18: Find the smallest value of $f(x) = \left|x + \dfrac{4}{x}\right|$.

Problem 19: If $|a| - |b| = 1$ and $3|a| = 4|b|$, find the distance between a and b.

Problem 20: (1988 AIME) Suppose that $|x_i| < 1$ for $i = 1, 2, \ldots, n$. Suppose further that $|x_1| + |x_2| + \ldots + |x_n| = 19 + |x_1 + x_2 + \cdots + x_n|$. What is the smallest possible value of n?

Problem 21: (1998 AIME) The graph of $y^2 + 2xy + 40|x| = 400$ partitions the plane into several regions. What is the area of the bounded region?

Problem 22: Find the smallest value of $(x+y)^3$ if $|x| = 3$, $|y| = 2$, and $|x-y| = y - x$.

Problem 23: Find if $|x-y|^3 + |y-z|^3 + |z-x|^3$, and $|x-y|^{2001} + |z-x|^{2002} = 1$. x, y, and z are integers.

Problem 24: (1979 AMC) Find the area of the smallest region bounded by the graphs of $y = |x|$ and $x^2 + y^2 = 4$.
(A) $\dfrac{\pi}{4}$ (B) $\dfrac{3\pi}{4}$ (C) π (D) $\dfrac{3\pi}{2}$ (E) 2π

Problem 25: (1963 AMC) Given points $P_1, P_2, \ldots, P_7$ on a straight line, in the order stated (not necessarily evenly spaced). Let P be an arbitrarily selected point on the line and let s be the sum of the undirected lengths
$$PP_1, \ PP_2, \ \cdots, \ PP_7.$$
Then s is smallest if and only if the point P is:
(A) midway between P_1 and P_7 \qquad (B) midway between P_2 and P_6
(C) midway between P_3 and P_6 \qquad (D) at P_4 \qquad (E) at P_1

Problem 26: Find the greatest value of $u = |x_1 - 1| + |x_2 - 2| + \ldots + |x_n - n|$ if $x_1, x_2, \ldots x_n$ are any arrangement of positive integers from 1 to n.

Problem 27: Find b if $\left|x^2 + 2x - 1\right| = b$ has four distinct solutions.

Problem 28: Find k if the graphs of $f(x) = \left|-x^2 + 4x - 3\right|$ and $y = kx$ have three points of intersection.

Problem 29: What is the greatest value of $y = |x+2| + |x-1| - |3x-6|$?

Problem 30: (1996 AIME) For each permutation $a_1, a_2, a_3, \ldots, a_{10}$, of the integers 1, 2, 3, ..., 10, form the sum $|a_1 - a_2| + |a_3 - a_4| + |a_5 - a_6| + |a_7 - a_8| + |a_9 - a_{10}|$.
The average value of all such sums can be written in the form $\dfrac{p}{q}$, where p and q are relatively prime positive integers. Find $p + q$.

SOLUTIONS

Problem 1: Solution: (C).
Since $x < 2$, it follows that $|x - 2| = 2 - x$. If $2 - x = p$, then $x = 2 - p$.
Thus $x - p = 2 - 2p$.

Problem 2: Solution: $1, 3, -1, -3$.
We need to get rid of the absolute value signs
$|a| = 1 \quad \Rightarrow \quad a = \pm 1$
$|b| = 2 \quad \Rightarrow \quad b = \pm 2$
When $a = 1$ and $b = 2$, $a + b = 3$
When $a = -1$ and $b = 2$, $a + b = 1$
When $a = 1$ and $b = -2$, $a + b = -1$
When $a = -1$ and $b = -2$, $a + b = -3$

Problem 3: Solution: $b + c$
Since $a < 0, b > 0, c > b. b > a$.
$|a| + |b| + |a + b| + |b - c| = (-a) + b + (b + a) + c - b = b + c$.

Problem 4: Solution: 16.
Since $|a - 2| \geq 0$ and $|3 + b| \geq 0$ and $|a - 2| + |3 + b| = 0$, so $|a - 2| = 0$ and $|3 + b| = 0$
$a = 2$ and $b = -3$
$a^2 - 2ab = 2^2 - 2 \times 2 \times (-3) = 16$

Problem 5: Solution:
Case I: $x < -3$.
$|x + 3| - |2x - 5| = -x - 3 + 2x - 5 = x - 8$.
Case II: $-3 \leq x < \dfrac{5}{2}$.
$|x + 3| - |2x - 5| = x + 3 + 2x - 5 = 3x - 2$.
Case III: $\dfrac{5}{2} \leq x$.
$|x + 3| - |2x - 5| = x + 3 - 2x + 5 = -x + 8$.

Problem 6: Simplifying $a + \left|\dfrac{1-2a+a^2}{a-1}\right|$, ($a < 1$).

Solution: 1.

$$a + \left|\dfrac{1-2a+a^2}{a-1}\right| = a + \left|\dfrac{(1-a)^2}{1-a}\right| = a + 1 - a = 1$$

Problem 7: Solution: (C).
Graph $y = |x|$ and $y = ax + 1$.

For $y = ax + 1$, only when the slope $a \geq 1$, it intercepts one branch of $y = |x|$ in the second quadrant and not intercepts another branch in the first quadrant.

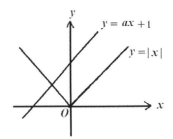

Problem 8: Solution:
We know that $|y| = x^2 - 1$ and $|y| \geq 0$. Hence $x^2 - 1 \geq 0$. Therefore there is no graph when $x^2 - 1 < 0$. That is, no solid line when $-1 < x < 1$. So we exclude the answers (A), (C), (E).
From $|y| = x^2 - 1$, we have $y = x^2 - 1$ and $-y = x^2 - 1$. The graphs of them are as follows:
Since there is no solid line when $-1 < x < 1$, we know that (D) is the answer.

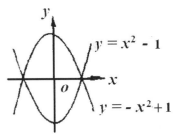

Problem 9: Solution:
Let $f_1(x) = |x^2 - 6x + 8|$. C_1 is the graph of $f_1(x)$:

Then the number of real solutions is the number of intersection points of C_1 and the line $l : y = m$.

When $m = 0$ or $m > 1$, C_1 and l have two points of intersection.

When $m < 0$, C_1 and l have no points of intersection.

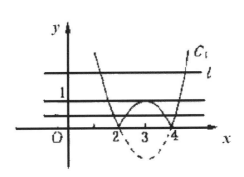

When $m = 1$, C_1 and l have three points of intersection.
When $0 < m < 1$, C_1 and l have four points of intersection.
Therefore we have the following expression for $f(m)$:

$$f(m) = \begin{cases} 0, & m < 0; \\ 2, & m = 0 \text{ or } m > 1; \\ 3, & m = 1 \\ 4, & 0 < m < 1. \end{cases}$$

Problem 10: Solution:
Let $f_1(x) = x^2 - 4|x| + 5$. C_1 is the graph of $f_1(x)$:

Then the number of real solutions is the number of intersection points of C_1 and the line l: $y = m$.

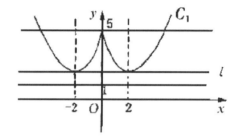

Therefore we have the following expression for $f(m)$:

$$f(m) = \begin{cases} 0, & m < 1; \\ 2, & m = 1 \text{ or } m > 5; \\ 3, & m = 5 \\ 4, & 1 < m < 5. \end{cases}$$

Problem 11: Solution: 2 and -5.

Problem 12: Solution: $x_{min} = 1001$, $x_{max} = 1002$.

Problem 13: Solution: (C).
Use the given information to obtain the equations $5 = -|2 - a| + b$, $5 = |2 - c| + d$, $3 = -|8 - a| + b$, and $3 = |8 - c| + d$. Subtract the third from the first to eliminate b and subtract the fourth from the second to eliminate d. The two resulting equations $|8 - a| - |2 - a| = 2$ and $|2 - c| - |8 - c| = 2$ can be solved for a and c. To solve the former, first consider all $a \leq 2$, for which the equation reduces to $8 - a - (2 - a) = 2$, which has no solutions. Then consider all a in the interval $2 \leq a \leq 8$, for which the equation reduces to $8 - a - (2 - a) = 2$, which yields $a = 4$. Finally, consider all $a \geq 8$, for which the equation

reduces to $a - 8 - (a - 2) = 2$, which has no solutions. The other equation can be solved similarly to show that $c = 6$. Thus $a + c = 10$.

Problem 14: Solution:
The equation can be written as $3|x|^2 - |x| - 4 = 0$.

∴ $(3|x| - 4)(|x| + 1) = 0$.

We know that $|x| + 1 > 0$, ∴ $3|x| - 4 = 0$.

∴ $|x| = \dfrac{4}{3}$ ⇒ $x_1 = \dfrac{4}{3}, \ x_2 = -\dfrac{4}{3}$.

∴ $\dfrac{x_1 + x_2 - 1}{x_1 x_2} = \dfrac{\dfrac{4}{3} + (-\dfrac{4}{3}) - 1}{\dfrac{4}{3}(-\dfrac{4}{3})} = \dfrac{9}{16}$.

Problem 15: Solution: (C).

We see that $\sqrt{a - 2002} \geq 0$. So $a \geq 2002$.
$|2001 - a| + \sqrt{a - 2002} = a$ can then be written as $a - 2001 + \sqrt{a - 2002} = a$, or
$\sqrt{a - 2002} = 2001$ ⇒ $a - 2002 = 2001^2$ ⇒ $a - 2001^2 = 2002$.

Problem 16: Solution: (A).
Since a, b, and c are sides of a triangle, the sum of any two will be greater than the third side. Thus we get:
$|a - b - c| = |a - (b + c)| = |(b + c) - a| = b + c - a$.
$|a - b + c| = |a + c - b| = a + c - b$.
$|a + b - c| = a + b - c$.
So $|a + b + c| - |a - b - c| - |a - b + c| - |a + b - c|$
$= a + b + c - (b + c - a) - (a + c - b) - (a + b - c) = 0$

Problem 17: Solution: 2004.
$1002x - 1002^2 = 1002^3$ ⇒ $x - 1002 = 1002^2$ ⇒ $x_1 = 1002^2 + 1002$
$1002x - 1002^2 = -1002^3$ ⇒ $x - 1002 = -1002^2$ ⇒ $x_2 = -1002^2 + 1002$
$x_1 + x_2 = 1002 + 1002 = 2004$.

Problem 18: Solution:

We know that x, $\dfrac{4}{x}$ have the same signs,

$$\therefore f(x) = \left|x + \dfrac{4}{x}\right| = |x| + \dfrac{4}{|x|} = \left(\sqrt{|x|} - \dfrac{2}{\sqrt{|x|}}\right)^2 + 4 \geq 4.$$

The equality holds when $\sqrt{|x|} - \dfrac{2}{\sqrt{|x|}} = 0 \Rightarrow x = \pm 2$.

Therefore $f(x)$ has the smallest value 4 when $x = \pm 2$.

Problem 19: Solution: 1 or 7.

From $|a| - |b| = 1$, we have $|a| = |b| + 1$ \hfill (1)

Substituting (1) into $3|a| = 4|b|$: $3|b| + 3 = 4|b|$ $\Rightarrow$ $|b| = 3$.

So $b = 3$ or $b = -3$.

Substituting $b = 3$ or $b = -3$ into (1): $|a| = 3 + 1 = 4 \Rightarrow$ $a = 4$ or $a = -4$.

So the distance between a and b is either 1 or 7.

Problem 20: Solution:

We have $|x_i| < 1$. $i = 1, 2, \ldots, n$.

We also know that $\left|\sum\limits_{i=1}^{n} x_i\right| \geq 0$.

$$\sum_{i=1}^{n}|x_i| - \left|\sum_{i=1}^{n} x_i\right| \leq \sum_{i=1}^{n}|x_i| < n$$

$$\sum_{i=1}^{n}|x_i| - \left|\sum_{i=1}^{n} x_i\right| = 19$$

So $n > 19$.

When $n = 20$, $x_i = \begin{cases} 0.95 & \text{even } i \\ -0.95 & \text{odd } i \end{cases}$, which satisfies the given conditions.

Thus the smallest n is 20.

Problem 21: Solution:

When $x \geq 0$, we have $y^2 + 2xy + 40x = 400$

$\Rightarrow$ $(y + 20)(y + 2x - 20) = 0$.

Therefore $y = -20$ or $y = -2x + 20$ $(x \geq 0)$.

When $x \leq 0$, we have $y^2 + 2xy - 40x = 400$

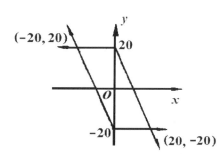

$\Rightarrow$ $(y - 20)(y + 2x + 20) = 0$.
We get $y = 20$ or $y = -2x - 20$ $(x \le 0)$.
The figure is a parallelogram with base 20 and height 40. The area is then 800.

Problem 22: Solution:
Since $|x - y| \ge 0$, $y - x \ge 0$, $y \ge x$.
We know that $|x| = 3$, $|y| = 2$, then $x < 0$.
Case I: $y = 2$, $x + y = -1$ $\Rightarrow$ $(x + y)^3 = -1$.
Case II: $y = -2$, $x + y = -5$ $\Rightarrow$ $(x + y)^3 = -125$.
The smallest value of $(x + y)^3$ is -125.

Problem 23: Solution:
Since x, y, and z are integers, $x - y$, $z - x$ are integers.
$|x - y|^{2001} \ge 0$ and $|z - x|^{2002} \ge 0$ are integers.
We know that $|x - y|^{2001} + |z - x|^{2002} = 1$.
Therefore we have

Case I: (1) $\begin{cases} |x - y|^{2001} = 0, \\ |z - x|^{2001} = 1, \end{cases}$ $\Rightarrow$ $\begin{cases} x = y \\ z - x = \pm 1 \end{cases}$ $\Rightarrow$ $|y - z| = |z - x| = 1$ $\Rightarrow$

$|x - y|^3 + |y - z|^3 + |z - x|^3 = 0^3 + 1^3 + 1^3 = 2$.

Case II: (2) $\begin{cases} |x - y|^{2001} = 1 \\ |z - x|^{2002} = 0 \end{cases}$ $\Rightarrow$ $\begin{cases} z = x \\ x - y = \pm 1 \end{cases}$ $\Rightarrow$ $|x - y| = |y - z| = 1$.

$|x - y|^3 + |y - z|^3 + |z - x|^3 = 2$.
Hence $|x - y|^3 + |y - z|^3 + |z - x|^3 = 2$.

Problem 24: Solution: (C).
The area of the smallest region bounded by $y = |x|$ and $x^2 + y^2 = 4$ is shown in the adjoining figure. Its area is
$\frac{1}{4}(\pi 2)^2 = \pi$.

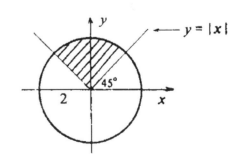

Problem 25: Solution: (D).
We conclude: If n is even, the point P that minimizes f may be taken anywhere on the segment $P_{n/2}P_{(n/2)+1}$, and if n is odd, P must be taken at $P_{(n+1)/2}$. In particular, if $n = 7$, choose P to coincide with P_4.

Problem 26: Solution:
The smaller the number subtracted, the greater the sum u.
When $n = 2k$, the greatest u is
$u = n + n + \ldots + (k+1) + (k+1) - k - k - \ldots - 1 - 1$
$= 2(1 + 2 + \ldots + n) - 4(1 + 2 + 3 + \ldots + k) = n(n+1) - 2k(k+1) = \dfrac{1}{2}n^2$.

When $n = 2k + 1$, the greatest u is
$u = n + n + \ldots + (k+2) + (k+2) + (k+1) - (k+1) - k - k - \ldots - 1 - 1$
$= 2(1 + 2 + \ldots + n) - 4(1 + 2 + 3 + \ldots + k) - 2(k+1) = (2k+2)k = \dfrac{1}{2}(n^2 - 1)$.

In summary, $u_{max} = \begin{cases} \dfrac{1}{2}n^2, & \text{even } n \\ \dfrac{1}{2}(n^2 - 1), & \text{odd } n \end{cases}$.

Problem 27: Solution:
Graph $y = |x^2 + 2x - 1|$ and $y = b$.
$y = |(x+1)^2 - 2| = \begin{cases} (x+1)^2 & \text{when } (x-1)^2 - 2 \geq 0 \\ 2 - (x+1)^2 & \text{when } (x-1)^2 - 2 < 0 \end{cases}$

The number of solutions of $|x^2 + 2x - 1| = b$ is the same as the number of intersections of $y = |x^2 + 2x - 1|$ and $y = b$.
We see from the graph that $0 < b < 2$.

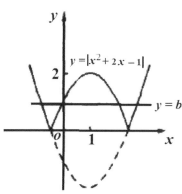

Problem 28: Solution:
If $f(x) = |-x^2 + 4x - 3|$ and $y = kx$ have three points of intersection, the graph of $y = kx$ in the region $[1, 3]$ needs to have only one pint of intersection, that is, the equation $-x^2 + 4x - 3 = kx$ have double roots. Hence $\Delta = (4-k)^2 - 12 = 0$. $k = 4 - 2\sqrt{3}$. Note that another value of k is extraneous.

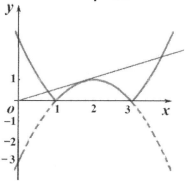

Thus the graph consists of four lines with slopes -3, -1, 1, and 3, and it has corners at $(a, b + c - 2a)$, $(b, c - a)$, and $(c, 2c - a - b)$. On the other hand, the graph of $2x + y = 2003$ is line whose slope is -2. If the graphs intersect at exactly one point, that point must be $(a, b + c - 2a)$. Therefore $2003 = 2a + (b + c - 2a) = b + c$.
Since $b < c$, the minimum value of c is 1002.

Problem 29: Solution: 5.
The greatest value is achieved when $|3x - 6|$ is zero. So $x = 2$.
$y = |x + 2| + |x - 1| - |3x - 6| = 4 + 1 - 0 = 5$.

Problem 30: Solution:

The average is just 5 times the average value of $|a_1 - a_2|$, because the average value of $|a_{2i-1} - a_{2i}|$ is the same for $i = 1, 2, 3, 4, 5$. When $a_1 = k$, the average value of $|a_1 - a_2|$ is

$$\frac{(k-1) + (k-2) + \ldots + 1 + 1 + 2 + \ldots + (10-k)}{9}$$

$$= \frac{1}{9}\left[\frac{k(k-1)}{2} + \frac{(10-k)(11-k)}{2}\right] = \frac{k^2 - 11k + 55}{9}.$$

Thus the average value of the sum is $5\frac{1}{10}\sum_{k=1}^{10}\frac{k^2 - 11k + 55}{9} = \frac{55}{3}$, and so $p + q = 58$.

PROBLEMS

Problem 1: Solve $x^2 - |x| - 1 = 0$.
(A) $\dfrac{1 \pm \sqrt{5}}{2}$.   (B) $\dfrac{-1 \pm \sqrt{5}}{2}$.   (C) $\dfrac{1 \pm \sqrt{5}}{2}$ or $\dfrac{-1 \pm \sqrt{5}}{2}$.   (D) $\pm\dfrac{1 + \sqrt{5}}{2}$.

Problem 2: How many distinct real roots are there for the equation $x|x| - 3|x-1| = 1$?
(A) 1   (B) 2   (C) 3   (D) 4

Problem 3: Solve for x: $|3x - 2| = 3 - 2x$.

Problem 4: Solve: $|x+1| + \dfrac{1}{2}|2x - 3| = 5x + 2$.

Problem 5: Solve for x: $|2x + 3| + |x - 1| = |3x + 2|$.

Problem 6: (1994 AMC) If x and y are non-zero real numbers such that $|x| + y = 3$ and $|x|y + x^3 = 0$, then the integer nearest to $x - y$ is
(A) -3 (B) -1 (C) 2 (D) 3 (E) 5

Problem 7: Find the sum of the roots of $x^2 - 2013|x| = 2013$.

Problem 8: Solve the following system of equations $\begin{cases} |x-2| + |y-5| = 7 \\ |x-2| = y - 6 \end{cases}$

Problem 9: Solve the following system of equations
$\begin{cases} |x+1| + |y-1| = 5 & (1), \\ |x+1| = 4y - 4 & (2). \end{cases}$

Problem 10: Solve $x^2 - |2x - 1| - 4 = 0$.

SOLUTIONS

Problem 1: Solution: (D).
$x^2 = |x|^2$. The given equation can be written as $|x|^2 - |x| - 1 = 0$.
So $|x| = \frac{1+\sqrt{5}}{2}$. (Note $x = \frac{1-\sqrt{5}}{2} < 0$ has been ignored).
$x = \pm \frac{1+\sqrt{5}}{2}$.

Problem 2: Solution: (B).
The original equation can be written as $x|x| = 3|x-1| + 1$. (1)
We know that $3|x-1| + 1 > 0$.
$\therefore x|x| > 0$, $\qquad \therefore x > 0$.

Equation (1) becomes: $x^2 = 3|x-1| + 1$.
$\therefore x^2 - 1 = 3|x-1|$, $\qquad \therefore x^2 - 1 \geq 0$.
$\therefore (x+1)(x-1) \geq 0$
Since $x > 0$, $x + 1 > 0 \Rightarrow x - 1 \geq 0$.
Hence the original equation can be written as $x^2 - 3(x-1) = 1$.
$\therefore x^2 - 3x + 2 = 0$, $\qquad \therefore x_1 = 1, x_2 = 2$.

Problem 3: Solution:
Squaring both sides:
$9x^2 - 12x + 4 = 9 - 12x + 4x^2$
$\therefore 5x^2 = 5$, $\qquad x = \pm 1$

Problem 4: Solution:
$[(x+1) + (x-\frac{3}{2}) + (5x+2)] \cdot [(x+1) - (x-\frac{3}{2}) + (5x+2)]$
$\cdot [(x+1) + (x-\frac{3}{2}) - (5x+2)] \cdot [(x+1) - (x-\frac{3}{2}) - (5x+2)] = 0$
$\Rightarrow (7x + \frac{3}{2})(5x + \frac{9}{2})(-3x - \frac{5}{2}) \cdot (-5x + \frac{1}{2}) = 0 \Rightarrow x = -\frac{3}{14}, -\frac{9}{10}, -\frac{5}{6}, \frac{1}{10}$.

Problem 5: Solution:
Method 1:

Case I: $x < -\dfrac{3}{2}$.

The original equation can be written as
$$-(2x+3) - (x-1) = -(3x+2).$$
Or $-3x - 2 = -3x - 2$.
$x < -\dfrac{3}{2}$.

Case II: $-\dfrac{3}{2} \leq x < -\dfrac{2}{3}$.

The original equation can be written as $2x + 3 - (x-1) = -(3x+2) \Rightarrow 4x = -6$.
$\therefore x = -\dfrac{3}{2}$.

Case III: $-\dfrac{3}{2} \leq x < 1$.

The original equation can be written as $2x + 3 - (x-1) = 3x + 2 \Rightarrow 2x = 2$.
$\therefore x = 1$ (extraneous solution).

Case IV: $1 \leq x$

The original equation can be written as $2x + 3 + x - 1 = 3x + 2 \Rightarrow 3x + 2 = 3x + 2$.
$\therefore x \geq 1$.

The solutions are then any real number satisfying $x \geq 1$ and $x \leq -\dfrac{3}{2}$.

Method 2:

We know that $(2x+3) + (x-1) = 3x + 2$ and $|2x+3| + |x-1| = |3x+2|$.

Based on the property $|A| + |B| \geq |A+B|$, the equality holds if and only if A and B have the same sign or one of them is zero.

(1) $2x + 3 = 0$, $\therefore x = -\dfrac{3}{2}$;

(2) $x - 1 = 0$, $\therefore x = 1$;

(3) $\begin{cases} 2x + 3 > 0, \\ x - 1 > 0, \end{cases}$ $\therefore x > 1$;

(4) $\begin{cases} 2x + 3 < 0, \\ x - 1 < 0, \end{cases}$ $\therefore x < -\dfrac{3}{2}$.

The solutions are then any real number satisfying $x \geq 1$ and $x \leq -\frac{3}{2}$.

Problem 6:
Solution: (A).
If $x > 0$, then $|x| = x$.
The original equations become:
$$\begin{cases} x + y = 3 & (1) \\ xy + x^3 = 0 & (2) \end{cases}$$
Substituting (1) into (2), we get: $x^3 - x^2 + 3x = 0$ \hfill (3)
Sinc x and y are non-zero real numbers, we can divided both sides of (3) by x:
$$x^2 - x + 3 = 0 \quad (4)$$
(4) has no real solutions since $\Delta = (-1)^2 - 4 \times 1 \times 3 = -11 < 0$.
If $x < 0$, then $|x| = -x$. $|x| + y = 3 \quad \Rightarrow \quad -x + y = 3 \quad \Rightarrow \quad x - y = -3$.

Problem 7: Solution:
If x_0 is a root, then $-x_0$ is also a root. So the sum of them is 0.

Problem 8: Solution:
We know that $y - 6 = |x - 2| \geq 0$, so $y \geq 6$. Then $y - 5 = \geq 0$ and $|y - 5| = y - 5$.
Therefore we have two cases:

Case I: when $x \geq 2$, the original equations can be written as:
$$\begin{cases} x - 2 + y - 5 = 7 \\ x - 2 = y - 6 \end{cases} \Rightarrow \begin{cases} x = 5 \\ y = 9 \end{cases}.$$

Case II: when $x < 2$, the original equations can be written as:
$$\begin{cases} -(x-2) + y - 5 = 7 \\ -(x-2) = y - 6 \end{cases} \Rightarrow \begin{cases} x = -1 \\ y = 9 \end{cases}.$$

The solutions are $\begin{cases} x = 5 \\ y = 9 \end{cases}$ and $\begin{cases} x = -1 \\ y = 9 \end{cases}$.

Problem 9: Solution:
Since $|x + 1| = 4(y - 1) \geq 0$,.
Substituting (2) into (1): $4y - 4 + y - 1 = 5$, $5y = 10$, $y = 2$.
Substituting $y = 2$ into (1): $|x + 1| = 4$.

Therefore $x = 3$, or $x = -5$.
The solutions are $(3, 2), (-5, 2)$.

Problem 10: Solution:
Case I: $2x - 1 \geq 0$.
We have $x \geq \dfrac{1}{2}$.
$x^2 - (2x - 1) - 4 = 0 \Rightarrow x^2 - 2x - 3 = 0$.
$x_1 = 3$ or $x_2 = -1$ (extraneous)

Case II: $2x - 1 < 0$.
We have $x < \dfrac{1}{2}$.
$x^2 + 2x - 1 - 4 = 0 \Rightarrow x^2 + 2x - 5 = 0$.
$x_3 = -1 + \sqrt{6}$ (extraneous), or $x_4 = -1 - \sqrt{6}$.
The solution is $x = 3$ or $x = -1 - \sqrt{6}$.

50 AMC Lectures Problems Book 1   (6) Vieta Theorem and Applications

PROBLEMS

Problem 1: (1960 AMC) For a given value of k the product of the roots of $x^2 - 3kx + 2k^2 - 1 = 0$ is 7. The roots may be characterized as:
(A) integral and positive   (B) integral and negative   (C) rational, but not integral
(D) irrational   (E) imaginary

Problem 2: (AMC 1955) If r and s are the roots of $x^2 - px + q = 0$, then $r^2 + s^2$ equals:
(A) $p^2 + 2q$ (B) $p^2 - 2q$ (C) $p^2 + q^2$ (D) $p^2 - q^2$ (E) p^2

Problem 3: (1963 AMC 14) Given the equations $x^2 + kx + 6 = 0$ and $x^2 - kx + 6 = 0$. If, when the roots of the equations are suitably listed, each root of the second equation is 5 more than the corresponding root of the first equation, then k equals:
(A) 5   (B) -5 (C) 7   (D) -7 (E) none of these

Problem 4: a and b are two roots of quadratic equation $x^2 + (m-2)x + 1 = 0$. The value of $(1 + ma + a^2)(1 + mb + b^2)$ is

(A) 1   (B) 2   (C) 3   (D) 4.

Problem 5: Find $\alpha^4 + 3\beta$ if α and β are two real roots of quadratic equation $x^2 - x - 1 = 0$.

Problem 6: Find integers p and q if two roots α and β of equation $x^2 - 3x + 1 = 0$ is also the roots of $x^6 - px + q = 0$.

Problem 7: Solve $2x^2 - 8nx + 10x - n^2 + 35n - 76 = 0$. n is positive integer and both of the roots of the equation are prime numbers.

Problem 8: The sum of two numbers is 20 and the product is 22. Find these two numbers.

Problem 9: Find k such that $x_1^2 + x_2^2$ is the smallest if x_1 and x_2 are two real roots of $x^2 - kx + 2k - 3 = 0$.

Problem 10: Find $\alpha^4 + \beta^4$ if α and β are two roots of the equation $x^2 + px + q = 0$.

Problem 11: Two roots of $2x^3 + 3x^2 - 23x - 12 = 0$ are 3 and -4. Find the third root.

Problem 12: If $f(2x+1) = 4x^2 + 14x$, find the sum of the roots of $f(x) = 0$. (2003 North Carolina State Mathematics Contest).

Problem 13: If a, b and c are the zeros, possibly complex, of the polynomial $5x^3 + 1440x^2 - 120x + 8$, what is the absolute value of $\dfrac{1}{a} + \dfrac{1}{b} + \dfrac{1}{c}$? (2007 North Carolina State Mathematics Contest).

Problem 14: Solve:

$$\begin{cases} x + y + z = 3, & (1) \\ x^2 + y^2 + z^2 = 3, & (2) \\ x^3 + y^3 + z^3 = 3. & (3) \end{cases}$$

Problem 15: Find q if the square of the difference of two roots for $x^2 - 2x + q = 0$ is 16.

Problem 16: Find $\dfrac{1}{\alpha^2} + \dfrac{1}{\beta^2}$ if α and β are two roots of the equation $x^2 - x - 3 = 0$

Problem 17: Find $\alpha^2 + \beta^2 + \gamma^2$ if α, β, and γ are three roots of the equation $x^3 - 2x^2 - 3x - 1 = 0$.

Problem 18: How many distinct ordered triples (x, y, z) satisfy the equations

$$x + 2y + 4z = 6$$
$$x^2 + 4y^2 + 9z^2 = 14$$
$$x^3 + 8y^3 + 27z^3 = 36$$

Problem 19: (1975 AMC 22) If p and q are primes and $x^2 - px + q = 0$ has distinct positive integral roots, then which of the following statements are true?
I. The difference of the roots is odd.
II. At least one root is prime.
III. $p^2 - q$ is prime.
IV. $p + q$ is prime.
(A) I only (B) II only (C) II and III only (D) I, II and IV only (E) All are true.

Problem 20: (1977 AMC 23) If the solutions of the equation $x^2 + px + q = 0$ are the cubes of the solutions of the equation $x^2 + mx + n = 0$, then
(A) $p = m^3 + 3mn$ (B) $p = m^3 - 3mn$ (C) $p + q = m^3$
(D) $(\frac{m}{n})^3 = \frac{p}{q}$ (E) none of these

Problem 21: (1991 AIME 8) For how many real numbers a does the quadratic equation $x^2 + ax + 6a = 0$ have only integer roots for x?

Problem 22: (1977 USAMO) If a and b are two of the roots of $x^4 + x^3 - 1 = 0$, prove that ab is a root of $x^6 + x^4 + x^3 - x^2 - 1 = 0$.

SOLUTIONS TO PROBLEMS

Problem 1: Solution:
The product of the roots, here, is equal to $2k^2 - 1$.
$\therefore 2k^2 - 1 = 7$, $k^2 = 4$.

Problem 2: Solution:
$r^2 + s^2 = (r+s)^2 - 2rs = p^2 - 2q$.

Problem 3: Solution:
(A) Let the roots of the first equation be r and s. Then $r + s = -k$ and $rs = 6$. Then, for the second equation, $r + 5 + s + 5 = k$ and $(r+5)(s+5) = 6$. Therefore $rs + 5(r+s) + 25 = 6$, $6 + 5(-k) + 25 = 6$, $k = 5$.

Problem 4: Solution: D.
We have $a^2 + (m-2)a + 1 = 0$ and $b^2 + mb + 1 = 2b$.
So $(1 + ma + a^2)(1 + mb + b^2) = 2a \cdot 2b = 4ab$.

According to Vieta Theorem, $ab = 1$
So $(1 + ma + a^2)(1 + mb + b^2) = 4$.

Problem 5: Solution:
Method 1:
From Vieta Theroem, $\alpha + \beta = 1$.
Since α is a root of $x^2 - x - 1 = 0$, $\alpha^2 - \alpha - 1 = 0$
$\therefore \alpha^4 + 3\beta = \alpha^4 + 3(1-\alpha) + 3 = \alpha^4 - 3\alpha + 3$
$= \alpha^2(\alpha^2 - \alpha - 1) + \alpha(\alpha^2 - \alpha - 1) + 2(\alpha^2 - \alpha - 1) + 5 = 5$.

Method 2:
By Vieta Theorem, α + β = 1.
Since α is a root of $x^2 - x - 1 = 0$, $\alpha^2 - \alpha - 1 = 0$.
$\therefore \alpha^4 + 3\beta = (\alpha+1)^2 + 3\beta = \alpha^2 + 2\alpha + 1 + 3\beta = (\alpha+1) + 2\alpha + 1 + 3\beta = 3(\alpha+\beta) + 2 = 5$.

Problem 6: Solution:
By Vieta Theorem, $\alpha + \beta = 3$, $\alpha\beta = 1$.
$\alpha^2 + \beta^2 = (\alpha+\beta)^2 - 2\alpha\beta = 7$
$\alpha^4 + \beta^4 = (\alpha^2 + \beta^2)^2 - 2\alpha^2\beta^2 = 47$

Since α and β are also roots of $x^6 - px + q = 0$,
$$\alpha^6 - p\alpha^2 + q = 0, \qquad (1)$$
$$\beta^6 - p\beta^2 + q = 0. \qquad (2)$$
$(1) - (2)$: $p = \dfrac{\alpha^6 - \beta^6}{\alpha^2 - \beta^2} = \alpha^4 + \alpha^2\beta^2 + \beta^4 = 48$.

$(2) \times \alpha^2 - (1) \times \beta^2$:
$(\alpha^2 - \beta^2)q + \alpha^2\beta^6 - \alpha^6\beta^2 = 0$
$q = \dfrac{\alpha^2\beta^2(\alpha^4 - \beta^4)}{\alpha^2 - \beta^2} = \alpha^2\beta^2(\alpha^2 + \beta^2) = 7$.

Problem 7: Solution:
Let α and β be the roots.
By Vieta Theorem
$$\alpha + \beta = -\dfrac{10 - 8n}{2} = 4n - 5. \qquad (1)$$
We know that α and β are prime numbers and $4n - 5$ is odd. One of α and β must be 2. Substituting 2 into the original equation:

$$2 \times 2^2 - 16n + 20 - n^2 + 35n - 76 = 0.$$

Simplifying to: $n^2 - 19n + 48 = 0$.
Solve for n: $n_1 = 16$, $n_2 = 3$.
When $n = 16$ $\Rightarrow$ $x_1 = 2, x_2 = 57$
When $n = 3$ $\Rightarrow$ $x_1 = 2, x_2 = 5$.

Problem 8: Solution:
We see these two numbers as the roots of an unknown equation.
By Converse of Vieta Theorem, $x^2 - 10x + 22 = 0$

Solve: $x_1 = 5 + \sqrt{3}$, $x_2 = 5 - \sqrt{3}$.

Problem 9: Solution:
If $x^2 - kx + 2k - 3 = 0$ has two real roots, $\Delta \geq 0$.
$k^2 - 4(2k - 3) \geq 0$

Solve the above inequality: $k \leq 2$ or $k \geq 6$.

$x_1^2 + x_2^2 = (x_1 + x_2)^2 - 2x_1 x_2$.

By Vieta Theorem,
$x_1 + x_2 = k$, $x_1 \cdot x_2 = 2k - 3$.
$\therefore \quad x_1^2 + x_2^2 = k^2 - 4k + 6$

In order for $x_1^2 + x_2^2$ to be the minimum, we have $k = -\dfrac{b}{2a} = \dfrac{4}{2} = 2$.

Problem 10: Solution:
$\alpha^4 + \beta^4 = (\alpha^2 + \beta^2)^2 - 2\alpha^2\beta^2 = [(\alpha + \beta)^2 - 2\alpha\beta]^2 - 2(\alpha\beta)^2$
$= [(-p)^2 - 2q]^2 - 2q^2 = p^4 - 4p^2 q + 2q^2$.

Problem 11: Solution:
Let the third root be x_3.

Method 1:
$3 + (-4) + x_3 = -\dfrac{3}{2}$

$\therefore \quad x_3 = -\dfrac{3}{2} - 3 + 4 = -\dfrac{1}{2}$.

Method 2:
$x_3 \cdot 3 \cdot (-4) = (-1)^3 \cdot (-\dfrac{12}{2})$.

$x_3 = \dfrac{6}{3(-4)} = -\dfrac{1}{2}$.

Problem 12: Solution:
$f(2x+1) = 4x^2 + 14x \Rightarrow f(x) = f[2(\dfrac{x-1}{2})+1]$

$f(x) = 4(\dfrac{x-1}{2})^2 + 14(\dfrac{x-1}{2}) = x^2 - 2x + 1 + 7x - 7 = x^2 + 5x - 6$

The sum of the root is $x_1 + x_2 = -\dfrac{5}{1} = -5$.

Problem 13: Solution: 15.
$1/a + 1/b + 1/c = (ab + ac + bc)/(abc) = (-120/5)/(-8/5) = 15$.

$$\frac{1}{a}+\frac{1}{b}+\frac{1}{c}=\frac{(ab+ac+bc)}{(abc)}=\frac{(-\frac{120}{5})}{(-\frac{8}{5})}=15.$$

Problem 14: Solution:

(1)² – (2): $xy+yz+zx=\frac{1}{2}[(x+y+z)^2-(x^2+y^2+z^2)]=3.$ \quad (4)

(2) – (4):
$x^2+y^2+z^2-(xy+yz+zx)=0.$ \quad (5)

(1) × (5):
$x^3+y^3+z^3-3xyz=0.$ \quad (6)

(6) – (3): $xyz=1.$ \quad (7)

From (1), (4), and (7), we know that x, y, and z are the three roots of the equation $u^3-3u^2+3u-1=0$.

Since $u^3-3u^2+3u-1=(u-1)^3$, $(u-1)^3=0$.
∴ $u_1=1$, $u_2=1$, $u_3=1$.
∴ $x=1$, $y=1$, $z=1$.

Problem 15: Solution:
Let x_1 and x_2 be the two roots of the equation.
$x_1+x_2=2$, $x_1x_2=q$.
We are given that $(x_1-x_2)^2=16$
By Vieta Theorem, $(x_1+x_2)^2-4x_1x_2=16$
∴ $2^2-4q=16$, $q=-3$.

Problem 16: Solution:
$\frac{1}{\alpha^2}+\frac{1}{\beta^2}=\frac{7}{9}$

Problem 17: Solution:

$\alpha^2+\beta^2+\gamma^2=10.$

Problem 18: Solution:

Let $x = X$, $2y = Y$, $3z = Z$.

$$\begin{cases} X + Y + Z = 6, & (1) \\ X^2 + Y^2 + Z^2 = 14, & (2) \\ X^3 + Y^3 + Z^3 = 36. & (3) \end{cases}$$

$(1)^2 - (2)$:
$$XY + YZ + ZX = 11. \quad (4)$$

$(2) - (4)$:
$$X^2 + Y^2 + Z^2 - XY - YZ - ZX = 3 \quad (5)$$
$(1) \times 5 - (3)$:

$$XYZ = 6. \quad (6)$$

From (1), (4), and (6), we know that X, Y, and Z are three roots of
$t^3 - 6t^2 + 11t - 6 = 0$.

Solve: $t_1 = 1$, $t_2 = 2$, $t_3 = 3$.

The solutions are:

$$\begin{cases} x = 1, \\ y = 1, \\ z = 1; \end{cases} \begin{cases} x = 1, \\ y = \dfrac{3}{2}, \\ z = \dfrac{2}{3}; \end{cases} \begin{cases} x = 2 \\ y = \dfrac{1}{2}, \\ z = 1; \end{cases} \begin{cases} x = 2, \\ y = \dfrac{3}{2}, \\ z = \dfrac{1}{3}; \end{cases} \begin{cases} x = 3, \\ y = \dfrac{1}{2}, \\ z = \dfrac{2}{3}; \end{cases} \begin{cases} x = 3, \\ y = 1, \\ z = \dfrac{1}{3}. \end{cases}$$

Problem 19: Solution: (E).
Since the product of the positive integral roots is the prime integer q, q must be positive and the roots must be 1 and q. Since $p = 1 + q$ is also prime, $q = 2$ and $p = 3$. Hence all four statements are true.

Problem 20: Solution: (B).
Let a and b be the solutions of $x^2 + ms + n = 0$; then
$$-m = a + b, \qquad -p = a^3 + b^3,$$

$$n = ab, \qquad q = a^3b^3.$$

Since $(a+b)^3 = a^3 + 3a^2b + 3ab^2 + b^3 = a^3 + b^3 + 3ab(a+b)$

We obtain $\quad -m^3 = -p + 3n(-m) \quad$ or $\quad p = m^3 - 3mn.$

Problem 21: Solution:

If the quadratic equation $x^2 + ax + 6a = 0$ has integer solutions m and n ($m \leq n$), by Vieta Theorem, we have: $a = -(m+n)$ and $6a = m \cdot n$.

Or

$m \cdot n + 6m + 6n + 36 = 36 \quad \Rightarrow \quad (m+6)(n+6) = 36.$

There are 10 pairs of solutions with $m \leq n$:

$(-42, -7)$, $(-24, -8)$, $(-18, -9)$,
$(-15, -10)$, $(-12, -12)$, $(-5, 30)$,
$(-4, 12)$, $(-3, 6)$, $(-2, 3)$, $(0, 0)$.

The corresponding values for $a = -(m+n)$ are

49, 32, 27, 25, 24, -25, -8, -3, -1, 0.

So there are 10 values of a.

Problem 22: Solution:

Let a, b, c, d be the roots of the given quartic equation, and also let $p = a + b$, $q = ab, r = c + d$, and $s = cd$. Then,

(1) $\qquad -1 = a + b + c + d = p + r,$
(2) $\qquad 0 = ab + ac + ad + bc + bd + cd = pr + q + s,$
(3) $\qquad 0 = abc + bcd + cda + dab = ps + qr,$
(4) $\qquad -1 = abcd = qs.$

We now eliminate p, r, and s from these equations. From (1) and (4), $r = -1 - p$, $s = -\dfrac{1}{q}$ and substituting these values in (2) and (3), gives

$$p(1+p) = q - \frac{1}{q} \quad \text{and} \quad p = \frac{-q^2}{q^2 + 1}.$$

Finally,

$$\frac{-q^2}{(q^2+1)} = \frac{q^2 - 1}{q} \quad \text{or} \quad q^6 + q^4 + q^3 - q^2 - 1 = 0.$$

50 AMC Lectures Problems Book 1 (7) Square Numbers

PROBLEMS

Problem 1: [MOSP 1998] Show that the sum of the squares of 5 consecutive integers is not a perfect square.

Problem 2: (1957 AMC) If the square of a number of two digits is decreased by the square of the number formed by reversing the digits, then the result is not always divisible by:
(A) 9 (B) the product of the digits (C) the sum of the digits (D) the difference of the digits (E) 11.

Problem 3: When 200 is added to a positive integer, the result is a square number. When 292 is added to the same positive integer, the result is a different square number. Find the positive integer.

Problem 4: Problem 1. (1999 AIME) Find the sum of all positive integers n for which $n^2 - 19n + 99$ is a perfect square.

Problem 5: Find the greatest n such that $n^2 + 1990n$ is a square number.

Problem 6: (1965 AMC) Let n be the number of integer values of x such that $P = x^4 + 6x^2 + 11x^2 + 3x + 31$ is the square of an integer. Then n is:
(A) 4   (B) 3   (C) 2   (D) 1   (E) 0

Problem 7: A list numbers are 1, 2, 3, 4, 5, 6, 7, 8, 9, 10, 11,…. All square numbers are deleted from the list to result in a new list: 2, 3, 5, 6, 7, 8, 10, 11,…. What is the number in 1992th position of the new list?

Problem 8: Find prime number p such that $17P + 1$ is a square number.

Problem 9: (1994 AIME) The increasing sequence 3, 15, 24, 48, ... consists of those positive multiples of 3 that are one less than a perfect square. What is the remainder when the 1994th term of the sequence is divided by 1000?

Problem 10: (2003 China Middle School Math Contest) Find the 4-digit number $\overline{abcd}$ such that $\overline{abcd} = (\overline{ab} + \overline{cd})^2$.

Problem 11: Twenty bored students take turns walking down a hall that contains a row of closed lockers, numbered 1 to 20. The first student opens all the lockers; the second student closes all the lockers numbered 2, 4, 6, 8, 10, 12, 14, 16, 18, 20; the third student operates on the lockers numbered 3, 6, 9, 12, 15, 18: if a locker was closed, he opens it, and if a locker was open, he closes it; and so on. For the ith student, he works on the lockers numbered by multiples of i: if a locker was closed, he opens it, and if a locker was open, he closes it. What is the number of the lockers that remain open after all the students finish their walks?

Problem 12: (1997 China Middle School Math Contest) Find $x + y$ if $x^2 + y^2 = 1997$. x and y are positive integers.

Problem 13: (1989 AIME) If $a < b < c < d < e$ are consecutive positive integers such that $b + c + d$ is a perfect square and $a + b + c + d + e$ is a perfect cube, what is the smallest possible value of c?

Problem 14: Find m if $x^2 - 2m(x - 4) - 15$ is a square number for any integers x.

Problem 15: (27th IMO) Let d be any positive integer not equal to 2, 5, or 13. Show that one can find distinct a, b in the set $\{2, 5, 13, d\}$ such that $ab - 1$ is not a square.

SOLUTIONS

Problem 1: Solution:
$(n-2)^2 + (n-1)^2 + n^2 + (n+1)^2 (n+2)^2 = 5(n^2 + 2)$.

If $5(n^2 + 2)$ is a square number, $(n^2 + 2)$ must be a multiple of 5, or the last digit of $5(n^2 + 2)$ must be 0 or 5.

We know that the last digit of a square number can only be 0, 1, 4, 5, 6, or 9. So the last digit of n^2 can only be 0, 1, 4, 5, 6, or 9. The last digit of $(n^2 + 2)$ can only be 2, 3, 6, 7, 8, or 1, and none of them is 0 or 5. Therefore $(n^2 + 2)$ is not a multiple of 5 and the sum of the squares of 5 consecutive integers is not a perfect square.

Problem 2: Solution: (B).
Let the two-digit number be $10m + n$.
$(10m + n)^2 - (10n + m)^2$
$= [(10m + n) + (10n + m)][(10m + n) - (10n + m)]$
$= 99(m + n)(m - n)$.
This is divisible by 9, 11, $m - n$, $m + n$. So (B) is the correct answer.

Problem 3: Solution: 284.
Let the number be n.
$n + 200 = a^2$
$n + 292 = b^2$
$b^2 - a^2 = 92$
$(b + a)(b - a) = 92$

Since $(b + a)$ and $(b - a)$ have the same parity.
$92 = 46 \times 2$.
$b + a = 46$, $b - a = 2$.
$a = 22$, $b = 24$
$n = 284$.

Problem 4: Solution: 38.
Method 1:
If $n^2 - 19n + 99 = m^2$ for positive integers m and n, then the quadratic equation $n^2 - 19n + 99 - m^2 = 0$ has the positive integer solutions and $\Delta = 19^2 - 4(99 - m^2)$ must be a perfect square.

We have: $19^2 - 4(99 - m^2) = k^2$ $\Rightarrow$ $(2m - k)(2m + k) = 35$.
$(m, k) = (9, 17)$ and $(3, 1)$.
When $m = 9$, $n^2 - 19n + 99 = 81$ $\Rightarrow$ $n = 1$ or 18.
When $m = 3$, $n^2 - 19n + 99 = 9$ $\Rightarrow$ $n = 9$ or 10.
The sum is $1 + 18 + 9 + 10 = 38$.

Method 2:
If $n^2 - 19n + 99 = m^2$ for positive integers m and n,
then $4n^2 - 76n + 396 = (2n - 19)^2 + 35 = 4m^2$. Thus $4m^2 - (2n - 19)^2 = 35$, or
$(2m + 2n - 19)(2m - 2n + 19) = 35$. The sum of the two factors is $4m$, a positive integer,
so the pair $(2m + 2n - 19, 2m + 2n + 19)$ can only be $(1, 35)$, $(5, 7)$, $(7, 5)$, or $(35, 1)$.
Therefore n can only be $1, 9, 10,$ or 18. The sum of all these integers is 38.

Problem 5: Solution: 494018.
Let $n^2 + 1990n = m^2$. m is positive integer and $m > n$.

Let $m = n + k$, k is positive integer.

$n^2 + 1990n = (n + k)^2 = n^2 + 2nk + k^2$
$1990n = 2nk + k^2$
$n = \dfrac{k^2}{1990 - 2k}$

We want the greatest n, so we let $2k$ be as close as possible to 1990. $k = 994$.

$n = \dfrac{1}{2} \times 994^2 = 494018$.

Problem 6: Solution: (D).
Let $P = x^4 + 6x^2 + 11x^2 + 3x + 31$
         $= (x^2 + 3x + 1)^2 - 3(x - 10) = y^2$.
When $x = 10$, $P = (x^2 + 3x + 1)^2 = 131^2 = y^2$.

To prove that 10 is the only possible value we use the following lemma:
If $|N| > |M|$, N, M integers, then $N^2 - M^2 \geq 2|N| - 1$.

Case I If $x > 10$, then

$3(x-10) = (x^2 + 3x + 1)^2 - y^2 \geq 2|x^2 + 3x + 1| - 1$, an impossibility.

Case II If $x < 10$, then

$3(x-10) = y^2 - (x^2 + 3x + 1)^2 \geq 2|y| - 1 > 2|x^2 + 3x + 1| - 1$.

This inequality holds for the integers
$x = 2, 1, 0, -1, -2, -3, -4, -5, -6$,
but none of these values makes P the square of an integer.

Problem 7: Solution:
Let $f(n)$ represents the nth non square number.

$f(1) = 2 = 1 + 1$
$f(2) = 3 = 2 + 1$
$f(3) = 5 = 3 + 2$
$f(4) = 6 = 4 + 2$
$f(5) = 7 = 5 + 2$
$f(6) = 8 = 6 + 2$
$f(7) = 10 = 7 + 3$
$f(8) = 11 = 8 + 3$
……

$f(n) = n + k$, where k is the square number nor exceeding $f(n)$.
Then $k^2 < n + k < (k+1)^2$
$k^2 + 1 < n + k < (k+1)^2 - 1$.
So $(k - \frac{1}{2})^2 + \frac{3}{4} = k^2 - k + 1 \leq n \leq k^2 + k = (k + \frac{1}{2})^2 - \frac{1}{4}$.
Therefore $k - \frac{1}{2} < \sqrt{n} < k + \frac{1}{2}$. That is, k is the closest integer to $\sqrt{n}$.
the integer closest to $\sqrt{1992}$ is 45.
Therefore $f(1992) = 1992 + 45 = 2037$.

Problem 8: Solution:
Let $17P + 1 = a^2$, a is positive integer.
$17P = (a + 1)(a - 1)$.
Since both $a + 1$ and $a - 1$ are not zeros.
We have $\begin{cases} 17 = a + 1, \\ p = a - 1 \end{cases}$ (1)
Or

$$\begin{cases} 17 = a-1, \\ p = a+1. \end{cases} \qquad (2)$$

Solving (1): $a = 16$ and $p = 15$ (not a prime).
Solving (2): $a = 18$ and $p = 19$.

Problem 9: Solution:
Any number that is one less than a perfect square has the form:
$n^2 - 1 = (n+1)(n-1)$, $n = 2, 3, \cdots$.
Only when n is not a multiple of 3, $n^2 - 1$ is divisible by 3.
So the $(2k-1)^{\text{th}}$ term is $(3k-1)^2 - 1$ and the $(2k^{\text{th}}$ term is $(3k+1)^2 - 1$.
So the 1994th term is $(3 \cdot 997 + 1)^2 - 1 = (3000 - 8)^2 - 1 = 3000^2 - 16 \times 3000 + 63$.
The remainder is 63 when divided by 1000.

Problem 10: Solution:
Let $m = \overline{ab}$ and $n = \overline{cd}$.

We have $(m+n)^2 = 100m + n$
$m^2 + 2(n-50)m + (n^2 - n) = 0$

In order to get the integer solutions, Δ must be a square number.
We have $\Delta = 4(n-50)^2 - 4(n^2 - n) = 4(2500 - 99n)$
When $n = 25$, $\Delta = 4(2500 - 99n = 100$.
Solve for m: $m = 25$ or 30.

The 4-digit number is 2025 or 3025.

Problem 11: Solution: 4.
Note that the ith locker will be operated by student j if and only if $j \mid i$. This can happen if and only if the locker will also be operated by student i
j. Thus, only the lockers numbered $1 = 1^2$, $4 = 2^2$, $9 = 3^2$, and $16 = 4^2$ will be operated on an odd number of times, and these are the lockers that will be left open after all the operations. Hence the answer is 4.

Problem 12: Solution:
Since 1997 is odd, one of x and y must be even and the other one odd.
Let x be odd and y be even.

The last digit of a square number can only be 0, 1, 4, 5, 6, or 9.
Since the last digit of 1997 is 7, the units digit of x and y must be 1, 4 or 1, 6 or 9, 4 or 9, 6.
Since y is even, the remainder is zero when y is divided by 4. When 1994 is divided by 4, the remainder is 1. So when x is divided by 4, the remainder is 1. Since $x^2 < 1997$, $x < 45$. Therefore x can be 1, 9, 21, 29, 41. We check each one of them and found that only when $x = 29$, $y = 34$, $29^2 + 34^2 = 1997$.
So $x + y = 63$.

Problem 13: Solution:
Let $a = x - 2$, $b = x - 1$, $c = x$, $d = x + 1$, $e = x + 2$.
Then $b + c + d = 3x$ and $a + b + c + d + e = 5x$.

In order for $3x$ to be a perfect square, x must be 3, 3^3, 3^5, 3^7, 3^9...

In order for $5x$ to be a perfect cube, x must be 5^2, 5^5, 5^8,....

In order for $3x$ to be a perfect square and $5x$ to be a perfect cube, x must be $3^3 \times 5^2$, $3^3 \times 5^8$,...., $3^9 \times 5^2$, $3^9 \times 5^8$, ...

The smallest value of x is $3^3 \times 5^2 = 675$.

Problem 14: Solution: $m = 3$ or $m = 5$.
We rewrite $x^2 - 2m(x - 4) - 15$ as $x^2 - 2mx + 8m - 15$.
We have $\Delta = (-2m)^2 - 4 \times (8m - 15) = 0$ or $4m^2 - 32m + 60 = 0$ $\Rightarrow m^2 - 8m + 15 = 0$.
Solving fro m: $m_1 = 3$, $m_2 = 5$.

Problem 15: Solution:
We have $\binom{4}{2} = 6$ ways to select two numbers from 2, 5, 13, and d:
(2, 5), (2, 13), (5, 13), (2, d), (5, d), and (13, d).

$2 \times 5 - 1 = 3^2$, $2 \times 13 - 1 = 5^2$ and $5 \times 13 - 1 = 8^2$ are all square numbers.
Therefore we need to show that at least one of $2d - 1$, $5d - 1$, and $13d - 1$ is not a square number.

We prove this problem by the way of contradiction.

Let all three are square number.

$2d - 1 = x^2$, (1)
$5d - 1 = y^2$, (2)
$13d - 1 = z^2$, (3)
x, y, and z are integers.

From (1) we know that x is odd and can be written as $x = 2k - 1$.

So $2d - 1 = (2k - 1)^2 \Rightarrow d = 2k^2 - 2k + 1$.

We know that d is odd.

From (2) and (3), we know that both y and z are even.
Let $y = 2m$ and $z = 2n$ substitute them into (2) and (3), respectively.
$5d - 1 = 4m^2$ (4)
$13d - 1 = 4n^2$ (5)
(4) – (5): $8d = 4n^2 - 4m^2 \Rightarrow 2d = n^2 - m^2 = (n + m)(n - m)$.
So $n^2 - m^2$ is even. Since $n + m$ and $n - m$ have the same parity, both $n + m$ and $n - m$ are even.

Therefore $2d$ is a multiple of 4 and d is even. d cannot be even and odd at the same time. So at least one of $2d - 1$, $5d - 1$, and $13d - 1$ is not a square number.

50 AMC Lectures Problems Book 1   (8) Divisibility

PROBLEMS

Problem 1. Find $N = 2^l 3^m$ such that the sum of all positive integral divisors of N is 403, where l and m are positive integers.

Problem 2. How many cubes are divisors of $2^3 \times 3^4$?

Problem 3. (2004 AIME 2 #8) How many positive integer divisors of 2004^{2004} are divisible by exactly 2004 positive integers?

Problem 4. Suppose a, b, and c are distinct digits for which the number $708,a6b,8c9$ is a multiple of 99. Find $a + b + c$.

Problem 5. (1954 AMC 12) The difference of the squares of two odd numbers is always divisible by 8. If $a > b$, and $2a + 1$ and $2b + 1$ are the odd numbers, to prove the given statement we put the difference of the squares in the form:
     (A) $(2a+1)^2 - (2b+1)^2$ (B) $4a^2 - 4b^2 + 4a - 4b$ (C) $4[a(a+1) - b(b+1)]$
     (D) $4(a-b)(a+b+1)$ (E) $4(a^2 + a - b^2 - b)$

Problem 6. (1959 AMC 12) A farmer divides his herd of n cows among his four sons so that one son gets one-half the herd, a second son, one-fourth, a third son, one-fifth, and the fourth son, 7 cows. Then n is:
     (A) 80   (B) 100   (C) 140   (D) 180   (E) 240

Problem 7. (1965 AMC 12) When $y^2 + my + 2$ is divided by $y - 1$ the quotient is $f(y)$ and the remainder is R_1. When $y^2 + my + 2$ is divided by $y + 1$ the quotient is $g(y)$ and the remainder is R_2. If $R_1 = R_2$ then m is:
(A) 0   (B) 1   (C) 2   (D) -1 (E) an undetermined constant

Problem 8. (1966 AMC 12) The number of positive integers less than 1000 divisible by neither 5 nor 7 is:
     (A) 688   (B) 686   (C) 684   (D) 658   (E) 630

50 AMC Lectures Problems Book 1 — (8) Divisibility

Problem 9. (1970 AMC 12) Let S be the set of all numbers which are the sum of the squares of three consecutive integers. Then we can say that
 (A) No member of S is divisible by 2
 (B) No member of S is divisible by 3 but some member is divisible by 11
 (C) No member of S is divisible by 3 or by 5
 (D) No member of S is divisible by 3 or by 7
 (E) None of these

Problem 10. (1970 AMC 12) If a number is selected at random from the set of all five-digit numbers in which the sum of the digits is equal to 43, what is the probability that this number will be divisible by 11?
 (A) $\dfrac{2}{5}$ (B) $\dfrac{1}{5}$ (C) $\dfrac{1}{6}$ (D) $\dfrac{1}{11}$ (E) $\dfrac{1}{15}$

Problem 11. (1972 AMC 12) When the number 2^{1000} is divided by 13, the remainder in the division is
(A) 1   (B) 2   (C) 3   (D) 7   (E) 11

Problem 12. (1974 AMC 12) 8. What is the smallest prime number dividing the sum $3^{11} + 5^{13}$?
(A) 2   (B) 3   (C) 5   (D) $3^{11} + 5^{13}$ (E) none of these

Problem 13. (1974 AMC 12) The number of distinct positive integral divisors of $(30)^4$ excluding 1 and $(30)^4$ is (A) 100   (B) 125   (C) 123   (D) 30   (E) none of these

Problem 14. (1981 AMC 12) How many of the first one hundred positive integers are divisible by all of the numbers 2, 3, 4, 5?
 (A) 0   (B) 1   (C) 2   (D) 3   (E) 4

Problem 15. (1984 AMC 12) Let n be the smallest nonprime integer greater than 1 with no prime factor less than 10. Then
(A) $100 < n \leq 110$ (B) $110 < n \leq 120$ (C) $120 < n \leq 130$
(D) $130 < n \leq 140$ (E) $140 < n \leq 150$

Problem 16. (1986 AMC 12) Let $N = 69^5 + 5 \cdot 69^4 + 10 \cdot 69^3 + 10 \cdot 69^2 + 5 \cdot 69 + 1$. How many positive integers are factors of N?
 (A) 3 (B) 5 (C) 69 (D) 125 (E) 216

Problem 17. (2002 AMC 12 B) For all positive integers n less than 2002, let

$$a_n = \begin{cases} 11, & \text{if } n \text{ is divisible by 13 and 14;} \\ 13, & \text{if } n \text{ is divisible by 14 and 11;} \\ 14, & \text{if } n \text{ is divisible by 11 and 13;} \end{cases}$$

Calculate $\sum_{n=1}^{2001} a_n$.

 (A) 448 (B) 486 (C) 1560 (D) 2001 (E) 2002.

Problem 18. (2005 AMC 12 B) A positive integer n has 60 divisors and $7n$ has 80 divisors. What is the greatest integer k such that $7k$ divides n?

 (A) 0 (B) 1 (C) 2 (D) 3 (E) 4

Problem 19. (2006 AMC 12 B) Elmo makes N sandwiches for a fundraiser. For each sandwich he uses B globs of peanut butter at 4¢ per glob and J blobs of jam at 5¢ per blob. The cost of the peanut butter and jam to make all the sandwiches is $2.53. Assume that B, J, and N are positive integers with $N > 1$. What is the cost of the jam Elmo uses to make the sandwiches?

 (A) $1.05 (B) $1.25 (C) $1.45 (D) $1.65 (E) $1.85

Problem 20. x, y, and z are integers. The remainder is zero when $7x + 2y - 5z$ is divided by 11. What is the remainder when $3x - 7y + 12z$ is divided by 5?

Problem 21. None of the three integers a, b, and $(a - b)$ is a multiple of 3. Find the remainder when $a^3 + b^3$ is divided by 9.

Problem 22. a is an odd number. Find the remainder when a^2 is divided by 8.

50 AMC Lectures Problems Book 1   (8) Divisibility

Problem 23. Find the remainder when $N = \underbrace{111....11}_{2011\ 1's}$ is divided by 7.

Problem 24. Show that $3 | n(n+1)(2n+1)$ if n is integer.

Problem 25. How many positive integers $a < 100$ are there such that $a^3 + 23$ is divisible by 24?
A. 4   B. 5   C. 9   D. 10

Problem 26. How many positive integers $n < 2013$ are there such that $2^n + 1$ is divisible by 3?

Problem 27. How many positive integers are there such that $(n-1)!$ is divisible by n if $n \leq 100$?

Problem 28. Find the remainder when the four-digit positive integer $\overline{abcd}$ is divided by 8 if $4b + 2c + d = 32$.

Problem 29. Find the remainder when $a^3 + b^3 + c^3$ is divided by 6 if $a + b + c$ is divisible by 6.

Problem 30. Find the integer n ($n \neq 1$) that will divide 92, 118, and 157 leaving the same remainder.

Problem 31. (1976 AMC 12) If r is the remainder when each of the numbers 1059, 1417 and 2312 is divided by d, where d is an integer greater than one, then $d - r$ equals
    (A) 1   (B) 15   (C) 179   (D) $d - 15$ (E) $d - 1$

Problem 32. How many values of n ($1 \leq n \leq 2015$) are there such that $2011^n + 2012^n + 2013^n + 2014^n + 2015^n$ is not divisible by 5?

(8) Divisibility

SOLUTIONS:

Problem 1. Solution: 144.
Since we know that the sum of the divisors of N is 403, we can write:

$$\frac{2^{l+1}-1}{2-1} \times \frac{3^{m+1}-1}{3-1} = 403 \quad \text{or} \quad (2^{l+1}-1) \times (3^{m+1}-1) = 2 \times 13 \times 31$$

We know that $2^{l+1} - 1$ is odd and $3^{m+1} - 1$ is even and greater than 8.
Therefore, $2^{l+1} - 1 = 13$ or $31 \quad \Rightarrow \quad 2^{l+1} = 14$ or 32.
Since there are no integer solutions if $2^{l+1} = 14$, we have: $2^{l+1} = 32$. $\Rightarrow l = 4, \ m = 2$.
The desired solution is $N = 144$.

Problem 2. Solution: **4.**
$2^3 \times 3^4 = 3 \, (2^3 \times 3^3) = 3(2^1 \times 3^1)^3$
The number of cubic divisors is the same as the number of divisors for $(2^1 \times 3^1)$, which can be calculated as $(1 + 1)(1 + 1) = 4$.

Problem 3. Solution: 54.
Method 1 Official Solution:
A positive integer N is a divisor of 2004^{2004} if and only if $N = 2^i 3^j 167^k$ with $0 \le i \le 4008$, $0 \le j \le 2004$, and $0 \le k \le 2004$. Such a number has exactly 2004 positive integer divisors if and only if $(i + 1)(j + 1)(k + 1) = 2004$. Thus the number of values of N meeting the required conditions is equal to the number of ordered triples of positive integers whose product is 2004. Each of the unordered triples {1002; 2; 1}; {668; 3; 1},{501; 4; 1}, {334; 6; 1}, {334; 3; 2}, {167; 12; 1},{167; 6; 2}, and {167; 4; 3} can be ordered in 6 possible ways, and the triples {2004; 1; 1} and {501; 2; 2} can each be ordered in 3 possible ways, so the total is $8 \times 6 + 2 \times 3 = 54$.

Method 2 Our solution:
The basic idea of our solution is the same as that of the official solution however without listing.

$2004 = 2 \times 2 \times 3 \times 167$

Case 1: If none of the factors are 1, we have the factors

       2,   2,   3,   167

We need to multiply two of these numbers together, to form the third factor, with the two remaining numbers being the other two factors.

For example, one possible combination could be:
{(2 × 2)   3   167}
There are four combinations:
(2 and 2), (2 and 3), (2 and 167), and (3 and 167). The triples are
{4; 167; 3}, {6; 167; 2}, {334; 3; 2}, {501; 2; 2}.
The number of ordered triples: $6 + 6 + 6 + 3 = 21$
Case 2. If one of the three factors is 1, we have the following numbers:
   1,   2,   2,   3,   167
Now we know that one factor must be one. That means that the other four numbers have to somehow group together to become two numbers.

In other words, we need to figure out how many ways the product $2 \times 2 \times 3 \times 167$ can be split into two factors.

$2004 = 2 \times 2 \times 3 \times 167$ has 12 factors, including 1 and itself. Now, we need to subtract 1 and $2 \times 2 \times 3 \times 167$ from the total number of factors to obtain 10 usable factors. Each factor corresponds to another factor, so we need to divide by 2.

Let d be the total number of factors. To find the number of usable pairs, we have

$$\left\lfloor \frac{d-2}{2} \right\rfloor = 10/2 = 5 \text{ total pairs.}$$

Below is a list of the 5 triples:
{668; 3; 1}, {501; 4; 1}, {334; 6; 1}, {167; 12; 1}, {1002; 2; 1};
The number of ordered triples: $6 + 6 + 6 + 6 + 6 = 30$

Case 3: If there are two 1's as the factors, then we have only one way:
{1   1   2002}
The number of ordered triples: 3.
The final answer will be $21 + 30 + 3 = 54$.

Problem 4. Solution: 16.
Since $99 = 9 \times 11$, in order for the number to be divisible by 99, the number must be divisible by both 9 and 11.
In order for a number to be divisible by 9, the sum of its digits must be divisible by 9:
$7 + 8 + a + 6 + b + 8 + c + 9 \equiv 0 \mod 9 \Rightarrow a + b + c \equiv 7 \mod 9$
This is equivalent to
$$a + b + c = 7$$
$$a + b + c = 16$$

$a + b + c = 25$.
In order for a number to be divisible by 11,
$7 + 8 + 6 + 8 + 9 - (a + b + c) \equiv 0 \bmod 11$.
This is equivalent to
$$a + b + c = 5.$$
$$a + b + c = 16.$$
$$a + b + c = 27.$$

If and only if $a + b + c = 16$, will the given number be divisible by both 9 and 11.
Note: Divisibility rule for 11: To find out if a number is divisible by eleven, add every other digit, and call that sum "x." Add together the remaining digits, and call that sum "y." Take the difference, $x - y$. If the difference is zero or a multiple of eleven, then the original number is a multiple of eleven.

Problem 5. Solution: (C).
$(2a + 1)^2 - (2b + 1)^2 = 4a^2 + 4a + 1 - 4b^2 - 4b - 1$
$= 4[a(a + 1) - b(b + 1)]$.
Since the product of two consecutive integers is divisible by 2, the last expression is divisible by 8.

Problem 6. Solution: (C).
$n = \frac{1}{2}n + \frac{1}{4}n + \frac{1}{5}n + 7. \qquad n = 140.$

Problem 7. Solution: (A).
Since $y^2 + my + 2 = (y-1)f(y) + R_1$. Similarly, since
$y^2 + my + 2 = (y-1)g(y) + R_2$.
for all values of y, we have, letting $y = -1$, $3 - m = R_2$. Since $R_1 = R_2$, $3 + m = 3 - m$.
$\therefore m = 0$.

Problem 8. Solution: (B).
$999 - \frac{999}{5} - \frac{999}{7} + \frac{999}{35} = 999 - 199 - 142 + 28 = 686$.

Problem 9. Solution: (A).
Three consecutive integers can always be expressed as $n - 1$, n, and $n + 1$, where n denotes the middle one. Thus each number of the set S is of the form
$(n - 1)^2 + n^2 + (n + 1)^2 = 3n^2 + 2$.

When n is even, $3n^2 + 2$ is divisible by 2, so choice (A) is false. We see that no member of S is divisible by 3, because the remainder in that division is always 2.

Problem 10. Solution: (B).
There are 15 5-digit numbers that have a digit sum of 43. Among them only 99979, 97999, and 98989 are divisible by 11. So the probability is $3/15 = 1/5$.

Problem 11. Solution: (A).
We make use of the following fact: If N_1, N_2 are integers whose remainders, upon division by D, are R_1 and R_2, then the products N_1N_2 and R_1R_2 have the same remainder upon division by D. In symbols: If $N_1 = Q_1D + R_1$ and $N_2 = Q_2D + R_2$, then
$N_1N_2 = (Q_1D + R_1)(Q_2D + R_2)$
$= (Q_1Q_2D + Q_1R_2 + Q_2R_1)D + R_1R_2,$

and the last expression clearly has the same remainder as R_1R_2.

Among the first few powers of two, we find that 2^6 has the convenient remainder 12 [or -1] upon division by 13, so $2^{12} = 2^6 \cdot 2^6$ has the same remainder as $12 \cdot 12$ [or $(-1)^2$], namely 1. We now write $2^{1000} = (2^{12})^{88} \cdot 2^4$, and conclude that the remainder upon division by 13 is $(1)^{88} \cdot 3 = 3$, since $2^4 = 16 = 1 \cdot 13 + 3$.
Using the notation of congruence, we have
$2^6 = 64 \equiv -1 \pmod{13}$,
$2^{1000} = (2^6)^{166} \cdot 2^4 \equiv (-1)^{166} \cdot 16 \pmod{13}$
$\equiv 1 \cdot 3 \pmod{13} \equiv 3 \pmod{13}$.

Problem 12. Solution: (A).
Since 3^{11} and 5^{13} are both odd, their sum is even.

Problem 13. (C).
Writing 30 as a product of prime factors, $30 = 2 \cdot 3 \cdot 5$, we obtain
$(30)^4 = 2^4 \cdot 3^4 \cdot 5^4$.
The divisors of $(30)^4$ are exactly the numbers of the form $2^i \cdot 3^j \cdot 5^k$, where I, j, k are non-negative integers between zero and four inclusively, so there are $(5)^3 = 125$ distinct divisors of $(30)^4$; excluding 1 and $(30)^4$ there are 123 divisors.

Problem 14. Solution: (B).
The least common multiple of 2, 3, 4 and 5 is 60. The numbers divisible by 2, 3, 4 and 5 are integer multiples of 60. There is only one such number (60 itself) from 1 to 100 divisible by 60.

Problem 15. Solution: (C).
The number n must be a prokuct of two or more primes gueater than 10, not necessarily dustubct. The smallest such prime is 11, so the smallest product is $11 \cdot 11 = 121$.

Problem 16. Solution: (E).
By the Binomial Theorem, $N = (69 + 1)^5 = (2 \cdot 5 \cdot 7)^5$. Thus a positive integer d is a factor of N if $d = 2^p 5^q 7^r$, where p, q, r are each one of the 6 integers 0, 1, 2, 3, 4, 5. Therefore there are $6^3 = 216$ choices for d.

Problem 17. Solution: (A).
Since $2002 = 11 \cdot 13 \cdot 14$, we have

$$a_n = \begin{cases} 11, \text{ if } n = 13 \cdot 14 \cdot i, \text{ where } i = 1, 2, \ldots, 10; \\ 13, \text{ if } n = 14 \cdot 11 \cdot j, \text{ where } j = 1, 2, \ldots, 12; \\ 14, \text{ if } n = 11 \cdot 13 \cdot k, \text{ where } k = 1, 2, \ldots, 13; \end{cases}$$

Therefore $\sum_{n=1}^{2001} a_n = 11 \cdot 10 + 13 \cdot 12 + 14 \cdot 13 = 448$.

Problem 18. Solution: (C).
Let $n = 7kQ$, where Q is the product of primes, none of which is 7. Let d be the number of divisors of Q. Then n has $(k+1)d$ divisors. Also $7n = 7k+1Q$, so $7n$ has $(k + 2)d$ divisors.
Thus $[(k + 2)d] / [(k + 1)d] = 80/60 = 4/3$ and $3(k + 2) = 4(k + 1)$.
Hence $k = 2$. Note that $n = 21972$ meets the conditions of the problem.

Problem 19. Solution: (D).
The total cost of the peanut butter and jam is $N(4B + 5J) = 253$ cents, so N and $4B + 5J$ are factors of $253 = 11 \cdot 23$. Because $N > 1$, the possible values of N are 11, 23, and 253. If $N = 253$, then $4B + 5J = 1$, which is impossible since B and J are positive integers. If $N = 23$, then $4B + 5J = 11$, which also has no solutions in positive integers. Hence $N = 11$ and $4B + 5J = 23$, which has the unique positive integer solution $B = 2$ and $J = 3$. So the cost of the jam is $11(3)(5¢) = \$1.65$.

Problem 20. Solution: 0.

Method 1:
$3x - 7y + 12z = 7x + 2y - 5z - 4x - 9y + 17z$
$= 7x + 2y - 5z - 4x - 9y + 17z + 11x + 11y - 22z = (7x + 2y - 5z) + (7x + 2y - 5z)$

Since the remainder is zero when $7x + 2y – 5z$ is divided by 11, the remainder when $3x – 7y + 12z$ is divided by 5 is also 0.

Method 2:
$4(3x – 7y + 12z) + 3(7x + 2y – 5z) = 11(3x – 2y + 3z)$
We know that $3(7x + 2y – 5z)$ is divisible by 11. We know that $11(3x – 2y + 3z)$ is also divisible by 11. Since $(11, 4) = 1$, $3x – 7y + 12z$ must be divisible by 11.
The remainder is zero when $3x – 7y + 12z$ is divided by 11.

Problem 21. Solution:

Since a, and $a – b$ are not multiples of 3, we have.
$a = 3m + 1$, $b = 3n – 1$ (m, n are integers)
$a^3 + b^3 = (3m+1)^3 + (3n-1)^3$
$= [(3m+1) + (3n-1)][(3m+1)^2 - (3m+1)(3n-1) + (3n-1)^2]$
$= 3(m+n)(9m^2 + 9n^2 - 9mn + 9m - 9n + 3)$
$= 9(m+n)(3m^2 + 3n^2 - 3mn + 3m - 3n + 1)$.

Since m and n are integers, both $m + n$ and $3m^2 + 3n^2 - 3mn + 3m - 3n + 1$ are integers. Therefore $a^3 + b^3$ is a multiple of 9.

Problem 22. Solution:
Let $a = 2k + 1$.
$a^2 = (2k+1)^2 = 4k^2 + 4k + 1 = 4k(k+1) + 1$.
k and $k + 1$ are consecutive integers. One of them must be even. Therefore $4k(k + 1)$ must be divisible by 8. So the remainder is 1 when a^2 is divided by 8.

Problem 23. Solution: **5.**
$111111 = 7 \times 15873$, so 111111 is divisible by 7.

2011 can be written as $334 \times 6 + 4$.
Let $N = 100p + 1111$, where p = 1111 $p = \underbrace{111....11}_{2007\ 1's}$.

The remainder when N is divided by 7 is equivalent to the remainder when 1111 is divided by 7. Since 1111 has the remainder 5 when divided by 7, the desired solution is 5.

Problem 24. Solution:
Method 1:
For any integer n, we have $n = 3k$, $n = 3k + 1$ or $n = 3k + 2$ where k is positive integer.

If $n = 3k$, $n(n+1)(2n + 1) = 3[k(3k + 1)(6k + 1)]$.
If $n = 3k + 1$, $n(n+1)(2n + 1) = 3[(3k + 1)(3k + 2)(2k + 1)]$.
If $n = 3k + 2$, $n(n+1)(2n + 1) = 3[(3k + 2)(k + 1)(6k + 5)]$.
In any case, we always have $3|n(n+1)(2n+1)$.

Method 2:
$n(n+1)(2n+1) = n(n+1)[(n-1)+(n+2)]$
$\qquad = (n-1)n(n+1) + n(n+1)(n+2)$
We know that both $(n-1)n(n+1)$ and $n(n+1)(n+2)$ are the product of three consecutive integers and each just have a factor of 3. Therefore $3|n(n+1)(2n+1)$.

Problem 25. Solution: (B).
We know that $24|a^3 + 23 = (a^3 - 1) + 24$..
$24|a^3 - 1 = (a - 1)[a(a+1)+1]$. $\qquad$ (1)
We know that $24 = 2^3 \times 3$ and $a(a + 1) + 1$ is odd.
Therefore we have $2^3|a-1$. $\qquad$ (2)
And $3|a-1$ $\qquad$ (3)
Otherwise, one of the three $a - 1, a, a + 1$ must be a multiple of 3.
So $a(a+1)$ is divisible by 3 and $a(a+1)+1$ is not divisible by 3, which is contradicted to (1). Therefore (3) is true.

Since $(2^3, 3) = 1$, $2^3 \times 3|a-1$.
And $a = 24k + 1$, k is nonnegative integer.
We know that $24k + 1 = a < 100$. So k can be 0, 1, 2, 3, 4.
Therefore $a = 1, 25, 49, 73, 97$.

Problem 26. Solution:
When n is odd, $2^n + 1 = 2^n + 1^n$ is divisible by $2 + 1 = 3$.
When n is even, $2^n + 1 = (3 - 1)^n + 1$ will have a remainder 2 when divided by 3.
There are k integers and $2013 = 1 + (k-1)2$ and $k = 1007$.

Problem 27. Solution:
If n is prime, $(n-1)!$ is not divisible by n.
If n is a composite number and $n = ab$, $a \neq b$, $1 < a < n$, and $(n-1)!$ is divisible by n since a and b are the factors of $(n-1)!$.

If n can only be written as $n = p^2$, where p is prime, when $p = 2$, $2^2 \nmid (4-1)!$; when $p > 2$, $n = p^2 > 2p$, $n-1 \geq 2p$.
p and $2p$ are factors of $(n-1)!$. Therefore $p^2 | (n-1)!$.

Hence $(n-1)!$ is divisible by any composite number except $n = 4$.

There are 25 prime numbers from 1 to 100 and $(n-1)!$ is divisible by $100 - 25 - 1 = 74$ numbers.

Problem 28. Solution: 0.
$$\overline{abcd} = a \cdot 10^3 + b \cdot 10^2 + c \cdot 10 + d = 1000a + 96b + 8c + (4b + 2c + d)$$
$$= 8(125a + 12b + c + 4)$$
Therefore $8 | \overline{abcd}$.

Problem 29. Solution: 0.
$a^3 + b^3 + c^3 - (a+b+c)$
$= (a^3 - a) + (b^3 - b) + (c^3 - c)$
$= (a-1)a(a+1) + (b-1)b(b+1) + (c-1)c(c+1)$

Since every term is the product of 3 consecutive integers, each term is divisible by $3! = 6$. Therefore $6 | a^3 + b^3 + c^3 - a - b - c$.

We know that $a + b + c$ is divisible by 6. Hence $a^3 + b^3 + c^3$ is divisible by 6.

Problem 30. Solution:
We know that $n | (118 - 92)$ or. $n | 26$
We also know that $n | (157 - 118)$ or $n | 39$.
Therefore divides the greatest common factor of 26 and 39, which is 13.
Since 13 is prime and $n \neq 1$, so $n = 13$.

Problem 31. Solution: (B).

Since each of the given numbers, when divided by d, has the same remainder, d divides the differences $2312 - 1417 = 895 = 5 \cdot 179$ and $1417 - 1059 = 378 = 2 \cdot 179$; and since 179 is prime, $d = 179$. Now $1059 = 5 \cdot 179 + 164$, $r = 164$, and $d - r = 179 - 164 = 15$.

Problem 32. Solution:
Since 2015^n is divisible by 5, we only need to find the values for n such that $2011^n + 2012^n + 2013^n + 2014^n$ is not divisible by 5. If $N = 2011^n + 2012^n + 2013^n + 2014^n$ is divisible by 5, the last digit of N should be 0 or 5. We classify n as $4k$, $4k+1$, $4k+2$, and $4k+3$, where k is positive integer.

When $n = 4k$, the last digit of 2011^n, 2012^n, 2013^n, and 2014^n are 1, 6, 1, and 6, respectively. The last digit of $2011^n + 2012^n + 2013^n + 2014^n$ is 4.

When $n = 4k + 1$, the last digit of 2011^n, 2012^n, 2013^n, and 2014^n are 1, 2, 3, and 4, respectively. The last digit of $2011^n + 2012^n + 2013^n + 2014^n$ is 0.

When $n = 4k + 2$, the last digit of 2011^n, 2012^n, 2013^n, and 2014^n are 1, 4, 9, and 6, respectively. The last digit of $2011^n + 2012^n + 2013^n + 2014^n$ is 0.

When $n = 4k + 3$, the last digit of 2011^n, 2012^n, 2013^n, and 2014^n are 1, 8, 7, and 4, respectively. The last digit of $2011^n + 2012^n + 2013^n + 2014^n$ is 0.

Therefore only when $n = 4k$, $2011^n + 2012^n + 2013^n + 2014^n + 2015^n$ is not divisible by 5.

$$\left\lfloor \frac{2014}{4} \right\rfloor = 503$$

Therefore there are 503 values of n.

PROBLEMS

Problem 1: In scalene triangle *ABC*, *D* and *E* are the midpoints of *AB* and *AC*, respectively. How many triangles have the same area as the triangle *ABE*?

(A) 0   (B) 1   (C) 2   (D) 3.

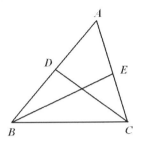

Problem 2: As shown in the figure, in isosceles $\triangle ABC$, $AB = AC$. *G* is the point where the three medians meet. How many pairs of congruent triangles are there?
(A) 5   (B) 6   (C) 7   (D) 8.

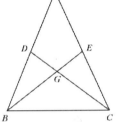

Problem 3: In $\triangle ABC$, *BC*, the angle bisector of $\angle A$ meets *AC* at *D*. $AB = AC + CD$, $\angle B = 40°$. Find $\angle C$.
(A) 60°.   (B) 80°.   (C) 100°.   (D) 120°.

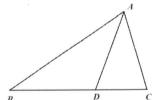

Problem 4: In $\triangle ABC$, $\angle C = 90°$. *DE* is the perpendicular bisector of *AB*. If $AB = 2AC$ and $BC = 18$ cm, find *BE*.

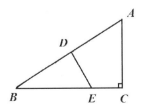

Problem 5: In △ABC, AD bisects ∠BAC. AB + BD = AC. Find ∠B : ∠C.

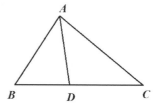

Problem 6: In △ABC, ∠BAC = 90°, ∠B = 2∠C. AD is the angle bisector of ∠BAC. If AB = 1, find BD.

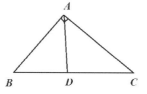

Problem 7: In quadrilateral ABCD, AB > AD, AC bisects ∠BAD. If ∠B + ∠D = 180°, prove that CD = CB.

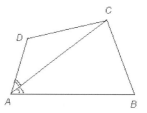

Problem 8: As shown in the figure, △ABC, AB = AC. ∠A = 100°. The angle bisector of ∠ABC meets AC at D. Prove: AD + BD = BC.

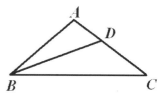

Problem 9: As shown in the figure, △ABC, AB > AC. ∠FBC = ∠ECB = ½ ∠A. Prove: BE = CF.

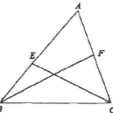

Problem 10: As shown in the figure, $\triangle ABC$. $\angle A = 90°$. $AB = AC$. D is the middle point of AC. $AE \perp BD$ at E. Extending AE to meet BC at F. Prove: $\angle ADB = \angle CDF$.

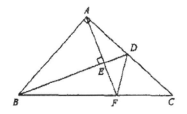

Problem 11. $\triangle ABC$ is a right triangle. $\angle ACB = 90°$. $CD \perp AB$ at D. AF is the angle bisector of $\angle CAB$ and meets CD at E, and CB at F, respectively. $EG//AB$ and meets CB at G. Prove: $CF = GB$.

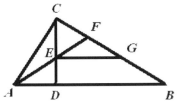

Problem 12. $\triangle ABC$ is an equilateral triangle. Extending BC to D, and extending BA to E such that $AE = BD$. If $CE = a$, find DE.

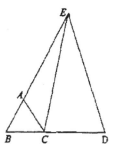

Problem 13: As shown in the figure, pentagon $ABCDE$ with $\angle ABC = \angle AED = 90°$. $AB = CD = AE = BC + DE = 1$. Find the area of the pentagon.

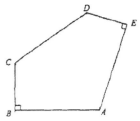

Problem 14: △ABC is an equilateral triangle. P is a point on AB and Q is a point on AC of △ABC. AP = CQ. M is the middle point of PQ. AM = 19. Find the length of PC.

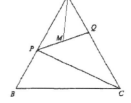

Problem 15: In rhombus ABCD, ∠BAD = 120°. M and N are points on BC and DC, respectively. Prove: if one interior angle of △AMN is 60°, then △AMN is an equilateral triangle.

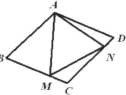

Problem 16: △ABC has ∠BCA = 90°. AC = BC. D is a point on C. E is a point on BC. CD = CE. CF ⊥ AE and meets AB at F. DG ⊥ AE and meets AB at G. Prove: BF = FG.

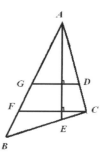

Problem 17. As shown in the figure, AB = AC. D, E, G, and H are the midpoints of AB, AC, AD, and AE, respectively. Connect BE, DH, GE, and DC. How many pairs of congruent triangles are there?
(A) 4   (B) 5   (C) 6   (D) None of these.

86

Problem 18. As shown in the figure, $\triangle ABC$, $\angle ACB = 90°$, $AD \perp AB$. $AD = AB$. $BE \perp DC$. $AF \perp AC$. Prove: CF is the angle bisector of $\angle ACB$.

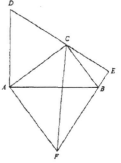

Problem 19. As shown in the figure is $\triangle ABC$. $\triangle ABD$ and $\triangle ACE$ are right triangles that are formed using AB and AC, respectively, as hypotenuses such that $\angle ABD = \angle ACE$, where M is the middle point of BC. Prove: $DM = EM$.

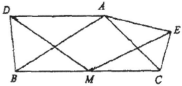

Problem 20: As shown in the figure, isosceles trapezoid $ABCD$ with $AB // DC$. Diagonals AC and BD meet at O. $\angle ACD = 60°$. Points S, P, and Q are the middle points of OD, OA, and BC, respectively.
(1) Prove: $\triangle PQS$ is an equilateral triangle.
(2) If $AB = 5$, $CD = 3$, find the area of $\triangle PQS$.

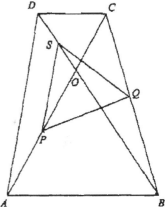

SOLUTIONS:

Problem 1:
Solution:
Let the area of triangle ABC be s.
$S_{\triangle ABE} = \dfrac{1}{2}S$

$S_{\triangle BEC} = S_{\triangle ADC} = S_{\triangle BDC} = \dfrac{1}{2}S$

The answer is (D).

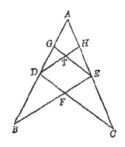

Problem 2: Solution: (C).
($\triangle ABF$, $\triangle ACF$); ($\triangle ABG$, $\triangle ACG$); ($\triangle GBF$, $\triangle GCF$); ($\triangle ABE$, $\triangle ACD$); ($\triangle ADG$, $\triangle AEG$);
($\triangle DGB$, $\triangle EGC$); ($\triangle DBC$, $\triangle ECB$).

Problem 3: Solution: (B).
Extend AC to E such that $CE = CD$. Connect DE.

In $\triangle ABD$ and $\triangle AED$, $AB = AC + CD = AC + CE = AE$, $\angle BAD = \angle EAD$, and $AD = AD$.
Therefore $\triangle ABD \cong \triangle AED$. $\angle B = \angle E$.

In $\triangle CDE$, $CD = DE$. So $\angle CDE = \angle E$.
We see that $\angle ACD$ is the exterior angle of $\triangle CDE$, so $\angle ACD = \angle CDE + \angle E$.
$\angle ACD = 2\angle E = 2\angle B$.
Since $\angle B = 40°$, $\angle ACB = 80°$.

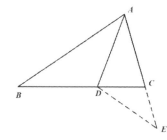

Problem 4: Solution:
Connect AE.
$\triangle BED \cong \triangle AED \cong \triangle AEC$.

We know that $\angle B = 30°$ and $EC = DE = \dfrac{1}{2}BE$.

$BC = BE + EC = BE + \dfrac{1}{2}BE$.

$\dfrac{3}{2}BE = 18 \text{cm} \qquad \Rightarrow \qquad BE = 12 \text{ cm}.$

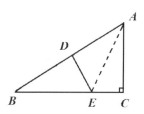

Problem 5: Solution:
Find point E on AC such that $AE = AB$. Connect DE.

In $\triangle ABD$ and $\triangle AED$, , $AB = AE$, $\angle BAD = \angle EAD$, $AD = AD$.

Therefore $\triangle ABD \cong \triangle AED$ $\Rightarrow BD = DE$, $\angle B = \angle AED$

We know that $AC = AB + BD$, $AE = AB$.

Therefore $EC = BD = DE$ and $\angle ECD = \angle C$.
$\angle B = \angle AED = \angle ECD + \angle C = 2\angle C$.
$\angle B : \angle C = 2:1$.

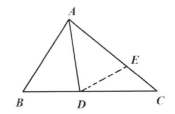

Problem 6: Solution:
Find point E on AC such that $AE = AB$. Connect DE.

Since $\angle BAD = \angle EAD$, and $AD = AD$, $\triangle ABD \cong \triangle AED$.

Therefore $AE = AB$, $BD = DE$.

In $\triangle ABC$, $\angle BAC = 90°$, $\angle B = 2\angle C$, so $\angle B = 60°$, $\angle C = 30°$.
We know that $AB = 1$. So $BC = 2$, $AC = \sqrt{3}$.
$EC = AC - AE = AC - AB = \sqrt{3} - 1$

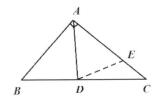

Problem 7: Proof:
Method 1: (our proof)
Extending AD to E. Draw $EC \perp DE$. Draw $CF \perp AB$.

Then $\triangle ACE \cong \triangle AFC$ ($AC=AC$, $\angle EAC = \angle EAB$ (given), $\angle E = \angle AFC = 90°$).

Then $EC = CF$.

$\angle B + \angle ADC = 180°$ (given), $\angle ADC = 90° + \angle DCE$, then $\angle B + \angle DCE = 90°$,
$\angle B + \angle FCB = 90°$, so $\angle DCE = \angle FCB$.
(or $\angle B + \angle ADC = 180°$, $\angle EDC + \angle ADC = 180°$, so $\angle EDC = \angle B$).

Then we know that $\triangle EDC \cong \triangle BCF$, then we know $CD = CB$.

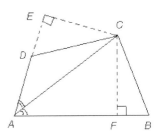

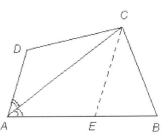

Method 2:
Since $AB > AD$, draw CE so that $AE = AD$.
$\triangle ACD \cong \triangle AEC$ (SAS). Then $CD = CE$, $\angle D = \angle AEC$.
Since $\angle B + \angle D = 180°$, $\angle B + \angle AEC = 180°$. $\angle CEB + \angle AEC = 180°$ (straight angle), so $\angle B = \angle CEB$.
Therefore $CE = CB = CD$.

Problem 8:
Proof:
Take a point F on BC such that $BF = BD$.
Since $\angle A = 100°$, $AB = AC$, so $\angle ABC = \angle C = \frac{1}{2}(180° - 100°) = 40°$,
and $\angle DBF = 20°$. But $BF = BD$, so $\angle BFD = \frac{1}{2}(180° - 20°) = 80°$.
So $\angle FDC = \angle BFD - \angle C = 40° = \angle C$. Therefore $FC = FD$.

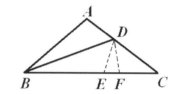

Take a point E on BF such that $\angle DEF = \angle DFE = 80°$. Then $DE = DF$, and $\angle BED = 180° - \angle DEF = 100° = \angle BAD$.
Since $\angle ABD = \angle EBD$, BD is a common side, so $\triangle ABD \cong \triangle EBD$. Thus $AD = DE$.
Since $DE = DF = FC$, $AD = FC$. Therefore $AD + BD = FC + BF = BC$.

Problem 9: Proof:
Method 1: Draw BG perpendicular to CG at G. Draw CH perpendicular to BF at
H. $\angle GCB = \frac{1}{2}\angle A = \angle HBC$, $\angle BGC = 90° = \angle CHB$, BC is the common side. So $\triangle GCB \cong \triangle HCB$. $GB = HC$.

Since $\angle GBE = \angle GBC - \angle ABC = 90° - \frac{1}{2}\angle A - \angle ABC$,

$\angle HCF = \angle ACB - \angle HCB = \angle ACB - (90° - \frac{1}{2}\angle A)$.

So $\angle GBE - \angle HCF = 90° - \frac{1}{2}\angle A - \angle ABC - \angle ACB + 90° - \frac{1}{2}\angle A = 180° - \angle A - \angle ABC - \angle ACB = 0°$.

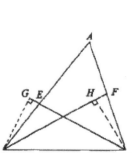

Therefore $\angle GBE = \angle HCF$.
Since $CB = HC$, $\angle BGE = \angle CHF = 90°$, so $\triangle BGE \cong \triangle CHF$. Thus, $BE = CF$.
Note that why BG meets the extension of CE and CH meets BF is because $AB > AC$, that is $\angle ACB > \angle ABC$. Since $\angle ABC + \angle ACB = 180° - \angle A$, so $\angle ACB > \frac{1}{2}(180° - \angle A) =$

$90° - \frac{1}{2}\angle A$. However $\angle ABC < \frac{1}{2}(180° - \angle A) = 90° - \frac{1}{2}\angle A$, so G is outside $\triangle ABC$ and H is inside $\triangle ABC$.

Method 2:
Since $AB > AC$, $\angle ACB > \angle ABC$. Draw $\angle BCG = \angle EBC$ inside $\triangle ABC$. CG meet BF at G.
Since $\angle BCG = \angle CBE$, $\angle GBC = \frac{1}{2}\angle A = \angle ECB$, BC is the common side, so $\triangle GBC \cong \triangle ECB$. $BE = CG$, $\angle BEG = \angle CGB$.
Let the intersection point of BF and CE be H, then $\angle EHF = \angle BHC = 180° - \angle HBC - \angle HCB = 180° - \angle A$.
Therefore, $\angle AEH + \angle AFH = 360° - \angle A - \angle EHF = 180°$.
So $\angle CFG = 180° - \angle AFH = \angle AEH = 180° - \angle BEH = 180° - \angle CGH = \angle CGF$.
We have $CG = CF$.
Since $BE = CG$, $BE = CF$.

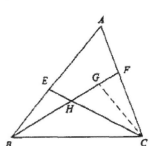

Problem 10:

Prove: Draw the angle bisector of $\angle BAC$ to meet BD at G.
$\angle BAG = 45° = \angle ACF$, $\angle ABG = 90° - \angle BAE = \angle CAF$, $AB = AC$. So $\triangle ABG \cong \triangle CAF$. We have $AG = CF$.
Since $AD = CD$ and $\angle GAD = 45° = \angle FCD$, $\triangle GAD \cong \triangle FCD$. So $\angle ADG = \angle CDF$ and $\angle ADB = \angle CDF$.

Note: through the relationship of congruence, one can also prove: $\angle AFB = \angle DFC$ and $AF + FD = BD$.

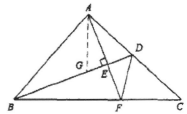

Problem 11. Prove:
Draw $FH \perp AB$ at H.
Since AF bisects $\angle CAB$, $FH = FC$. $\angle CEF = \angle AED = 90° - \angle EAD$, $\angle CFE = 90° - \angle CAF$, $\angle EAD = \angle CAF$.
So $\angle CEF = \angle CFE$, $CE = CF$. $CE = FH$.
Since $\angle CEG = 90° = \angle FHB$, and $\angle CGE = \angle FBH$, so $\triangle CEG \cong \triangle FHB$. $CG = FB$. $CF = GB$.

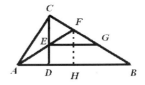

91

Problem 12. Solution :
Extend CD to F such that $DF = AB$. Connect EF.
Since $AE = BD$, $AB = DF$, $BE = AE + AB = BD + DF = BF$.
Since $\angle B = 60°$, $\triangle BEF$ is an equilateral triangle.
So $BE = FE$, $\angle F = \angle B = 60°$.
Since $BC = FD$, $\triangle BCE \cong \triangle FDE$.
Therefore $DE = CE = a$.

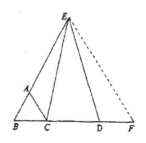

Problem 13: Solution:
Extend CB to F such that $BF = DE$. Connect AF.
We see that $AB = AE = 1$, $BF = ED$ and $\angle FBA = 90° = \angle DEA$.
$\therefore \triangle FBA \cong \triangle DEA$
$\therefore AF = AD$.

We also see that $CF = CB + BF = CB + DE = 1 = CD$. $AC = AC$
$\therefore \triangle ACF \cong \triangle ACD$.
$\therefore S_{\triangle ACF} = S_{\triangle ACD}$.
$S_{ABCDE} = S_{\triangle ADCB} + S_{\triangle AED} = S_{\triangle ADCB} + S_{\triangle ABF}$
$\qquad = S_{ADCF} = S_{\triangle ACD} + S_{\triangle ACF}$
$\therefore S_{ABCDE} = 2S_{\triangle ACF} = 2 \times \dfrac{1}{2} \times 1 \times 1 = 1$.

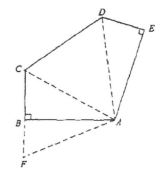

Problem 14: Solution:
Draw $QD//AB$ and meets BC at D. Then $\angle QDC = \angle B = 60°$.

Since $\angle C = 60°$, so $\triangle QDC$ is an equilateral triangle. Therefore, $DQ = CQ = AP$. $DQ//AP$. $APQD$ is a parallelogram. So A, M, D lie on the same line with $AM = \dfrac{1}{2} AD$.
We know that $AP = QD = CD$, $\angle PAC = 60° = \angle DCA$, $AC = AC$.
Therefore $\triangle APC \cong \triangle CDA$. So $PC = DA$. $PC = 2AM = 38$ cm.

Problem 15:
Proof:
Method 1:
Let $\angle MAN = 60°$. We connect AC and we then have $\angle BAM = 60° - \angle MAC = \angle MAN - \angle MAC = \angle CAN$.

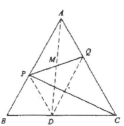

We know that $AB = AC$, $\angle ABM = 60° = \angle ACN$, so $\triangle ABM \cong \triangle ACN$.
$AM = AN$.

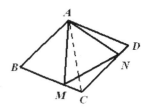

Since $\angle MAN = 60°$, $\triangle AMN$ is an equilateral triangle.

Method 2:
Let $\angle MAN = 60°$. We draw that $ME//AC$ and meets AB at E.
Then $\angle AME = \angle AMB - 60° = (180° - \angle AMN - \angle NMC) - 60° = 60° - \angle NMC$.
But $\angle NMC + \angle MNC + \angle MCN = 180°$, $\angle MCN = 120°$.
So $\angle NMC = 60° - \angle MNC$. $\angle AME = \angle MNC$.
We know that $\angle AEM = 120° = \angle MCN$, $AE = MC$, so $\triangle AEM \cong \triangle MCN$.
$AM = MN$. Since $\angle AMN = 60°$, $\triangle AMN$ is an equilateral triangle.

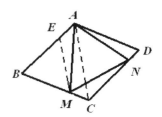

Problem 16:

Proof:
Draw $BH//CF$ to meet the extension of AC at H.
Then $\angle CBH = \angle BCF = 90° - \angle AEC = \angle CAE$,
$\angle BCH = 90° = \angle ACE$,
$BC = AC$.
So $\triangle BCH \cong \triangle ACE$.
$CH = CE = CD$.
Therefore $BF = FG$.

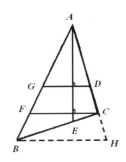

Problem 17. Solution: (B).

Problem 18. Solution:
$\angle DAC + \angle CAB = \angle DAB = 90°$, $\angle BAF + \angle CAB = \angle CAF = 90°$.
$\therefore \angle DAC = \angle BAF$.
We know that $\angle D + \angle DAB + \angle BEB + \angle ABE = 360°$, $\angle DAB = \angle DEB = 90°$.
$\therefore \angle D + \angle ABE = 180°$.
Since $\angle ABF + \angle ABE = 180°$ $\therefore \angle D = \angle ABF$.
Since $\angle DAC = \angle BAF$, $\angle ADC = \angle ABF$, $AD = AB$, so $\triangle DAC \cong \triangle BAF$
and $AC = AF$.
Since $\angle CAF = 90°$, $\angle ACF = 45°$. Therefore we know that CF bisects $\angle ACB$.

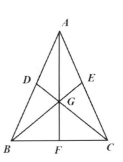

Problem 19. Proof:

Take the midpoints F of AB, and G of AC. Connect DF, EG, FM, and GM.
Since $DF = \frac{1}{2} AB$, $GM \parallel AB$ and $GM = \frac{1}{2} AB$, then $DF = MG$.

Since $FM \parallel AC$ and $FM = \frac{1}{2} AC$, $GE = \frac{1}{2} AC$, so $FM = GE$.

However $\angle DFM = \angle DFB + \angle BFM = (180° - 2\angle DBF) + \angle BAC = (180° - 2\angle GCE) + \angle MGC = \angle CGE + \angle MGC = \angle MGE$. So $\triangle DFM \cong \triangle MGE$ and $DM = EM$.

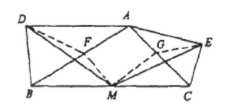

Problem 20: Solution

(1). Connect SC and PB. Since $AD = BC$, $\angle ADC = \angle BCD$, $DC = CD$, so $\triangle ADC \cong \triangle BCD$. $\angle BDC = \angle ACD = 60°$.

So triangle CDO is an equilateral triangle. $CD = CO$.
Since S is the midpoint of DO, $CS \perp DO$. That is, $\triangle CSB$ is a right triangle. $SQ = \frac{1}{2} BC$.

Similarly we can prove that $PQ = \frac{1}{2} BC$. We also know that $PS = \frac{1}{2} AD = \frac{1}{2} BC$, so $PS = QS = PQ$, that is, $\triangle PQS$ is an equilateral triangle.

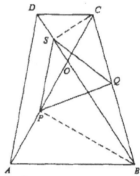

(2) Since $CS = \frac{\sqrt{3}}{2} CD = \frac{3\sqrt{3}}{2}$, and $SB = SO + OB = \frac{1}{2} DO + OB = \frac{1}{2} CD + AB = \frac{13}{2}$,
$BC = \sqrt{CS^2 + SB^2} = 7$.

So $\triangle PQS$ has the side length of $\frac{7}{2}$. Therefore $S_{\triangle PQS} = \frac{\sqrt{3}}{4} \times (\frac{7}{2})^2 = \frac{49\sqrt{3}}{16}$.

PROBLEMS

Problem 1: $ABCD$ is a square with the side length of a. Half circles are drawn inside the square with BC and CD as diameters, respectively. Find the shaded area.

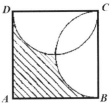

Problem 2: As shown in the figure, circle O has the radius of 1. The inscribed angle $\angle ABC = 30°$. Find the shaded area.

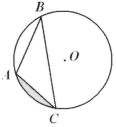

Problem 3: As shown in the figure, isosceles right triangle ABC with $BC = 8$ cm. BDC is a half circle with the diameter BC. Find the sum of two shaded areas I and II.

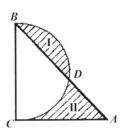

Problem 4: Two diameters of circle O are perpendicular. Using AO, BO, CO, and DO as diameters to draw circles as shown in the figure. Show that the areas of four regions inside the big circle but outside the small circles equal the areas of four regions shared by every two small circles.

Problem 5: Two squares with the side lengths of 10 cm and 12 cm, respectively. Find the shaded area.

Problem 6: (1983 AMC #28) Triangle *ABC* in the figure has area 10. Points *D*, *E*, and *F*, all distinct from *A*, *B*, and *C*, are on sides *AB*, *BC* and *CA* respectively, and $AD = 2$, $DB = 3$. If triangle *ABE* and quadrilateral *DBEF* have equal areas, find that area.

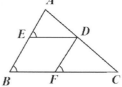

Problem 7: *D*, *E*, and *F* are three vertices of rhombus *BFDE* which are on the sides *AC*, *AB*, and *BC* of triangle *ABC*, respectively, as shown in the figure. If $AB = a$ and $BC = b$, find the perimeter of the rhombus *BFDE*.

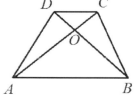

Problem 8: As shown in the figure, trapezoid *ABCD* has the area of *S*. $AB = b$, $CD = a$ with $a < b$ and $AB // CD$. Two diagonals meet at *O*. The area of $\triangle BOC$ is $\frac{2}{9}S$. Find $\frac{a}{b}$.

Problem 9: In $\triangle ABC$, *D* is the midpoint of side *BC*, *E* is the midpoint of *AD*, *F* is the midpoint of *BE*, and *G* is the midpoint of *FC*. What part of the area of $\triangle ABC$ is the area of $\triangle EFG$?

96

Problem 10: As shown in the figure, $\triangle ABC$ is divided into six smaller triangles by lines drawn from the vertices through a common interior point. The areas of four of these triangles are as indicated. Find the area $\triangle ABC$.

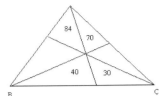

Problem 11. (1988 AIME) Let P be an interior point of $\triangle ABC$ and extend lines from the vertices through P to the opposite sides. Let a, b, c, and d denote the lengths of the segments indicated in the figure. Find the product abc if $a + b + c = 43$ and $d = 3$.

Problem 12: (1997 China Middle School Math Competition) As shown in the figure, P is a point inside the equilateral triangle ABC. The distances from P o each side are $PD = 1$, $PE = 3$, and $PF = 5$. Find the area of the equilateral triangle ABC.

Problem 13: The area of $\triangle ABC$ is 60. As shown in the figure, E and F trisect BC. D is the midpoint of CA. BD intersects AE at G, AF at H. Find the area of quadrilateral $\triangle AGH$.

Problem 14: (2001 AMC 12) In rectangle $ABCD$, points F and G lie on AB so that $AF = FG = GB$ and E is the midpoint of DC. Also, AC intersects EF at H and EG at J. The area of rectangle $ABCD$ is 70. Find the area of triangle EHJ.

(A) $\dfrac{5}{2}$ (B) $\dfrac{35}{12}$ (C) 3 (D) $\dfrac{7}{2}$ (E) $\dfrac{35}{8}$

Problem 15: As shown in the figure, D, E, and F are points on BC, CA, and AB of an acute triangle ABC. AD, BE, and CF meet at P. $AP = BP = CP = 6$. If $PD = x$, $PE = y$, $PF = z$, and $xy + yz + zx = 28$. Find the value of xyz.

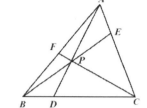

Problem 16: As shown in the figure, $ABCD$ is a rectangle. BD is the diagonal. AE and CF are perpendicular to BD. Find the area of $ABCD$ if $BE = 1$, and $EF = 2$.

$4\sqrt{3}$, (B) $3\sqrt{5}$ (C) 6 (D) Undetermined.

Problem 17: As shown in the figure, $ABCD$ is a square. Find the shaded area.

(A) 17 (B) $\dfrac{290}{17}$ (C) 18 (D) $10\sqrt{3}$

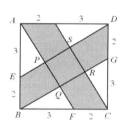

Problem 18: As shown in the figure, the area of parallelogram $ABCD$ is 1. E and F are the midpoints of AB and BC, respectively. AF meets CE at G and DE at H. Find the area of $\triangle EGH$.

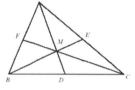

Problem 19: M is the centroid of $\triangle ABC$. $AM = 3$, $MB = 4$, $MC = 5$. Find the area of $\triangle ABC$.

Problem 20: (1984 AIME) A point P is chosen in the interior of $\triangle ABC$ so that when lines are drawn through P parallel to the sides of $\triangle ABC$, the resulting smaller triangles, t_1, t_2 and t_3 in the figure, have areas 4, 9 and 49, respectively. Find the area of $\triangle ABC$.

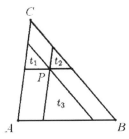

Problem 21: As shown in the figure, in $\triangle ABC$, points D, E, and F are on BC, AC, and AB, respectively. AD, BE, and CF meet at G. $BD = 2CD$. The area $S_1 = 3$, and $S_2 = 4$. Find S_{ABC}, the area of $\triangle ABC$.

Problem 22: As shown in the figure, $S_{\triangle ABC} = 1$. $AD = \dfrac{1}{3}AB$, $BE = \dfrac{1}{3}BC$ and $CF = \dfrac{1}{3}CA$. CD, AE, BF meet pair wisely at X, Y, and Z. Find the area of $\triangle XYZ$.

Problem 23: For triangle ABC, extend AB to F such that $AB = BF$, extend BC to D such that $BC = CD$, and extend CA to E such that $CA = AE$. The ratio of the area of triangle ABC to the area of triangle DEF is 1/7.

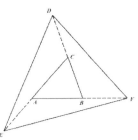

SOLUTIONS TO PROBLEMS

Problem 1: Solution:

Draw $OM \perp CD$, $ON \perp BC$ through O, the center of the square.

The unshaded area consists of one smaller square and two quarter circles.

The shaded area is S, and $S = a^2 - [(\frac{1}{2}a)^2 + 2 \times \frac{1}{4}\pi(\frac{a}{2})^2] = \frac{(6-\pi)a^2}{8}$

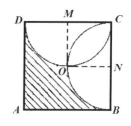

Problem 2: Solution:

Connect CO to meet the circle at D. Connect AD and AO.

We see that $\angle AOC = 60°$.

The shaded are is the same as the area of the sector OAC – the area of $\triangle OAC = \frac{1}{6}\pi - \frac{\sqrt{3}}{4}$

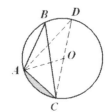

Problem 3: Solution:
Connect CD. Triangle CDB is also an isosceles right triangle with $CD = BD$. So I and III have the same areas.

We also see that D is the midpoint of AB. Therefore the sum of the shaded areas is $\frac{1}{2}S_{\triangle ABC} = \frac{1}{2} \times \frac{1}{2} \times 8^2 = 16$

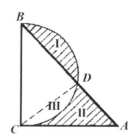

Problem 4: Solution:

We label each region as shown in the figure.

We have:

$\begin{cases} 2x + y = \pi a^2 & (1) \\ 4x + 4y + 4z = \pi(2a)^2 & (2) \end{cases}$

$4 \times (1) - (2)$: $4x - 4z = 0$ $\Rightarrow$ $4x = 4z$

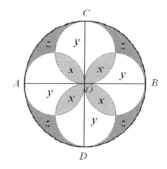

Problem 5: Solution: 50.

We connect BF and we know that AC//BF. So the area of triangle ABH is the same as the area of triangle CHF (**Theorem 4(a)**).

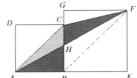

The shaded area is the area of triangle ACF, which is the same as the area of triangle ABC, which is $10 \times 10 \div 2 = 50$.

Problem 6: Solution: 6.

Since triangle ABE and quadrilateral DBEF have equal areas, we know that triangle ADG has the same area as triangle EFG (**Theorem 4(b))**.

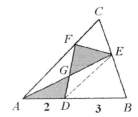

Therefore, AF//DE and $\triangle ABC$ is similar to $\triangle DBE$.

$$\frac{AD}{CE} = \frac{DB}{BE} \Rightarrow \frac{2}{CE} = \frac{3}{BE} \Rightarrow \frac{2}{3} = \frac{CE}{BE} \Rightarrow \frac{2}{3} = \frac{S_{\triangle ACE}}{S_{\triangle ABE}}$$

$$S_{\triangle ABE} = \frac{3}{3+2} \times 10 = 6.$$

Problem 7: Solution:
Let the side of the rhombus be x.
We write the equation of the areas:
$\triangle ABC = \triangle AED + \triangle DFC + S_{BFDE}$.
Since $\angle AED = \angle DFC = \angle B$, we have:
$\frac{1}{2} ac \sin B = \frac{1}{2} x(c-x) \sin B + \frac{1}{2} x(a-x) \sin B + x^2 \sin B.$
$ac = x(c-x) + x(a-x) + 2x^2 = (a+c)x.$
Solving for x: $x = \frac{ac}{a+c}$.

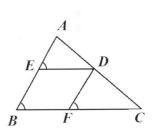

Therefore the perimeter is $\frac{4ac}{a+c}$.

Problem 8: Solution:

Let the areas of $\triangle DOC = S_1$ and $\triangle AOB = S_2$.

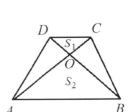

$$\begin{cases} S_1 + S_2 = \dfrac{5}{9}S, \\ S_1 S_2 = (\dfrac{2}{9}S)^2. \end{cases}$$

Solving we get $\begin{cases} S_1 = \dfrac{4}{9}S, \\ S_2 = \dfrac{1}{9}S. \end{cases}$ or $\begin{cases} S_1 = \dfrac{1}{9}S, \\ S_2 = \dfrac{4}{9}S. \end{cases}$

Since, $a < b$, $S_1 < S_2$. Therefore $\dfrac{a}{b} = \sqrt{\dfrac{S_1}{S_2}} = \dfrac{1}{2}$.

Problem 9: Solution: 1/8.

Draw EC. Since the altitude of $\triangle BEC$ is $\dfrac{1}{2}$ the altitude of $\triangle BAC$, and both triangles share the same base, the area of $\triangle BEC = \dfrac{1}{2}$ area of $\triangle BAC$. Area of $\triangle EFC = \dfrac{1}{2}$ area of $\triangle BEC$, and area of $\triangle EGF = \dfrac{1}{2}$ area of $\triangle EFC$; therefore area of $\triangle EGF = \dfrac{1}{4}$ area of $\triangle BEC$. Thus, since area of $\triangle BEC = \dfrac{1}{2}$ area of $\triangle ABC$, area of $\triangle EGF = \dfrac{1}{8}$ area of $\triangle ABC$.

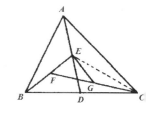

Problem 10: Solution: 315.

Let x and y be the areas for the small triangles as shown in the figure.

$\dfrac{S_{\triangle ABO}}{S_{\triangle ACO}} = \dfrac{S_{\triangle BOD}}{S_{\triangle COD}} \Rightarrow \dfrac{84+x}{70+y} = \dfrac{40}{30}$

Similarly, we have $\dfrac{S_{\triangle ABO}}{S_{\triangle BCO}} = \dfrac{S_{\triangle AEO}}{S_{\triangle CEO}} \Rightarrow \dfrac{84+x}{40+30} = \dfrac{70}{y}$

Or $\dfrac{70+y}{70} = \dfrac{3}{4}\dfrac{70}{y}$.

$x = 56$ and $y = 35$. The total area is $84 + 70 + 40 + 30 + 35 + 56 = 315$.

Problem 11. Solution:
By **Theorem 9,** we have

$$\frac{S_{\triangle BPC}}{S_{\triangle BAC}} = \frac{d}{d+a} \quad (1)$$

$$\frac{S_{\triangle CPA}}{S_{\triangle CBA}} = \frac{d}{d+b} \quad (2)$$

$$\frac{S_{\triangle APB}}{S_{\triangle ACB}} = \frac{d}{d+c} \quad (3)$$

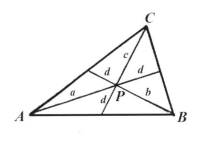

We also know that $S_{\triangle BPC} + S_{\triangle CPA} + S_{\triangle APB} = S_{\triangle ABC}$

Adding (1), (2), and (3), we get: $\frac{d}{d+a} + \frac{d}{d+b} + \frac{d}{d+c} = 1$.

Simplifying into: $2d^3 + (a+b+c)d^2 - abc = 0$.

Therefore $abc = 2d^3 + (a+b+c)d^2 = 2 \times 3^2 + 43 \times 3^2 = 441$.

Problem 12: Solution:
Connect PD, PE, and PF.

We have $S_{\triangle ABC} = \frac{1}{2}(PD + PE + PF) \cdot BC = \frac{9}{2} BC$.

We know that $S_{\triangle BPC} = \frac{1}{2} PD \cdot BC = \frac{1}{2} BC$.

Let the height on BC be h. We have $\frac{PD}{h} = \frac{S_{\triangle PBC}}{S_{\triangle ABC}} = \frac{1}{9}$.

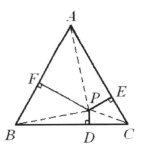

So we get $h = 9$.

Then the side of triangle ABC is $9 \times \frac{2\sqrt{3}}{3} = 6\sqrt{3}$.

Therefore $S_{\triangle ABC} = \frac{\sqrt{3}}{4} \times (6\sqrt{3})^2 = 27\sqrt{3}$.

Problem 13: Solution:
Connect FG and FD. Since AD = DC, EF = FC, we know that DF is parallel to AE. $S_{\triangle ADH} = S_{\triangle HFG}$.

We also know that $S_{\triangle BDC} = \frac{1}{2} S_{\triangle ABC} = 30$ and $S_{\triangle BFD} = \frac{2}{3} S_{\triangle BDC} = 20$.

Since BE = EF and DF // GE, BG = GD, $S_{\triangle BEG} = \frac{1}{4} S_{\triangle BFD} = 5$, and

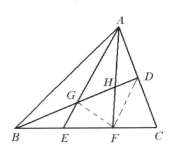

$S_{\triangle BEFG} = S_{\triangle BEG} = 5$, and $S_{\triangle BGA} = S_{\triangle ABE} - S_{\triangle BEG} = \frac{1}{3}S_{\triangle ABC} - 5 = 20 - 5 = 15$.

Let $S_{\triangle AHG} = a$, $S_{\triangle HdJ} = b$, and $S_{\triangle ADH} = c$.
So $c + b = 20 - 10 = 10$, and $a + c = 30 - 15 = 15$.
From Theorem 8, we have $\frac{a+c}{b+c} = \frac{GH}{HD} = \frac{15}{10} = \frac{3}{2}$.

So by Theorem 6 we have $\frac{a}{c} = \frac{3}{2} \Rightarrow 2a = 3c$

We already know that $a + c = 15$. Therefore $a = 9$ and $b = 6$.

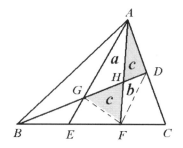

Problem 14: Solution: (C).
The area of triangle EFG is $(1/6)(70) = 35/3$.

Triangles AFH and CEH are similar, so $3/2 = EC/AF = EH/HF$ and $EH/EF = 3/5$.

Triangles AGJ and CEJ are similar, so $3/4 = EC/AG = EJ/JG$ and $EJ/EG = 3/7$.

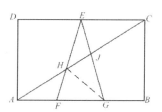

Since the areas of the triangles that have a common altitude are proportional to their bases, the ratio of the area of $\triangle EHJ$ to the area of $\triangle EHG$ is $3/7$, and the ratio of the area of $\triangle EHG$ to that of $\triangle EFG$ is $3/5$.

Therefore, the ratio of the area of $\triangle EHJ$ to the area of $\triangle EFG$ is $(3/5)(3/7) = 9/35$.
Thus, the area of $\triangle EHJ$ is $(9/35)(35/3) = 3$.

Problem 15: Solution:
Draw $PM \perp BC$ at M, $AN \perp BC$ at N.
We know that $S_{\triangle PBC} = \frac{1}{2} PM \cdot BC$ and $S_{\triangle ABC} = \frac{1}{2} AN \cdot BC$.

Therefore $\frac{S_{\triangle PBC}}{S_{\triangle ABC}} = \frac{PM}{AN} = \frac{PD}{AD} = \frac{x}{x+6}$.

Similarly $\frac{S_{\triangle PAC}}{S_{\triangle ABC}} = \frac{y}{y+6}$ and $\frac{S_{\triangle PAB}}{S_{\triangle ABC}} = \frac{z}{z+6}$.

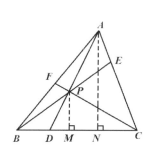

Adding them together we get:

$$\frac{x}{x+6} + \frac{y}{y+6} + \frac{z}{z+6} = \frac{S_{\triangle PBC} + S_{\triangle PAC} + S_{\triangle PAB}}{S_{\triangle ABC}} = 1 \quad \Rightarrow$$

$$1 - \frac{6}{x+6} + 1 - \frac{6}{y+6} + 1 - \frac{6}{z+6} = 1 \quad \Rightarrow \quad \frac{3}{x+6} + \frac{3}{y+6} + \frac{3}{z+6} = 1.$$

Simplifying:
$3(yz + zx + xy) + 36(x + y + z) + 324 = xyz + 6(xy + yz + zx) + 36(x + y + z) + 216.$
We are given that $xy + yz + zx = 28$.
Hence $xyz = 108 - 3(xy + yz + zx) = 24$.

Problem 16: Solution: (A).
Since $AB = CD$, $\angle ABD = \angle CDB$, Rt$\triangle ABE \cong$ Rt$\triangle CDF$.
$\therefore BE = DF$.

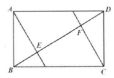

We know that $BE = 1$, $EF = 2$.
$\therefore FD = 1$, $ED = EF + FD = 2 + 1 = 3$
$BD = BE + ED = 1 + 3 = 4$.
$AE^2 = EB \cdot DE = 1 \times 3 = 3 \quad \Rightarrow \quad AE = \sqrt{3}$.
$S_{ABCD} = 2 S_{\triangle ABD} = 2 \cdot \frac{1}{2} BD \cdot AE = 4\sqrt{3}$

Problem 17: Solution: (B).
Both $BGDE$ and $CHAF$ are parallelograms. $PQRS$ is also a parallelogram.

Since $\triangle ADE \cong \triangle BAF$, $DE = AF$, $\angle ADE = \angle BAF$.

Therefore $\angle QPS = \angle PAD + \angle ADP = \angle PAD + \angle BAF = 90°$.

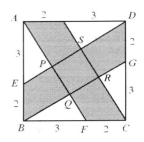

So $PQRS$ is a rectangle.
In Rt$\triangle ABF$, $AF = \sqrt{AB^2 + BF^2} = \sqrt{34}$.
In parallelogram $AFCH$, $S_{AFCH} = FC \times AB = AF \times PS$.
So $PS = \frac{10}{\sqrt{34}}$.

Similarly, $PQ = \frac{10}{\sqrt{34}}$.

So $PQRS$ is a square. $S_{PQRS} = PS^2 = \frac{50}{17}$.

Therefore the shaded area is: $S_{AFCH} + S_{BGDE} - S_{PQRS} = 2 \times 5 + 2 \times 5 - \frac{50}{17} = \frac{290}{17}$.

Problem 18: Solution:

Connect BG and DG.

Since $S_{\triangle ABF} = \frac{1}{2} S_{\triangle ABC} = S_{\triangle EBC}$, $S_{\triangle AEG} = S_{\triangle CFG}$.

Therefore $S_{\triangle BEG} = S_{\triangle AEG} = S_{\triangle CFG} = S_{\triangle BFG} = \frac{1}{3} S_{\triangle ABF} = \frac{1}{6} S_{\triangle ABC} = \frac{1}{12} S_{ABCD} = \frac{1}{12}$.

We also know that $S_{\triangle ADG} + S_{\triangle BCG} = \frac{1}{2} S_{ABCD}$. So $S_{\triangle ADG} = \frac{1}{3}$.

So $\frac{HE}{DH} = \frac{S_{\triangle AEH}}{S_{\triangle ADH}} = \frac{S_{\triangle GEH}}{S_{\triangle GDH}} = \frac{S_{\triangle AEH} + S_{\triangle GEH}}{S_{\triangle ADH} + S_{\triangle GDH}} = \frac{S_{\triangle AEG}}{S_{\triangle ADG}} = \frac{\frac{1}{12}}{\frac{1}{3}} = \frac{1}{4}$.

$S_{\triangle AEH} = \frac{1}{5} S_{\triangle DAE} = \frac{1}{5} \times (\frac{1}{4} S_{ABCD}) = \frac{1}{20}$.

Therefore $S_{\triangle EGH} = S_{\triangle AEG} - S_{AEH} = \frac{1}{12} - \frac{1}{20} = \frac{1}{30}$.

Problem 19: Solution:

Extend AD to G such that $MD = DG$. Connect CG.
So we have $MG = 2MD = AM = 3$, $GC = BM = 4$, and $MC = 5$.
So $\angle MGC = 90°$.

We also have $S_{\triangle MGC} = \frac{1}{2} MG \cdot GC = 6$.

$S_{\triangle MDC} = \frac{1}{2} S_{\triangle MGC} = 3$

Thus $S_{\triangle ABC} = 6 S_{\triangle MDC} = 18$.

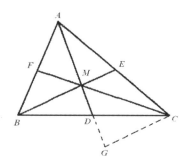

Problem 20: Solution:
Let $MP = P$, $PN = q$, $RT = r$, $AB = c$, and the area of $\triangle ABC$ be S.

Three small triangles are similar to $\triangle ABC$. The ratio of the square roots of their areas is the same as the ratio of their corresponding sides.

So we have $\dfrac{2}{\sqrt{S}} = \dfrac{q}{c}$ (1)

$\dfrac{3}{\sqrt{S}} = \dfrac{p}{c}$ (2)

$\dfrac{7}{\sqrt{S}} = \dfrac{r}{c}$ (3)

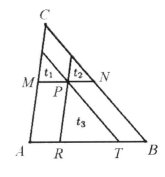

Adding (1), (2), and (3) together we get:

$\dfrac{2+3+7}{\sqrt{S}} = \dfrac{p+q+r}{c} = \dfrac{c}{c} = 1$

Therefore $\sqrt{S} = 12$ and $S = 144$.

Note: $\sqrt{S} = \sqrt{t_1} + \sqrt{t_2} + \sqrt{t_3}$

Problem 21: Solution:

Since $BD = 2CD$, $\dfrac{S_3}{S_2} = 2$.

So $S_3 = 8$.

Therefore $\dfrac{BG}{GE} = \dfrac{S_2 + S_3}{S_1} = 4$.

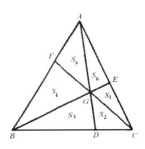

$\dfrac{S_4 + S_5}{S_6} = 4$. (1)

We also know that

$\dfrac{S_4 + S_5}{S_6 + S_1} = \dfrac{S_3}{S_2} = 2$, (2)

And $\dfrac{S_6 + S_1}{S_3 + S_2} = \dfrac{S_5}{S_4} = \dfrac{AF}{FB}$ (3)

Solving the system of equations (1), (2), and (3), we have
$S_4 = 8$, $S_5 = 4$, $S_6 = 3$.
So $S_{\triangle ABC} = S_1 + S_2 + S_3 + S_4 + S_5 + S_6 = 3 + 4 + 8 + 8 + 4 + 3 = 30$.

Problem 22: Solution:

Connect CY and let $S_{\triangle BEY} = S$.

Then we have $\dfrac{S_{\triangle YBE}}{S_{\triangle YBC}} = \dfrac{BE}{BC} = \dfrac{1}{3}$.

So $S_{\triangle YBC} = 3S$.

Since $\dfrac{S_{\triangle YCF}}{S_{\triangle YAF}} = \dfrac{CF}{FA}$ and $\dfrac{S_{\triangle BCF}}{S_{\triangle BAF}} = \dfrac{CF}{FA}$,

$\dfrac{S_{\triangle BAY}}{S_{\triangle BCY}} = \dfrac{S_{\triangle BAF} - S_{\triangle YAF}}{S_{\triangle BCF} - S_{\triangle YCF}} = \dfrac{FA}{CF} = 2$.

So $S_{\triangle BAY} = 6S$.

Therefore we have $S_{\triangle ABE} = S_{\triangle BAY} + S_{\triangle BEY} = 7S$.

Since $\dfrac{S_{\triangle ABE}}{S_{\triangle ABC}} = \dfrac{1}{3}$, $S_{\triangle ABC} = 21S = 1$.

So we get $S = \dfrac{1}{21}$.

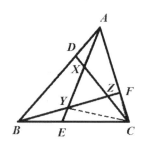

$S_{\triangle BAY} = \dfrac{6}{21}$. Similarly, we have $S_{\triangle CAX} = S_{\triangle BCZ} = \dfrac{6}{21}$.

Therefore $S_{\triangle XYZ} = S_{\triangle ABC} - (S_{\triangle BAY} + S_{\triangle CAX} + S_{\triangle BCZ}) = 1 - \dfrac{6}{21} \times 3 = \dfrac{1}{7}$.

Problem 23: Proof:
Connect FC, DA, and EB as shown in the figure. All the seven triangles have the same areas.

Therefore, the ratio of the area of triangle ABC to the area of triangle DEF is 1/7.

50 AMC Lectures Problems Book 1   (11) Eight Methods To Draw Auxiliary Lines

PROBLEMS

Problem 1: $\triangle ABC$, AD is the median. Show that $AD < \frac{1}{2}(AB + AC)$.

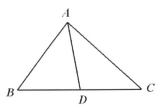

Problem 2: (1971 AMC #26) In triangle ABC, point F divides side AC in the ratio 1:2. Let E be the point of intersection of sides BC and AG where G is the midpoint of BF. Then point E divides side BC in the ratio
(A) 1:4   (B) 1:3   (C) 2:5   (D) 4:11   (E) 3:8

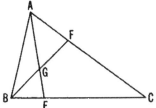

Problem 3: (1980 AMC) In triangle ABC, $\angle CBA = 72°$, E is the midpoint of side AC, and D is a point on side BC such that $2BD = DC$; AD and BE intersect at F. The ratio of the area of $\triangle BDF$ to the area of quadrilateral $FDCE$ is

(A) $\frac{1}{5}$ (B) $\frac{1}{4}$ (C) $\frac{1}{3}$ (D) $\frac{2}{5}$

(E) none of these

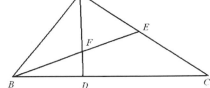

Problem 4: As shown in the figure, $\angle EAF = \angle EDC$. Prove $\dfrac{BD}{BE} = \dfrac{AF}{EF}$.

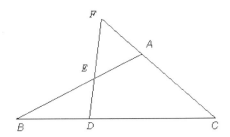

Problem 5: The measure of the longer base of a trapezoid is b. The measure of the line segment joining the midpoints of the diagonals is d. Find the measure of the shorter base.

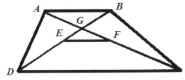

109

Problem 6: In $\triangle ABC$, D is a point on side BA such that $BD:DA = 1:2$. E is a point on side CB so that $CE:EB = 1:4$. Segments DC and AE intersect at F. Express $CF:FD$ in terms of two positive relatively prime integers.

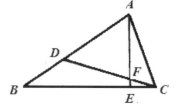

Problem 7: In $\triangle ABC$, BE is a median and O is the midpoint of BE. Draw AO and extend it to meet BC at D. Draw CO and extend it to meet BA at F. If $CO = 15$, $OF = 5$, and $AO = 12$, find the measure OD.

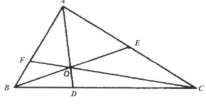

Problem 8: Can you establish a relationship for problem 7 between OD and AO?

Problem 9: (1970 AMC) In a triangle, the area is numerically equal to the perimeter. What is the radius of the inscribed circle?
(A) 2　　(B) 3　　(C) 4　　(D) 5　　(E) 6.

Problem 10: (2004 AMC 12) Circles A, B, and C are externally tangent to each other and internally tangent to circle D. Circles B and C are congruent. Circle A has radius 1 and passes through the center of D. What is the radius of circle B?

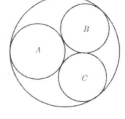

(A) $\dfrac{2}{3}$　　(B) $\dfrac{\sqrt{3}}{2}$　　(C) $\dfrac{7}{8}$　　(D) $\dfrac{8}{9}$　　(E) $\dfrac{1+\sqrt{3}}{3}$

Problem 11: In triangle ABC lines CE and AD are drawn so that $\dfrac{CD}{DB} = \dfrac{3}{1}$ and $\dfrac{AE}{EB} = \dfrac{3}{2}$. Let $r = \dfrac{CP}{PE}$, where P is the intersection point of CE and AD. Then r equals:

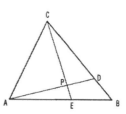

(A) 3　　(B) $\dfrac{3}{2}$　　(C) 4　　(D) 5　　(E) $\dfrac{5}{2}$

110

Problem 12: Triangle *ABC*, *D*, *E* are the points on *BC*, and *AB*, respectively. If $\angle 1 = \angle 2$, $DA = DB$, prove: $\dfrac{BD}{DC} = \dfrac{AE}{BE}$.

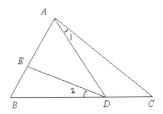

Problem 13: In a triangle *ABC*, *BD* = *CE*, *DM* = *ME*. Prove triangle *ABC* is an isosceles triangle.

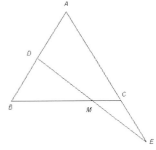

Problem 14: In $\triangle ABC$, $AB > AC$, Prove $\angle C > \angle B$.

Problem 15. (2011 AIME I) In triangle *ABC*, *AB* = 125, *AC* = 117 and *BC* = 120. The angle bisector of angle *A* intersects *BC* at point *L*, and the angle bisector of angle *B* intersects *AC* at point *K*. Let *M* and *N* be the feet of the perpendiculars from *C* to *BK* and *AL*, respectively. Find *MN*.

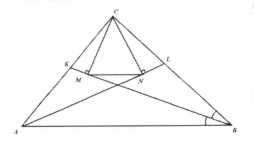

Problem 16: Diagonals *AC* and *BD* of quadrilateral *ABCD* meet at *E*. If *AE* = 2, *BE* = 5, *CE* = 10, *DE* = 4, and $BC = \dfrac{15}{2}$, find *AB*.

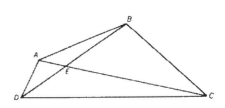

Problem 17. (1983 AMC) Distinct points A and B are on a semicircle with diameter MN and center C. The point P is on CN and $\angle CAP = \angle CBP = 10°$. If $\widehat{MA} = 40°$, then $\widehat{BN}$ equals
(A) 10°   (B) 15°   (C) 20°   (D) 25°   (E) 30°

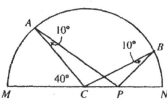

Problem 18: In $\triangle ABC$, $\angle A = 2\angle B$. CD bisects $\angle C$. Show that $BC = AC + AD$.

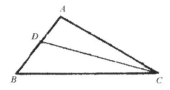

Problem 19: $\triangle ABC$. AD bisects $\angle A$. $AD = AB$. $CM \perp AD$.
Prove: $AM = \dfrac{1}{2}(AB + AC)$.

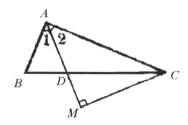

Problem 20: In $\triangle ABC$, $\angle B = 2\angle A$.
Show that $AC^2 = BC^2 + BC \times AB$.

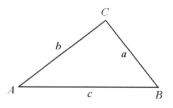

Problem 21: In $\triangle ABC$, $\angle B = 2\angle C$. $AD \perp BC$ at D. M is the midpoint of BC. Show that $MD = \dfrac{1}{2}AB$.

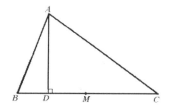

SOLUTIONS

Problem 1: Solution:
Method 1:
Extending AD to E such that $DE = AD$. Connecting BE.
In $\triangle ADC$ and $\triangle EDB$,
$AD = DE$, $CD = BD$, $\angle ADC = \angle EDB$,
$\quad \therefore \triangle ADC \cong \triangle EDB$.
$\quad \therefore BE = AC$.
In $\triangle ABD$, $AB + BE > AE$.

$\therefore AB + AC > 2AD \Rightarrow AD < \dfrac{1}{2}(AB + AC)$

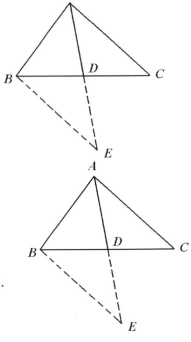

Method 2:

Draw $BE \parallel AC$ and $BE = AC$.
Since $BE \parallel AC$, $\angle ACB = \angle EBC$.
Since $BE = AC$, $BD = DC$, $\triangle BED \cong \triangle CAD$.
Therefore $\angle BDE = \angle CDA$, $DE = AD$.
We know that $\angle BDE + \angle EDC = 180°$ and $\angle CDA + \angle EDC = 180°$.
Therefore A, D, and E lie in the same line with $AE = 2AD$.
In $\triangle ABE$, $AB + BE > AE$, $\therefore 2AD < AB + AC$
$\Rightarrow AD < \dfrac{1}{2}(AB + AC)$.

Method 3:
Connecting DE such that E is the midpoint of AB.
In $\triangle ADE$, $AD < AE + ED \quad \Rightarrow$
$AD < \dfrac{AB}{2} + \dfrac{AC}{2} = \dfrac{1}{2}(AB + AC)$

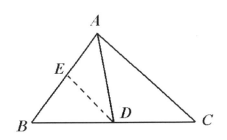

Problem 2: Solution: (B).

Draw *FH* parallel to line *AGE* (see figure). Then *BE* = *EH* because *BG* = *GF* and a line (*GE*) parallel to the base (*HF*) of a triangle (*HFB*) divides the other tow sides proportionally. By the same reasoning applied to triangle *AEC* with line *FH* parallel to base *AE*, we see that *HC* = 2*EH*, because *FC* = 2*AF* is given. Therefore *EC* = *EH* + *HC* = 3*EH* = 3*BE*, and *E* divides side *BC* in the ratio 1:3.

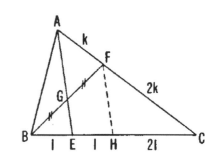

Problem 3: Solution: (A).

In the adjoining figure the line segment from *E* to *G*, the midpoint of *DC*, is drawn. Then

area $\triangle EBG = (\frac{2}{3})$ (area $\triangle EBC$),

area $\triangle BDF = (\frac{1}{4})$ (area $\triangle EBG$) = $(\frac{1}{6})$ (area $\triangle EBC$).

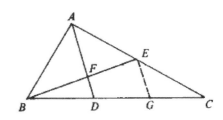

(Note that since *EG* connects the midpoints of sides *AC* and *DC* in $\triangle ACD$, *EG* is parallel to *AD*.) Therefore, area *FDCE* = $(\frac{5}{6})$ (area $\triangle EBC$) and $\frac{\text{area}\triangle BDF}{\text{area} FDCE} = \frac{1}{5}$. The measure of $\angle CBA$ was not needed.

Problem 4: Proof:

Method 1. Extending *FD* to *G*. Draw *BG* = *BD*.
Since *BD* = *BG*, so $\angle 3 = \angle 4$.

Since $\angle 1 = \angle 2$ (given), $\angle 2 = \angle 3$ (vertical angles)
So $\angle 1 = \angle 4$.
Since $\angle 5 = \angle 6$, so $\triangle BCE \sim \triangle FAE$.

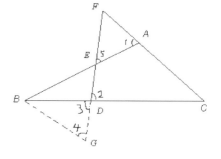

So $\dfrac{BF}{BE} = \dfrac{AF}{EF}$ Or $\dfrac{BD}{BE} = \dfrac{AF}{EF}$

Method 2. Draw *AG*//*BC*.
So $\triangle BDE \sim \triangle AGE$. So $\dfrac{BD}{BE} = \dfrac{AG}{AE}$. Since $\angle EAF = \angle EDC$
And $\angle EDC = \angle FGA$, so $\angle EAF = \angle FGA$ and
$\angle F = \angle F$. So $\triangle FGA \sim \triangle FAE$.

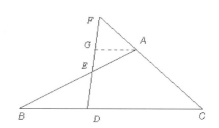

So $\dfrac{AF}{EF} = \dfrac{AG}{AE}$ Or $\dfrac{BD}{BE} = \dfrac{AF}{EF}$

Method 3. Since ∠EAF = ∠EDC, so A, E, D, C are in the same circle. So ∠1 = ∠2, ∠F = ∠F, △AFD ~ △EFC. So $\dfrac{AF}{EF} = \dfrac{AD}{EC}$. Similarly, $\dfrac{BD}{BE} = \dfrac{AD}{EC}$. Therefore $\dfrac{BD}{BE} = \dfrac{AF}{EF}$.

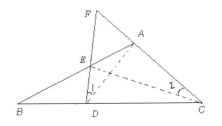

Problem 5: ANSWER: $b - 2d$, where b is the length of the longer base and d is the length of the line joining the midpoints of the diagonals.

Problem 6: Solution:
Draw $DG \parallel BC$.
△ADG ~ △ABE, and $\dfrac{AD}{AB} = \dfrac{DG}{BE} = \dfrac{2}{3}$. Then $DG = \dfrac{2}{3}(BE)$.
But △DGF ~ △CEF, and $\dfrac{CF}{FD} = \dfrac{EC}{DG}$.
Since $EC = \dfrac{1}{4}(BE)$, $\dfrac{CF}{FD} = \dfrac{\dfrac{1}{4}(BE)}{\dfrac{2}{3}(BE)} = \dfrac{3}{8}$.

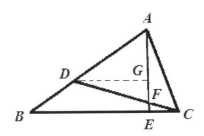

Problem 7: Solution:

Draw EH parallel to AD. Since E is the midpoint of AC, $EG = \dfrac{1}{2}(AO) = 6$. Since H is the midpoint of CD, $GH = \dfrac{1}{2}(OD)$. In △BEH, OD is parallel to EH and O is the midpoint of BE; therefore, $OD = \dfrac{1}{2}(EH)$.

Then $OD = \dfrac{1}{2}(EG + GH)$, so $OD = \dfrac{1}{2}(6 + \dfrac{1}{2}OD) = 4$.

Note that the measures of CO and OF were not necessary for the solution of this problem.

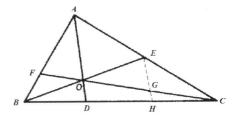

Problem 8: ANSWER: $OD = \frac{1}{3}AO$, regardless of the measures of CO, OF, and AO.

Problem 9: Solution: (A).
Let the given triangle be ABC with perimeter $p = AB + BC + CA$, and denote the center and radius of its inscribed circle by O and r; see figure. Then the area of $\triangle ABC$ is the sum of the areas of $\triangle AOB$, $\triangle BOC$, and $\triangle COA$, whose bases are AB, BC and CA respectively, and whose altitudes have length r. Therefore

$$\text{Area of } \triangle ABC = \frac{1}{2}rAB + \frac{1}{2}rBC + \frac{1}{2r}CA$$

$$= \frac{1}{2}r(AB + BC + CA) = \frac{1}{2}rp,$$

Which is given to be equal to the perimeter p of $\triangle ABC$:
$\frac{1}{2}rp = p$. Hence $r = 2$.

Problem 10: Solution: (D).
Let E, H, and F be the centers of circles A, B, and D, respectively, and let G be the point of tangency of circles B and C. Let $x = FG$ and $y = GH$. Since
the center of circle D lies on circle A and the circles have a common point of tangency, the radius of circle D is 2, which is the diameter of circle A. Applying the Pythagorean Theorem to right triangles EGH and FGH gives
$(1 + y)^2 = (1 + x)^2 + y^2$ and $(2 - y)^2 = x^2 + y^2$; from which it follows that

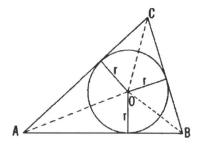

$$y = x + \frac{x^2}{2} \quad \text{and} \quad y = 1 - \frac{x^2}{4}.$$

$$y - x + \frac{x^2}{2} \quad \text{and} \quad y = 1 - \frac{x^2}{4}.$$

The solutions of this system are $(x, y) = (2/3, 8/9)$ and $(x, y) = (-2, 0)$. The radius of circle B is the positive solution for y, which is 8/9.

Problem 11: Solution: (D).
Draw DR //AB. $\frac{CR}{RE} = \frac{CD}{DB} = \frac{3}{1}$, $\frac{RD}{EB} = \frac{CD}{CB} = \frac{3}{4}$;

$\therefore CR = 3RE = 3RP + 3PE$ and $RD = \dfrac{3}{4}EB$,

$\therefore CP = CR + RP = 4RP + 3PE$.

Since $\triangle RDP \sim \triangle EAP$,

$\dfrac{RP}{PE} = \dfrac{RD}{AE}$, $\therefore RD = \dfrac{RP \times AE}{PE}$.

But $AE = \dfrac{3}{2}EB$. $\therefore RD = \dfrac{RP}{PE} \cdot \dfrac{3}{2}EB$.

$\therefore \dfrac{3}{4}EB = \dfrac{3}{2}EB \cdot \dfrac{RP}{PE}$, $RP = \dfrac{1}{2}PE$,

$CP = 4 \cdot \dfrac{1}{2}PE + 3PE = 5PE$; $\therefore \dfrac{CP}{PE} = 5$.

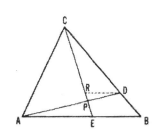

Problem 12: Proof:
Method 1.
Since $\angle 1 + \angle 3 = \angle 2 + \angle 4$, and $\angle 1 = \angle 2$, so $\angle 3 = \angle C$. Since $DA = DB$, so $\angle 4 = \angle B$ and $\triangle ADE \sim \triangle BCA$.

So $\dfrac{AD}{BC} = \dfrac{AE}{AB}, \dfrac{BD}{BC} = \dfrac{AE}{AB}$

So $\dfrac{BD}{BC - BD} = \dfrac{AE}{AB - AE}$, i.e. $\dfrac{BD}{DC} = \dfrac{AE}{BE}$

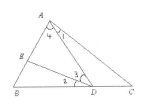

Method 2. Draw $BM//DE$.

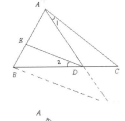

Method 3. Draw $BM//AD$.

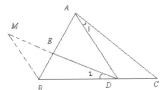

Method 4. Draw $AM//BC$.

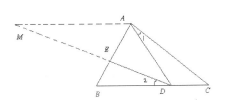

Method 5. Draw *AM//DE*.

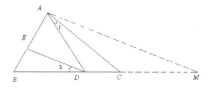

Method 6. Draw *DM//AB*.

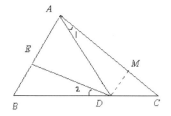

Problem 13: Proof :
Draw *DG//BC*. Since *MC//DG* and cuts *DE* into two equal parts, it also cuts *GE* into two equal parts.

Therefore we know *GC = CE = DB*, or *DBCG* is an isosceles trapezoid. Therefore $\angle DBC = \angle GCB$. Hence triangle *ABC* is an isosceles triangle.

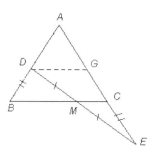

Problem 14: Proof:

Method 1:
Since *AB > AC*, we find appoint E on AB such that *AE = AC*. Therefore $\angle 1 = \angle 2$.

Since $\angle 2 = \angle B + \angle BCE$, $\angle 2 > \angle B$. Therefore $\angle 1 > \angle B$.
Since $\angle C > \angle 1$, $\angle C > \angle B$.

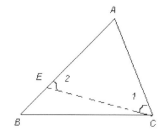

Method 2: (*AF = AB*)
Since *AB > AC*, we extend AC to F such that *AF = AB*. Therefore $\angle ABF = \angle AFB$.
Since $\angle ACB = \angle CFB + \angle FBC$, $\angle C > \angle F$.
Since $\angle F = \angle ABF > \angle ABC$, $\angle F > \angle B$.
Therefore $\angle C > \angle B$.

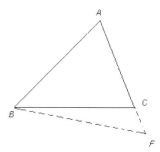

Problem 15. Solution:

Extend *MN* such that it intersects lines *AC* and *BC* at point *O* and *Q*, respectively.

Extend *CM* to meet *AB* at, say, *S*. then triangle *BCM* and triangle *BSM* are congruent. Hence *BS* = *BC* = 120. Similarly, extend *CN* to meet *AB* at, say, *R*, and triangle *ACN* and triangle *ARN* are congruent. Hence *AR* = *AC* = 117. So *CM* = *MS*, and *CN* = *NR*. So *MN* is the midline of triangle *CSR* (and *OQ* is the midline of *AB*).

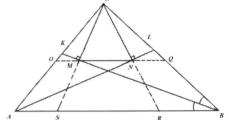

$$MN = \frac{AB}{2} - \frac{AS}{2} - \frac{BR}{2} = \frac{AB}{2} - \frac{AB-BS}{2} - \frac{AB-AR}{2}$$
$$= \frac{BS}{2} + \frac{AR}{2} - \frac{AB}{2} = \frac{BC+AC-AB}{2} = \frac{120+117-125}{2} = 56$$

Problem 16: Solution:
Since $\frac{BE}{AE} = \frac{CE}{DE} = \frac{15}{2}$,   (1)

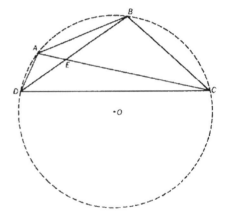

$\triangle AED \sim \triangle BEC$. Therefore, $\frac{BE}{AE} = \frac{BC}{AD}$, or $\frac{5}{2} = \frac{\frac{15}{2}}{AD}$.

Thus, *AD* = 3.
Similarly, from (1), $\triangle AEB \sim \triangle DEC$.   (2)
Therefore, $\frac{AE}{DE} = \frac{AB}{DC}$, or $\frac{1}{2} = \frac{AB}{DC}$. Thus, *DC* = 2(*AB*).
Also, from (2), ∠*BAC* = ∠*BDC*. Therefore, quadrilateral *ABCD* is cyclic.

Now, applying Ptolemy's Theorem to cyclic quadrilateral *ABCD*,
(*AB*)(*DC*) = (*AD*)(*BC*) = (*AC*)(*BD*).
Substituting, we find $AB = \frac{1}{2}\sqrt{171}$.

Problem 17. Solution: (official solution): (C).
In $\triangle ACP$ and $\triangle BCP$ we have (in the order given) the condition angle-side-side.
Since these triangles are not congruent (∠*CPA* ≠ ∠*CPB*), we must have that ∠*CPA* and ∠*CPB* are supplementary.
From $\triangle ACP$ we compute
∠*CPA* = 180° − 10° − (180° − 40°) = 30°.
Thus ∠*CPB* = 150° and $\widehat{BN}$ = ∠*PCB* = 180° − 10° − 150° = 20°.

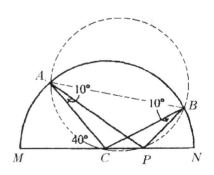

Method 2 (our solution)
∠CPA = 30° (arc AC)
∠CBA = 30° (arc AC)
∠CAB = ∠CBA (arc BC = arc AC)
∠PAB = 30° − 10 ° = 20°.
∠BCP = ∠PAB = 20° (same arc PB).

Problem 18: Solution:
Since $\angle A = 2\angle B$, BC is the longest side in $\triangle ABC$.
Let E be a point in BC such that $EC = AC$. Connect DE.
Since $AC = EC$, $DC = DC$, and $\angle ACD = \angle ECD$, $\triangle ADC$ and
$\triangle EDC$ are congruent.
Therefore $AD = DE$, and $\angle A = \angle DEC$.
Since $\angle A = 2\angle B$, $\angle DEC = 2\angle B = \angle B + \angle BDE$. We see that $\angle B = \angle BDE$. Therefore $DE = BE$.
$BC = EC + BE = EC + DE = AC + AD$

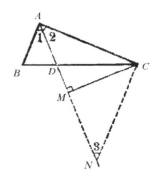

Problem 19: Solution:
Extend AM to N such that $AM = MN$ and connect C.
$AN = 2AM$
Since $CM \perp AM$, $AC = CN$
Since $\angle 2 = \angle 3$ and $\angle 1 = \angle 2$, so $\angle 1 = \angle 3$ and $AB // CN$.
So $\angle B = \angle DCN$.
Now we know that $\angle B = \angle ADB = \angle CDN$.
Therefore $\angle CDN = \angle DCN$, $DN = CN$
$AN = 2AM = DN + AD = CN + AB \Rightarrow AM = \frac{1}{2}(AB + AC)$

Problem 20: Solution:
Extend AB to D such that $BD = BC$.
Both triangles ADC and DBC are isosceles triangles.
$\triangle ACD \sim \triangle DBC$
$\dfrac{AD}{CD} = \dfrac{AC}{BC} \Rightarrow \dfrac{c+a}{b} = \dfrac{b}{a}$
That is $AC^2 = BC^2 + BC \times AB$.

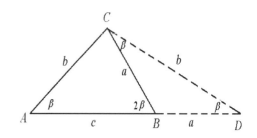

Problem 21: Solution:
Connect ML and DL such that L is the midpoint of AC. We see that DL is the median of right triangle ADC on the hypotenuse AC. ML is the midline of $\triangle ABC$ and $ML // BA$

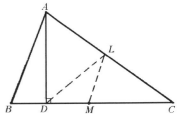

Therefore $ML = \frac{1}{2} AB$.

We also see that $\angle MLD = \angle CML - \angle MDL = \angle B - \angle C = \angle C = \angle MDL$.

Therefore $ML = MD$.

That is $MD = \frac{1}{2} AB$.

PROBLEMS

Problem 1: Find the value for $\tan\alpha$ if $\cos\alpha - \sin\alpha = \dfrac{1}{5}$ ($0° < \alpha < 90°$).

(A) $\dfrac{4}{3}$. (B) $\dfrac{3}{4}$. (C) $\dfrac{3}{5}$. (D) $\dfrac{4}{5}$.

Problem 2: Calculate $\dfrac{\sin^3 x + 2\cos x}{\sin x - \cos x}$ if $\tan x = 2$.

Problem 3: Calculate $\sin(-1200°)\cos 1290° + \cos(-1020°)\sin(-1050°) + \tan 945°$

Problem 4: Find the value of $\sin^3\theta + \cos^3\theta$ if $\sin\theta, \cos\theta$ are the two roots of the equation $25x^2 - 5x - 12 = 0$.

Problem 5: Find the value of $a^2 + b^2$ if
$\quad a\sec x - 2\tan x = 1$ $\qquad\qquad$ (1)
and $\quad b\sec x + \tan x = 2$ $\qquad\qquad$ (2)

Problem 6: Find $\tan 80°$ if $\cos(-100°) = k$.

A. $\dfrac{\sqrt{1-k^2}}{k}$ B. $-\dfrac{\sqrt{1-k^2}}{k}$ C. $\dfrac{\sqrt{1+k^2}}{k}$ D. $-\dfrac{\sqrt{1+k^2}}{k}$

Problem 7: Find $\sin\alpha + \cos\alpha$ if
$\quad \sin\alpha + \sin\beta = 1$ $\qquad\qquad$ (1)
$\quad \cos\alpha + \cos\beta = 1$ $\qquad\qquad$ (2)

Problem 8: Find sum of $\tan^2\alpha + \cot^2\alpha$ and $\tan^3\alpha + \cot^3\alpha$ if $\tan\alpha + \cot\alpha = 10$

Problem 9: Show $\sin^4\alpha + \cos^4\alpha = 1 - 2\sin^2\alpha\cos^2\alpha$.

Problem 10: Find $\dfrac{\sin 79°}{\cos 11°} + \dfrac{\tan(45° - \alpha)}{\cot(45° + \alpha)}$.

Problem 11: (2007 AMC 12 II) Rhombus $ABCD$, with side length 6, is rolled to form a cylinder of volume 6 by taping AB to DC. What is $\sin(\angle ABC)$?

(A) $\frac{\pi}{9}$ (B) $\frac{1}{2}$ (C) $\frac{\pi}{6}$ (D) $\frac{\pi}{4}$ (E) $\frac{\sqrt{3}}{2}$.

Problem 12: What is the first quadrant angle x in terms of π that solves the equation $\frac{\sqrt{2}}{2}\cos x = \sin x$?

Problem 13: (2000 NC Math Contest) The function $f(x)$ is defined by $f(x) = \cos^4 x + k\cos^2(2x) + \sin^4 x$, where k is a constant. If the function $f(x)$ is a constant function, what is the value of k?

(a) -1 (b) $-\frac{1}{2}$ (c) 0   (d) $\frac{1}{2}$ (e) 1

Problem 14: (2000 NC Math Contest) Evaluate the product of $\tan 1° \cdot \tan 3° \cdot \tan 5° \cdots \tan 179°$.
a. 1   b. -1 c. 0   d. $+\infty$ e. none of these.

Problem 15: (NC Math Contest) In the diagram if $QR = d$, then PS equals

a. $\dfrac{\sin(\beta)}{\sin(\alpha - \beta)}d$

b. $\dfrac{\tan(\beta)}{\tan(\alpha) - \tan(\beta)}d$

c. $\dfrac{d}{\tan(\alpha) - \tan(\beta)}$

d. $\dfrac{d}{\cot(\beta) - \cot(\alpha)}$

e. $\dfrac{\sin(\alpha)\sin(\beta)}{\cos(\alpha)(\sin(\alpha) - \sin(\beta))}d$.

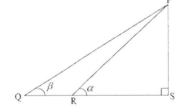

Problem 16: Using radian measure, what is the value of the sum
$\cos(\dfrac{\pi}{6}) + \cos(\dfrac{2\pi}{6}) + \cos(\dfrac{3\pi}{6}) + \cdots + \cos(\dfrac{2006\pi}{6})$?

a) 0   b) 1003   c) $1003\sqrt{3}$ d) $\dfrac{1+\sqrt{3}}{2}$ e) None of a) through d) is correct.

Problem 17: (1973 AMC) A sector with acute central angle θ is cut from a circle of radius 6. The radius of the circle circumscribed about the sector is

(A) $3\cos\theta$ (B) $3\sec\theta$ (C) $3\cos\frac{1}{2}\theta$ (D) $3\sec\frac{1}{2}\theta$ (E) 3

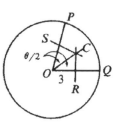

Problem 18: (1974 AMC) If (a, b) and (c, d) are two points on the line whose equation is $y = mx + k$, then the distance between (a, b) and (c, d), in terms of a, c and m, is

(A) $|a-c|\sqrt{1+m^2}$ (B) $|a+c|\sqrt{1+m^2}$ (C) $\dfrac{|a-c|}{\sqrt{1+m^2}}$ (D) $|a-c|(1+m^2)$

(E) $|a-c||m|$.

Problem 19: (1979 AMC) Sides AB, BC and CD of convex quadrilateral $ABCD$ have lengths 4, 5 and 20, respectively. If vertex angles B and C are obtuse and $\sin C = -\cos B = \dfrac{3}{5}$, then side AD has length

A (24) (B) 24.5 (C) 24.6 (D) 24.8 (E) 25

Problem 20: (1980 AMC) Line segments drawn from the vertex opposite the hypotenuse of a right triangle to the points trisection the hypotenuse have lengths $\sin x$ and $\cos x$, where x is a real number such that $0 < x < \dfrac{\pi}{2}$. The length of the hypotenuse is

(A) $\dfrac{4}{3}$ (B) $\dfrac{3}{2}$ (C) $\dfrac{3\sqrt{5}}{5}$ (D) $\dfrac{2\sqrt{5}}{3}$

(E) not uniquely determined by the given information.

Problem 21: (1986 AMC) In the configuration below, θ is measured in radians, C is the center of the circle, BCD and ACE are line segments, and AB is tangent to the circle at A.
A necessary and sufficient condition for the equality of the two shaded areas, given $0 < \theta < \dfrac{\pi}{2}$, is

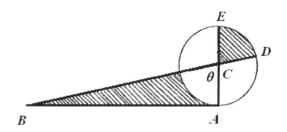

(A) $\tan\theta = \theta$ (B) $\tan\theta = 2\theta$ (C) $\tan\theta = 4\theta$

(D) $\tan 2\theta = \theta$ (E) $\tan\dfrac{\theta}{2} = \theta$.

Problem 22: (1989 AMC) Two strips of width 1 overlap at an angle of α as shown. The area of the overlap (shown shaded) is

(A) $\sin \alpha$ (B) $\dfrac{1}{\sin \alpha}$ (C) $\dfrac{1}{1-\cos \alpha}$ (D) $\dfrac{1}{\sin^2 \alpha}$ (E) $\dfrac{1}{(1-\cos \alpha)^2}$

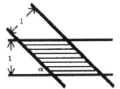

Problem 23: Right triangle ABC has the hypotenuse c and $a - b = \dfrac{c}{4}$. Find all the values of the trigonometric function of the acute angle A.

Problem 24. (1991 AIME) Suppose that $\sec x + \tan x = \dfrac{22}{7}$ and that $\csc x + \cot x = \dfrac{m}{n}$, where $\dfrac{m}{n}$ is in lowest terms. Find $m + n$.

Problem 25. If α is an angle in the second quadrant, what quadrants are $\dfrac{\alpha}{2}$ in?

Problem 26. Find $\tan \alpha$ if $\sin \alpha \cos \alpha = \dfrac{60}{169}$ and $\dfrac{\pi}{4} < \alpha < \dfrac{\pi}{2}$.

50 AMC Lectures Problems Book 1   (12) Trigonometry Six Functions

SOLUTIONS

Problem 1: Solution: (B).

We know that $\cos\alpha > \sin\alpha$ because $\cos\alpha - \sin\alpha = \dfrac{1}{5}$ (1)

Squaring both sides of (1): $(\cos\alpha - \sin\alpha)^2 = (\dfrac{1}{5})^2$

$25(\cos^2\alpha - 2\cos\alpha\sin\alpha + \sin^2\alpha) = 1 \quad\Rightarrow\quad 25(1 - 2\cos\alpha\sin\alpha) = 1 \quad\Rightarrow$

$-25\cos\alpha\sin\alpha + 12 = 0 \quad\Rightarrow\quad 12\cos^2\alpha - 25\cos\alpha\sin\alpha + 12\sin^2\alpha) = 0.$

Factoring we get: $(4\cos\alpha - 3\sin\alpha)(3\cos\alpha - 4\sin\alpha) = 0.$

Since $\cos\alpha > \sin\alpha$, $4\cos\alpha - 3\sin\alpha \neq 0$.

Therefore $4\cos\alpha - 3\sin\alpha = 0 \Rightarrow \quad \tan\alpha = \dfrac{\sin\alpha}{\cos\alpha} = \dfrac{3}{4}$.

Problem 2: Solution:

$$= \dfrac{\sin^3 x + 2\cos x(\sin^2 x + \cos^2 x)}{(\sin x - \cos x)(\sin^2 x + \cos^2 x)} = \dfrac{\sin^3 x + 2\sin^2 x \cos x + 2\cos^3 x}{\sin^3 x - \sin^2 x \cos x + \sin x \cos^2 x - \cos^3 x}$$

$$= \dfrac{\tan^3 x + 2\tan^2 x + 2}{\tan^3 x - \tan^2 x + \tan x - 1} = \dfrac{2^3 + 2\times 2^2 + 2}{2^3 - 2^2 + 2 - 1} = \dfrac{18}{5}.$$

Problem 3: Solution:

$\sin(-1200°)\cos 1290° + \cos(-1020°)\sin(-1050°) + \tan 945°$
$= \sin(-120°)\cos(210°) + \cos(-300°)\sin(-330°) + \tan 225°$
$= -\sin(120°)\cos 210° - \cos 300° \sin 330° + \tan 225°$
$= -\sin(90° + 30°)\cos(180° + 30°) - \cos(360° - 300°)\sin(360° - 30°) + \tan(180° + 45°)$
$= -\cos 30°(-\cos 30°) - \cos 60°(-\sin 30°) + \tan 45°$
$= \dfrac{\sqrt{3}}{2}\cdot\dfrac{\sqrt{3}}{2} + \dfrac{1}{2}\cdot\dfrac{1}{2} + 1 = 2.$

Problem 4: Solution:

From the Vieta Theorem, we know that $\sin\theta + \cos\theta = \dfrac{1}{5}$, and $\sin\theta\cdot\cos\theta = -\dfrac{12}{25}$

Therefore $\sin^3\theta + \cos^3\theta = (\sin\theta + \cos\theta)(\sin^2\theta - \sin\theta\cos\theta + \cos^2\theta)$

$$= (\sin\theta + \cos\theta)(1 - \sin\theta\cos\theta) = \dfrac{1}{5}\times(1 + \dfrac{12}{25}) = \dfrac{37}{125}$$

Problem 5: Solution:
Solving the system of equations (1) and (2) gives
$a = \cos x + 2\sin x$, $b = 2\cos x - \sin x$ $\Rightarrow$ $a^2 + b^2 = 5$.

Method 2:
Solving the system equations (1) and (2) by the method of elimination:
$$\sec x = \frac{5}{2a+b} \tag{3}$$
$$\tan x = \frac{2a-b}{a+2b} \tag{4}$$
We know that $\sec^2 x - \tan^2 x = 1$ \hfill (5)
Substituting (3) and (4) into (5): $a^2 + b^2 = 5$.

Problem 6: Solution: (B).
Since $\cos(-100°) = \cos(-180° + 80°) = -\cos 80° = k$, $\cos 80° = -k$.
$\therefore \sin 80° = \sqrt{1 - \cos^2 80°} = \sqrt{1-k^2}$.

Problem 7: Solution:
Rewrite (1) as $\sin \beta = 1 - \sin \alpha$ \hfill (3)
Rewrite (2) as $\cos \beta = 1 - \cos \alpha$ \hfill (4)
$(3)^2 + (4)^2$: $(1 - \sin \alpha)^2 + (1 - \cos \alpha)^2 = 1$ or $2 - 2(\sin \alpha + \cos \alpha) + (\sin^2 \alpha + \cos^2 \alpha) = 1$
Therefore $\sin \alpha + \cos \alpha = 1$.

Problem 8: Solution: 1068.
$\tan^2 \alpha + \cot^2 \alpha = (\tan \alpha + \cot \alpha)^2 - 2\tan \alpha \cot \alpha = 10^2 - 2 = 98$.
$\tan^3 \alpha + \cot^3 \alpha = (\tan \alpha + \cot \alpha)^3 - 3\tan \alpha \cot \alpha (\tan \alpha + \cot \alpha) = 10^3 - 30 = 970$.
The sum is $98 + 970 = 1068$.

Problem 9: Solution:
LHS = $\sin^4 \alpha + 2\sin^2 \alpha \cos^2 \alpha + \cos^4 \alpha - 2\sin^2 \alpha \cos^2 \alpha$
$= (\sin^2 \alpha + \cos^2 \alpha)^2 - 2\sin^2 \alpha \cos^2 \alpha = 1 - 2\sin^2 \alpha \cos^2 \alpha =$ RHS.

Problem 10: Solution:
$$\frac{\sin 79°}{\cos 11°} + \frac{\tan(45° - \alpha)}{\cot(45° + \alpha)} = \frac{\sin(90° - 11°)}{\cos 11°} + \frac{\tan[90° - (45° - \alpha)]}{\cot(45° + \alpha)}$$
$$= \frac{\cos 11°}{\cos 11°} + \frac{\cot(45° + \alpha)}{\cot(45° + \alpha)} = 2.$$

Problem 11: Solution: (A).
Let $\theta = \angle ABC$. The base of the cylinder is a circle with circumference 6, so the radius of the base is $\frac{6}{2\pi} = \frac{3}{\pi}$. The height of the cylinder is the altitude of the rhombus, which is 6 sin θ. Thus the volume of the cylinder is $6 = \pi(\frac{3}{\pi})^2 (6 \sin \theta) = \frac{54}{\pi} \sin\theta$, so $\sin\theta = \frac{9}{\pi}$.

Problem 12:

Solution $\frac{\pi}{4}$.

$\frac{\sqrt{2}}{2}\cos(x) = \sin(x) \Rightarrow \frac{\sqrt{2}}{2} = \frac{\sin(x)}{\cos(x)} = \tan(x) \Rightarrow x = \frac{\pi}{4}$.

The degree measure of this angle approximately 63.4°.

Problem 13: Solution: (B).
The easy way is to substitute in two values for x and force them to be equal, since the function is to be constant. Any multiples of $\frac{\pi}{2}$ result in $1 + K$, so we need to put in one value that is not a multiple of $\frac{\pi}{2}$. Try $\frac{\pi}{4}$. This gives us

$\cos^4(\frac{\pi}{4}) + K\cos^2(\frac{\pi}{2}) + \sin^4(\frac{\pi}{4}) = \frac{1}{4} + K \cdot 0 + \frac{1}{4} = \frac{1}{2}$. So now we know that $1 + K = \frac{1}{2}$, so $K = -\frac{1}{2}$. This does in fact give us the function $f(x) = (\cos^2 x + \sin^2 x)^2 - \frac{1}{2} = \frac{1}{2}$.

Problem 14: Solution: b.
Note that (tan 1° · tan 89°)·(tan 3° · tan 87°)·(tan 5° · tan 85°)·....·(tan 91° · tan 179° = 1. This pairing will not include tan 45° = 1 or tan 135° = − 1.

Problem 15: Solution: d.
Let $x = PS$. Ten $x = (d + x \cot(\alpha)) \tan(\beta)$. Solving for

$x = \frac{d \tan(\beta)}{1 - \cot(\alpha)\tan(\beta)} = \frac{d}{\cot(\beta) - \cot(\alpha)}$

Problem 16: Solution: d.

Every twelve consecutive terms sum to 0 and 2006 = 12(267) + 2 so we get
$$\cos(\frac{\pi}{6}) + \cos(\frac{2\pi}{6}) = \frac{1+\sqrt{3}}{2}.$$

Problem 17: (1973 AMC) Solution: (D).
The center of the circle which circumscribes sector POQ is at C, the intersection of the perpendicular bisectors SC and RC. Considering $\triangle ORC$, we see that $\sec\frac{\theta}{2} = \frac{OC}{3}$ or $OC = 3\sec\frac{\theta}{2}$.

Problem 18: Solution:

Let θ be the angle between the line and the x-axis; then $(\tan\theta)^2 = m^2 = \frac{(b-d)^2}{(a-c)^2}$, so
$(b-d)^2 = m(a-c)^2$, and the square of the desired distance is
$(a-c)^2 + (b-d)^2 = (a-c)^2 + m^2(a-c)^2 = (a-c)^2(1+m^2)$.

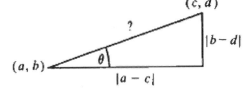

Problem 19: Solution: (E).
Let E be the intersection of lines AB and CD, and let β and θ be the measures of $\angle EBC$ and $\angle ECB$, respectively; see figure.
Since $\cos\beta = -\cos B = \sin C = \sin\theta$, $\beta + \theta = 90°$, so $\angle BEC$ is a right angle, and $BE = BC \sin\theta = 3$; $CE = BC \sin\beta = 4$.
Therefore, $AE = 7$ $DE = 24$ and AD, which is the hypotenuse of right triangle ADE, is $\sqrt{7^2 + 24^2} = 25$.

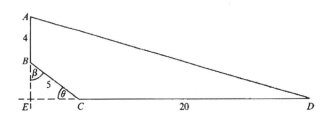

Problem 20: Solution: (C).
Applying the Pythagorean theorem to $\triangle CDF$ and $\triangle CEG$ in the adjoining figure yields
$4a^2 + b^2 = \sin^2 x$, $a^2 + 4b^2 = \cos^2 x$.
Adding these equations, we obtain
$5(a^2 + b^2) = \sin^2 x + \cos^2 x = 1$ Hence
$AB = 3\sqrt{a^2 + b^2} = 3\sqrt{\dfrac{1}{5}} = 3\dfrac{\sqrt{5}}{5}$.

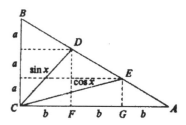

Problem 21: Solution: (B).
The area of the shaded sector is $\dfrac{\theta}{2}(AB)^2$. This must equal half the area of $\triangle ABC$, which is $\dfrac{1}{2}(AC)(AB)$. Hence the shaded regions have equal area if
$\dfrac{\theta}{2}(AC)^2 = \dfrac{1}{4}(AC)(AB)$, which is equivalent to $2\theta = \dfrac{AB}{AC} = \tan\theta$.

Problem 22: Solution: (B).
Method 1:
The shaded figure in the problem is a rhombus. Each side has length $\dfrac{1}{\sin\alpha}$. Which can be observed in the right triangle indicated in the figure. The height of the rhombus is 1, which is the width of each strip. The area of the rhombus is $base \cdot height = 1 \cdot \dfrac{1}{\sin\alpha}$.

Method 2:
The area of a parallelogram is the product of the lengths of two adjacent sides and the sine of the angle between them. Therefore, the area of this rhombus is $(\dfrac{1}{\sin\alpha})^2 \cdot \sin\alpha$.

Problem 23: Solution:
Solve a and b from $a^2 + b^2 = c^2$ $a - b = \dfrac{c}{4}$.
$a = \dfrac{1}{8}(\sqrt{31} + 1)c$, $b = \dfrac{1}{8}(\sqrt{31} - 1)c$.
$\sin A = \dfrac{a}{c} = \dfrac{1}{8}(\sqrt{31} + 1)$, $\cos A = \dfrac{b}{c} = \dfrac{1}{8}(\sqrt{31} - 1)$,

$$\tan A = \frac{a}{b} = \frac{\sqrt{31}+1}{\sqrt{31}-1} = \frac{16+\sqrt{31}}{15}, \quad \cot A = \frac{b}{a} = \frac{\sqrt{31}-1}{\sqrt{31}+1} = \frac{16-\sqrt{31}}{15},$$

$$\sec A = \frac{c}{b} = \frac{8}{\sqrt{31}-1} = \frac{4(\sqrt{31}+1)}{15}, \quad \csc A = \frac{c}{a} = \frac{8}{\sqrt{31}+1} = \frac{4(\sqrt{31}-1)}{15}.$$

Problem 24. Solution:

Let $p = \frac{22}{7}$

$$\sec x + \tan x = p \quad (1)$$

$$\sec^2 x - \tan^2 x = 1,$$

We know $\sec^2 x - \tan^2 x = 1$, so $\sec x - \tan x = \frac{1}{p}$, $\quad (2)$

Solving the system of equations (1) and (2):

$$2\sec x = p + \frac{1}{p}, \qquad 2\tan x = p - \frac{1}{p}.$$

Or $\cos x = \frac{2p}{p^2+1}, \quad \sin x = \frac{p^2-1}{p^2+1}$.

Therefore $\csc x + \cot x = \frac{p+1}{p-1} = \frac{29}{15}$.

$m + n = 29 + 15 = 44$.

Problem 25. Solution:

Since α is an angle in the second quadrant, $k \cdot 360° + 90° < \alpha < k \cdot 360° + 180°$ $(k \in z)$. k is integer.

Therefore $k \cdot 180° + 45° < \frac{\alpha}{2} < k \cdot 180° + 90°$ $(k \in z)$.

When k is even, $\frac{\alpha}{2}$ is in the first quadrant.

When k is odd, $\frac{\alpha}{2}$ is in the third quadrant.

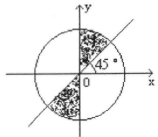

Problem 26. Solution:

$$\sin\alpha\cos\alpha = \frac{60}{169} \quad \Rightarrow \quad 2\sin\alpha\cos\alpha = \frac{2\cdot 60}{169} \Rightarrow 1 + 2\sin\alpha\cos\alpha = 1 + \frac{2\cdot 60}{169} = \frac{289}{169}$$

$$\Rightarrow \quad \sin^2\alpha + 2\sin\alpha\cos\alpha + \cos^2\alpha = \frac{289}{169} \Rightarrow (\sin\alpha + \cos\alpha)^2 = \frac{289}{169}.$$

Since $\dfrac{\pi}{4} < \alpha < \dfrac{\pi}{2}$, $\sin\alpha + \cos\alpha = \dfrac{17}{13}$ \hfill (1)

Similarly we have $\sin\alpha - \cos\alpha = \dfrac{7}{13}$ \hfill (2)

(1) – (2): $\cos\alpha = \dfrac{5}{13}$.

$$\tan\alpha = \frac{\sin\alpha}{\cos\alpha} = \frac{\sin\alpha\cos\alpha}{\cos^2\alpha} = \frac{\frac{60}{169}}{(\frac{5}{13})^2} = \frac{\frac{60}{169}}{\frac{25}{169}} = \frac{60}{25} = \frac{12}{5}$$

PROBLEMS

Problem 1: Factor: $(2x-3y)^3 + (3x-2y)^3 - 125(x-y)^3$.

Problem 2: Factor: $(x+2y-3z)^3 + (y+2z-3x)^3 + (z+2x-3y)^3$.

Problem 3: Factor: $(x^2+y^2)^3 + (z^2-x^2)^3 - (y^2+z^2)^3$.

Problem 4: Calculate: $\sqrt[3]{20+14\sqrt{2}} + \sqrt[3]{20-14\sqrt{2}}$.

Problem 5: Calculate: $\sqrt[3]{18+5\sqrt{13}} + \sqrt[3]{8-5\sqrt{13}}$.

Problem 6: Find $x^3 + 12x$ if $x = \sqrt[3]{4(\sqrt{5}+1)} + \sqrt[3]{4(\sqrt{5}-1)}$.

Problem 7: Find the integer n such that $\sqrt[3]{n+\sqrt{n^2+8}} + \sqrt[3]{n-\sqrt{n^2+8}} = 8$.

Problem 8: a, b, and c are integers with $3+a^2+b^2+c^2 < ab+3b+2c$, find the value of $\left(\dfrac{1}{a}+\dfrac{1}{b}+\dfrac{1}{c}\right)^{abc}$.

Problem 9: If $a+b+c=0$, show that $\dfrac{1}{b^2+c^2-a^2} + \dfrac{1}{c^2+a^2-b^2} + \dfrac{1}{a^2+b^2-c^2} = 0$.

Problem 10: Find all real values of x that satisfy $(16x^2-9)^3 + (9x^2-16)^3 = (25x^2-25)^3$.

Problem 11: If *a, b,* and *c* satisfy the condition: $a(\frac{1}{b}+\frac{1}{c})+b(\frac{1}{c}+\frac{1}{a})+c(\frac{1}{a}+\frac{1}{b})+3=0$,
Show that either $a+b+c=0$ or $ab+bc+ca=0$.

Problem 12: If $\frac{1}{a}+\frac{1}{b}+\frac{1}{c}=0$, prove that $(a+b+c)^2 = a^2+b^2+c^2$.

Problem 13: Let x, y, z be integers such that $(x-y)^2+(y-z)^2+(z-x)^2 = xyz$.
Find the remainder when $x^3+y^3+z^3$ is divided by $x+y+z+6$.

Problem 14: (1977 AMC). Find the smallest integer n such that
$(x^2+y^2+z^2)^2 \leq n(x^4+y^4+z^4)$ for all real numbers x, y, and z.
(A) 2   (B) 3   (C) 4   (D) 6   (E) There is no such integer n.

SOLUTIONS TO PRORLEMS

Problem 1: Solution:
$a = 2x - 3y$, $b = 3x - 2y$, and $c = 5(x - y) = 5x - 5y$.
Since $a + b + c = 2x - 3y + 3x - 2y + 5x - 5y = 0$, we have:
$(2x - 3y)^3 + (3x - 2y)^3 - 125(x - y)^3$
$= 3(2x - 3y)(3x - 2y)(5y - 5x) = 15(2x - 3y)(3x - 2y)(y - x)$

Problem 2: Solution:
$a = x + 2y - 3z$, $b = y + 2z - 3x$, and $c = z + 2x - 3y$.
Since $a + b + c = x + 2y - 3z + y + 2z - 3x + z + 2x - 3y = 0$, we have:
$(x + 2y - 3z)^3 + (y + 2z - 3x)^3 + (z + 2x - 3y)^3$
$= 3(x + 2y - 3z)(y + 2z - 3x)(z + 2x - 3y)$

Problem 3: Solution:
$a = x^2 + y^2$, $b = z^2 - x^2$, and $c = y^2 + z^2$.
Since $a + b + c = = 0$, we have:
$(x^2 + y^2)^3 + (z^2 - x^2)^3 - (y^2 + z^2)^3 = 3(x^2 + y^2) \cdot (z^2 - x^2) \cdot [-(y^2 + z^2)]$
$= -3(x^2 + y^2)(z - x)(z + x)(y^2 + z^2) = 3(x^2 + y^2)(x - z)(x + z)(y^2 + z^2)$

Problem 4: Solution: 4.
Let $\sqrt[3]{20 + 14\sqrt{2}} + \sqrt[3]{20 - 14\sqrt{2}} = x$, then $\sqrt[3]{20 + 14\sqrt{2}} + \sqrt[3]{20 - 14\sqrt{2}} - x = 0$.
So $\left(\sqrt[3]{20 + 14\sqrt{2}}\right)^3 + \left(\sqrt[3]{20 - 14\sqrt{2}}\right)^3 - x^3 = 3 \cdot (\sqrt[3]{20 + 14\sqrt{2}}) \cdot (\sqrt[3]{20 - 14\sqrt{2}}) \cdot (-x)$.
The above equation becomes: $x^3 - 6x - 40 = 0$
Or $(x - 4)(x^2 + 4x + 40) = 0$.
Since $(x^2 + 4x + 40) = (x + 2)^2 + 6^2 > 0$, so $x - 4 = 0$, or $x = 4$.
$\sqrt[3]{20 + 14\sqrt{2}} + \sqrt[3]{20 - 14\sqrt{2}} = 4$.

Problem 5: Solution: 3.
Let $\sqrt[3]{18 + 5\sqrt{13}} + \sqrt[3]{8 - 5\sqrt{13}} = x$, then $\sqrt[3]{18 + 5\sqrt{13}} + \sqrt[3]{8 - 5\sqrt{13}} - x = 0$.
So $\left(\sqrt[3]{18 + 5\sqrt{13}}\right)^3 + \left(\sqrt[3]{8 - 5\sqrt{13}}\right)^3 - x^3 = 3 \cdot (\sqrt[3]{18 + 5\sqrt{13}}) \cdot (\sqrt[3]{18 - 5\sqrt{13}}) \cdot (-x)$.
$\sqrt[3]{18 + 5\sqrt{13}} + \sqrt[3]{8 - 5\sqrt{13}} - x = 0..$

The above equation becomes: $x^3 + 3x - 36 = 0$
Or $(x-3)(x^2 + 3x + 12) = 0$.
Since $(x^2 + 3x + 12) = (x + \frac{3}{2})^2 + \frac{39}{4} > 0$, so $x - 3 = 0$, or $x = 3$.
$\sqrt[3]{18 + 5\sqrt{13}} + \sqrt[3]{8 - 5\sqrt{13}} = 3$.

Problem 6: Solution: 8.
Write $x = \sqrt[3]{4(\sqrt{5}+1)} + \sqrt[3]{4(\sqrt{5}-1)}$ as $\sqrt[3]{4(\sqrt{5}+1)} + \sqrt[3]{4(\sqrt{5}-1)} - x = 0$.
So $\left(\sqrt[3]{4(\sqrt{5}+1)}\right)^3 + \left(\sqrt[3]{4(\sqrt{5}-1)}\right)^3 - x^3 = 3 \cdot \left(\sqrt[3]{4(\sqrt{5}+1)}\right) \cdot \left(\sqrt[3]{4(\sqrt{5}-1)}\right) \cdot (-x)$.
$4(\sqrt{5}+1) + 4(\sqrt{5}-1) - x^3 = -3 \cdot \left(\sqrt[3]{4(\sqrt{5}+1)4(\sqrt{5}-1)}\right) \cdot x$
$8 - x^3 = -3 \cdot \left(\sqrt[3]{-64}\right) \cdot x = 12x$
$x^3 + 12x = 8$

Problem 7: Solution: 280.
The original equation can be written as $\sqrt[3]{n + \sqrt{n^2 + 8}} + \sqrt[3]{n - \sqrt{n^2 + 8}} - 8 = 0$.
Therefore
$\left(\sqrt[3]{n + \sqrt{n^2+8}}\right)^3 + \left(\sqrt[3]{n - \sqrt{n^2+8}}\right)^3 - 8^3 = 3 \cdot (\sqrt[3]{n + \sqrt{n^2+8}}) \cdot (\sqrt[3]{n - \sqrt{n^2+8}}) \cdot (-8)$.
$(n + \sqrt{n^2+8}) + n - \sqrt{n^2+8}^3 - 512^3 = -24 \cdot (\sqrt[3]{(n + \sqrt{n^2+8})(n - \sqrt{n^2+8})})$
$2n - 512 = -24 \cdot (\sqrt[3]{(n + \sqrt{n^2+8})(n - \sqrt{n^2+8})}) = -24 \cdot \sqrt[3]{-8} = 48$.
Solve for n: $2n - 512 = 48$, and $n = 280$.

Problem 8: Solution: $\frac{25}{4}$.

$3 + a^2 + b^2 + c^2 < ab + 3b + 2c \quad \Rightarrow \quad a^2 + b^2 + c^2 - ab - 3b - 2c + 4 < 1$.
Because a, b, and c are integers, $a^2 + b^2 + c^2 - ab - 3b - 2c + 4 \leq 0$.
Or $(a - \frac{b}{2})^2 + 3(\frac{b}{2} - 1)^2 + (c - 1)^2 \leq 0$.
We also know that:
$(a - \frac{b}{2})^2 + 3(\frac{b}{2} - 1)^2 + (c - 1)^2 \geq 0$,

So $(a-\frac{b}{2})^2 + 3(\frac{b}{2}-1)^2 + (c-1)^2 = 0$.

$a - \frac{b}{2} = 0$, $\frac{b}{2} - 1 = 0$, $c - 1 = 0$.

Therefore $a = 1$, $c = 2$, $c = 1$.

So $\left(\frac{1}{a} + \frac{1}{b} + \frac{1}{c}\right)^{abc} = \left(\frac{1}{1} + \frac{1}{2} + \frac{1}{1}\right)^{1 \times 2 \times 1} = \frac{25}{4}$.

Problem 9: Solution:

$b^2 + c^2 - a^2 = b^2 + c^2 - (-b-c)^2 = -2bc$

$c^2 + a^2 - b^2 = c^2 + a^2 - (-a-c)^2 = -2ac$

$a^2 + b^2 - c^2 = a^2 + b^2 - (-a-b)^2 = -2ab$

$\frac{1}{b^2+c^2-a^2} + \frac{1}{c^2+a^2-b^2} + \frac{1}{a^2+b^2-c^2}$

$= -\frac{1}{2bc} - \frac{1}{2ac} - \frac{1}{2ab} = -\frac{a+b+c}{2abc} = 0$

Problem 10: Solution:

Rewrite the given equation as $(16x^2 - 9)^3 + (9x^2 - 16)^3 - (25x^2 - 25)^3 = 0$

Since $(16x^2 - 9) + (9x^2 - 16) + [-(25x^2 - 25)] = 0$, we have

$(16x^2 - 9)^3 + (9x^2 - 16)^3 - (25x^2 - 25)^3 = 3(16x^2 - 9)(9x^2 - 16)[-(25x^2 - 25)] = 0$.

Or $-3(16x^2 - 9)(9x^2 - 16)(25x^2 - 25) = 0 \Rightarrow (16x^2 - 9)(9x^2 - 16)(25x^2 - 25) = 0$.

The solutions are

$(16x^2 - 9) = 0 \qquad \Rightarrow \qquad x = \pm\frac{3}{4}$.

$(9x^2 - 16) = 0 \qquad \Rightarrow \qquad x = \pm\frac{4}{3}$.

$(25x^2 - 25) = 0 \qquad \Rightarrow \qquad x = \pm 1$.

Problem 11: Solution:

$a(\frac{1}{b} + \frac{1}{c}) + b(\frac{1}{c} + \frac{1}{a}) + c(\frac{1}{a} + \frac{1}{b}) + 3 = 0$ can be written as:

$a^2b + a^2c + b^2c + b^2a + ac^2 + bc^2 + 3abc = 0$.

Or
$$ab(a+b+c)+ac(a+b+c)+bc(a+b+c) = (a+b+c)(ab+bc+ca) = 0.$$
That is either $a + b + c = 0$ or $ab + bc + ca = 0$.

Problem 12:
Solution:
We know that $ab + bc + ca = 0$.
$$(a+b+c) - a^2 - b^2 - c^2$$
$$= a^2 + b^2 + c^2 + 2ab + 2bc + 2ca - a^2 - b^2 - c^2$$
$$= 2(ab + bc + ca) = 0.$$

Problem 13: Solution:
We know that $x^3 + y^3 + z^3 - 3xyz = \frac{1}{2}(x+y+z)[(x-y)^2 + (y-z)^2 + (z-x)^2]$.
Since $(x-y)^2 + (y-z)^2 + (z-x)^2 = xyz$
$$x^3 + y^3 + z^3 - 3xyz = \frac{1}{2}(x+y+z)xyz$$
$$x^3 + y^3 + z^3 = \frac{1}{2}(x+y+z)xyz + 3xyz = \frac{1}{2}(x+y+z)xyz + \frac{6xyz}{2} = \frac{xyz}{2}(x+y+z+6).$$
Notice that at least one of x, y, and z is even (if they are all odd, the left hand side of $(x-y)^2 + (y-z)^2 + (z-x)^2 = xyz$ is even but the right hand side is odd but even ≠ odd), that is, $\frac{xyz}{2}$ is an integer.
So the remainder is zero when $x^3 + y^3 + z^3$ is divided by $x + y + z + 6$.

Problem 14: (B)
Let $a = x^2, b = y^2$ and $c = z^2$, Noting that $(a-b)^2 \geq 0$ implies $a^2 + b^2 \geq 2ab$, we see that
$$(a+b+c)^2 = a^2 + b^2 + c^2 + 2ab + 2ac + 2bc$$
$$\leq a^2 + b^2 + c^2 + (a^2 + b^2) + (a^2 + c^2) + (b^2 + c^2) = 3(a^2 + b^2 + c^2).$$
Therefore $n \leq 3$. Choosing $a = b = c > 0$ shows n is not less than three.

PROBLEMS

Problem 1. In an arithmetic sequence a_n, the sum of the first n terms is S_n. If $S_3 = 3$, $S_6 = 24$, find a_9.

Problem 2. In an arithmetic sequence a_n, the common difference is not zero. If $a_1 = 1$, and a_1, a_3, and a_9 form a geometric sequence. Find a_n.

Problem 3: In an arithmetic sequence a_n, the sum of first m terms is 30, the sum of first 2m terms is 100. Find S_{3m}, the sum of first 3m terms.
(A)   130   (B) 170   (C)210   (D)260

Problem 4. In an arithmetic sequence a_n, $a_1 = 0$, and $a_2 = 2$. For any positive integers m and n, $a_{2m-1} + a_{2n-1} = 2a_{m+n-1} + 2(m-n)^2$. Find a_3 and a_5.

Problem 5. In an arithmetic sequence an, $a_3 = 7$, $a_5 + a_7 = 26$, The sum of first n terms is S_n. Find a_n.

Problem 6. In an arithmetic sequence a_n, the sum of first n terms is S_n. If $a_5 = 5a_3$, then $\dfrac{S_9}{S_5} = ?$

Problem 7. In an arithmetic sequence a_n, the sum of first n terms is S_n. If $a_5 = 5a_3$, $6S_5 - 5S_3 = 5$, then $a_4 = ?$

Problem 8. In an arithmetic sequence a_n, s_n is the sum of first n terms. If $\dfrac{a_{2n}}{a_n} = \dfrac{4n-1}{2n-1}$, then $\dfrac{S_{2n}}{S_n} = \underline{\qquad}$.

Problem 9. In an arithmetic sequence a_n, the sum of first n terms is S_n. If $a_1 = -11, a_4 + a_6 = -6$, find n when S_n is the smallest.
  A. 6 B. 7 C. 8 D. 9

Problem 10. In an arithmetic sequence a_n, the first term a_1 and the common difference d are real numbers. The sum of first n terms is S_n. If $S_5 S_6 + 15 = 0$, find the interval for d.

Problem 11. In an arithmetic sequence a_n, $a_3 = 5$, $a_{10} = -9$, and the sum of first n terms is S_n. Find n such that the sum of first n terms is the greatest possible.

Problem 12. In an arithmetic sequence a_m, find odd number m if $a_1 + a_3 + \cdots + a_m = 44$, and $a_2 + a_4 + \cdots + a_{m-1} = 33$.

Problem 13. The side lengths of a right triangle are all integers and form an arithmatic sequence. One possible length is
  (A) 13. (B) 41. (C) 81. (D) 91.

Problem 14. In an arithmetic sequence a_n, the sum of first n terms is S_n. If $a_{16} = 41$, find S_{31}.

Problem 15. In an arithmetic sequence a_n, the sum of first n terms is S_n. If $a_3 = \frac{1}{5}$, $a_5 = \frac{1}{3}$, find S_{15}.

Problem 16. In an arithmetic sequence a_n, the sum of first 4 terms is 40, the sum of last 4 terms is 80, and the sum of all terms is 210. Find n.
  A. 12 B. 14 C. 16 D. 18

Problem 17. (1958 AMC) The first term of an arithmetic series of consecutive integers is $k^2 + 1$. The sum $2k + 1$ terms of this series may be expressed as:

(A) $k^3 + (k+1)^3$ (B) $(k-1)^3 + k^3$ (C) $(k+1)^3$ (D) $(k+1)^2$

Problem 18. (1961 AMC) Thirty-one books are arranged from left to right in order of increasing prices. The price of each book differs by $2 from that of each adjacent book. For the price of the book at the extreme right a customer can buy the middle book and an adjacent one. Then:
(A). The adjacent book referred to is at the left of the middle book.
(B). The middle book sells for $36.   (C). The cheapest book sells for $4.
(D). The most expensive book sells for $64.   (E). None of these is correct.

Problem 19: (1965 AMC) For every n the sum S_n of n terms of an arithmetic progression if $2n + 3n^2$. The rth term is:
(A) $3r^2$ (B) $3r^2 + 2r$ (C) $6r - 1$ (D) $5r + 5$ (E) $6r + 2$

Problem 20. (1966 AMC) Let s_1 be the sum of the first n terms of the arithmetic sequence 8, 12, ... and let s_2 be the sum of the first n terms of the arithmetic sequence 17, 19, ... Assume $n \neq 0$. The $s_1 = s_2$ for:
(A) no value of n (B) one value of n (C) two values of n
(D) four values of n (E) more than four values of n

Problem 21. (1969 AMC) Let S_n and T_n be the respective sums of the first n terms of two arithmetic series. If $S_n : T_n = (7n+1) : (4n+27)$ for all n, the ratio of the eleventh term of the first series to the eleventh term of the second series is:
(A) 4 : 3   (B) 3 : 2   (C) 7 : 4   (D) 78 : 71   (E) undetermined

Problem 22. (1970 AMC) If the sum of the first $3n$ positive integers is 150 more than the sum of the first n positive integers, then the sum of the first $4n$ positive integers is
(A) 300   (B) 350   (C) 400   (D) 450   (E) 600

Problem 23. (1975 AMC) Let $a_1, a_2, \ldots$ and $b_1, b_2, \ldots$ be arithmetic progressions such that $a_1 = 25$, $b_1 = 75$ and $a_{100} + b_{100} = 100$. Find the sum of the first one hundred terms of the progression $a_1 + b_1, a_2 + b_2, \ldots$.
(A) 0   (B) 100   (C) 10,000   (D) 505,000
(E) not enough information given to solve the problem

Problem 24. (1993 AMC) Let $a_1, a_2, \ldots, a_k$ be a finite arithmetic sequence with $a_4 + a_7 + a_{10} = 17$ and $a_4 + a_5 + a_6 + a_7 + a_8 + a_9 + a_{10} + a_{11} + a_{12} + a_{13} + a_{14} = 77$. If $a_k = 13$, then $k =$
(A) 16 (B) 18 (C) 20 (D) 22 (E) 24

Problem 25. (1987 AMC) The first four terms of an arithmetic sequence are $a, x, b, 2x$. The ratio of a to b is
(A) $\frac{1}{4}$ (B) $\frac{1}{3}$ (C) $\frac{1}{2}$ (D) $\frac{2}{3}$ (E) 2

Problem 26. (1980 AMC) If the sum of the first 10 terms and the sum of the first 100 terms of a given arithmetic progression are 100 and 10, respectively, then the sum of the first 110 terms is
(A) 90 (B) –90 (C) 110 (D) –110 (E) –100

Problem 27. An arithmetic sequence starts with terms 2, 6, 10, 14,…. And a second sequence begins 2, 8, 14, 20,…, find the sum of the terms common to both sequences.

Problem 28. Find the number of terms common to both sequences listed below:
2, 5, 8, 11, 14, 17, … , $2 + (200 – 1) \times 3$;
5, 9, 13, 17, 21, 25, … , $5 + (200 – 1) \times 4$.

Problem 29. An arithmetic sequence with first term 1 has a common difference of 6. A second sequence begins with 4 and has a common difference of 7. In the range of 1 to 2009, find the number of terms common to both sequences.

Problem 30. Find the number of terms common to both sequences listed below:
1, 3, 5, 7, … , 1991; 1, 6, 11, 16, …, 1991.

Problem 31. In an arithmetic sequence a_n, the sum of first n terms is S_n. If $a_1 = 1$, $S_{n+1} = 4a_n + 2$, find a_n.

Problem 32. (1997 China High School Math Contest) The sum of n terms of an arithmetic progression is 97^2, and the common difference and first term are all nonnegative integers with $n > 2$. How many such arithmetic progressions are there?

Problem 33. (1986 AIME) The pages of a book are numbered 1 though n. When the page numbers of the book were added, one of the page numbers was mistakenly added twice, resulting in the incorrect sum of 1986. What was the number of the page that was added twice?

Problem 34. (2003 AIME I) Find the eighth term of the sequence 1440, 1716, 1848, ..., whose terms are formed by multiplying the corresponding terms of two arithmetic sequences.

Problem 35. (2004 AIME) Set A consists of m consecutive integers whose sum is $2m$, and set B consists of $2m$ consecutive integers whose sum is m. The absolute value of the difference between the greatest element of A and the greatest element of B is 99. Find m.

SOLUTIONS

Problem 1. Solution: 15.
We can write the following equations:
$$\begin{cases} S_3 = 3a_1 + \frac{3\times 2}{2}d = 3 \\ S_6 = 6a_1 + \frac{6\times 5}{2}d = 24 \end{cases},$$
Solving we get: $\begin{cases} a_1 = -1 \\ d = 2 \end{cases}$, $\therefore a_9 = a_1 + 8d = 15$.

Problem 2. Solution: $a_n = n$.
We know that $d \neq 0$. We also know that a_1, a_3, and a_9 form a geometric sequence.
Therefore we have $\frac{1+2d}{1} = \frac{1+8d}{1+2d}$,
Solving we get: $d = 1$ or $d = 0$ (extranous).
Hence $a_n = 1 + (n-1)\times 1 = n$.

Problem 3. Solution: (C).
Since $\frac{S_n}{n}$ is also an arithmetic sequence, $\frac{S_m}{m}, \frac{S_{2m}}{2m}$, and $\frac{S_{3m}}{3m}$ form an arithmetic sequence.
Then we have $\frac{S_m}{m} + \frac{S_{3m}}{3m} = 2 \times \frac{S_{2m}}{2m}$.
Therefore $S_{3m} = 3(S_{2m} - S_m) = 3(100 - 30) = 210$.

Problem 4. Solution:
We know that the following relationship is true for any positive integers m and n: $a_{2m-1} + a_{2n-1} = 2a_{m+n-1} + 2(m-n)^2$.
Let $m = 2, n = 1$, we get $a_3 = 2a_2 - a_1 + 2 = 6$
Let $m = 3, n = 1$, we get $a_5 = 2a_3 - a_1 + 8 = 20$.

Problem 5. Solution:
Let the common diffrence be d.
We know that $a_3 = 7$, $a_5 + a_7 = 26$.
Therefore:
$$\begin{cases} a_1 + 2d = 7 \\ 2a_1 + 10d = 26 \end{cases}$$

Solving we get: $a_1 = 3$, $d = 2$.
$a_n = 3 + 2(n-1) = 2n + 1$.

Problem 6. Solution:
We know that a_n is an arithmetic sequence, $\therefore \dfrac{S_9}{S_5} = \dfrac{9a_5}{5a_3} = 9$

Problem 7. Solution:
We know that $S_n = na_1 + \dfrac{1}{2}n(n-1)d$.
Therefore $S_5 = 5a_1 + 10d$, $S_3 = 3a_1 + 3d = 5$.
$6S_5 - 5S_3 = 30a_1 + 60d - (15a_1 + 15d) = 15a_1 + 45d = 15(a_1 + 3d) = 15a_4$
$15a_4 = 5 \quad \Rightarrow \quad a_4 = \dfrac{1}{3}$.

Problem 8. Solution:
$\dfrac{a_{2n}}{a_n} = \dfrac{4n-1}{2n-1}$, that is, $\dfrac{a_n + nd}{a_n} = \dfrac{4n-1}{2n-1} \Rightarrow a_n = \dfrac{2n-1}{2}d, a_1 = \dfrac{d}{2}$.
$S_n = \dfrac{n(a_1 + a_n)}{2} = \dfrac{n^2 d}{2}$, $S_{2n} = \dfrac{(2n)^2 d}{2} = 4S_n$. Therefore $\dfrac{S_{2n}}{S_n} = 4$.

Problem 9. Solution: A.
Let the common difference be d. Then $a_4 + a_6 = 2a_1 + 8d = 2 \times (-11) + 8d = -6$.
Solving we get $d = 2$.
Therefore $S_n = -11n + \dfrac{n(n-1)}{2} \times 2 = n^2 - 12n = (n-6)^2 - 36$.
When $n = 6$, S_n is the smallest.

Problem 10. Solution:
Since $S_5 S_6 + 15 = 0$, $(5a_1 + 10d)(6a_1 + 15d) = 0 \Rightarrow 2a_1^2 + 9a_1 d + 10d^2 + 1 = 0$.
Therefore $(4a_1 + 9d)^2 = d^2 - 8 \geq 0, \therefore d^2 \geq 8$,
The intervals for d are $d \leq -2\sqrt{2}$ or $d \geq 2\sqrt{2}$.

Problem 11. Solution: 5.
We know that $a_3 = 5$, $a_{10} = -9$.

According to $a_n = a_1 + (n-1)d$, we have $\begin{cases} a_1 + 2d = 5 \\ a_1 + 9d = -9 \end{cases}$

Solving we get $\begin{cases} a_1 = 9 \\ d = -2 \end{cases}$

The sum of first n terms:
$S_n = na_1 + \dfrac{n(n-1)}{2}d = 10n - n^2$.
$S_n = -(n-5)^2 + 25$.
When $n = 5$, S_n has the greatest value 25.

Problem 12. Solution:
Let the common difference be d.
$$a_1 + (a_3 - a_2) + (a_5 - a_4) + \cdots + (a_m - a_{m-1}) = a_1 + \dfrac{m-1}{2}d = 11 \qquad (1)$$

We add two given equations given together:
$$a_1 + a_2 + a_3 + \cdots + a_m = \dfrac{(a_1 + a_m)m}{2} = \dfrac{2a_1 + (m-1)d}{2} \cdot m = 77 \qquad (2)$$

$(2) \div (1)$: $m = 7$.

Problem 13. Solution:
Let the lengths be $x - d, x, x + d$.
By the Pythagorean theorem, $(x-d)^2 + x^2 = (x+d)^2$.
Simplifying into $x(x - 4d) = 0$.

Since $x \neq 0$, $x = 4d$.
The ratio of three sides is $3 : 4 : 5$.
The possible length should be a multiple of 3, 4, or 5. Only 81 is the correct answer.

Problem 14. Solution:
Method 1:
$a_{16} = a_1 + (16-1)d = a_1 + 15d = 41$
$S_{31} = \dfrac{31}{2}[2a_1 + (31-1)d] = 31(a_1 + 15d) = 31a_{16} = 1271$.

Method 2:
We know that $S_{2n-1} = (2n-1)a_n$.

Therefore $S_{2 \times 16 - 1} = (2 \times 16 - 1)a_{16} = 29 \times 41 = 1271$.

Problem 15. Solution:

We look at a general case where $a_m = \frac{1}{n}$, $a_n = \frac{1}{m}$, where $m \neq n$.

$$a_1 + (m-1)d = \frac{1}{n} \quad (1)$$

$$a_1 + (n-1)d = \frac{1}{m} \quad (2)$$

(1) – (2): $(m-n)d = \frac{1}{n} - \frac{1}{m} = \frac{m-n}{mn}$.

Since $m \neq n$, $d = \frac{1}{mn}$.

Substituting this into (1): $a_1 = \frac{1}{n} - (m-1)\frac{1}{mn} = \frac{1}{mn}$.

$\therefore S_{mn} = \frac{mn}{2}[\frac{2}{mn} + (mn-1) \cdot \frac{1}{mn}] = \frac{mn}{2}(\frac{1}{mn} + 1) = \frac{mn+1}{2}$.

Therefore $S_{15} = (3 \times 5 + 1)/2 = 8$.

Problem 16. Solution: B.

$\begin{cases} a_1 + a_2 + a_3 + a_4 = 40 & (1) \\ a_{n-3} + a_{n-2} + a_{n-1} + a_n = 80 & (2) \end{cases}$

(1) + (2): $(a_1 + a_n) + (a_2 + a_{n-1}) + (a_3 + a_{n-2}) + (a_4 + a_{n-3}) = 120$.

We also have: $4(a_1 + a_n) = 120 \Rightarrow a_1 + a_n = 30$.

Since $S_n = \frac{n(a_1 + a_n)}{2} = 210$, $\frac{n \times 30}{2} = 210$.

$n = 14$.

Problem 17. Solution: (A).

$s = \frac{n}{2}[2a + (n-1)d]$; $a = k^2 + 1$, $n = 2k + 1$, $d = 1$,

$s = (2k+1)(k^2 + k + 1) = 2k^3 + 3k^2 + 3k + 1$
$= k^3 + 3k^2 + 3k + 1 + k^3 = (k+1)^3 + k^3$.

Problem 18. Solution: (A).

Let the prices, arranged in order from left to right be $P, P + 2, P + 4, \ldots, P + 58$, $P + 60$. The price of the middle book is $P + 30$. Then either
$P + 30 + P + 32 = P + 60$ or $P + 30 + P + 28 = P + 60$.
The first equation yields a negative value for P, an impossibility. The second equation leads to $P = 2$, so that (A) is the correct choice.

Problem 19: Solution: (C).
Method 1:
By the formula (2.6), we know that the rth term equals $a_r = S_r - S_{r-1}$ (1)
We have $S_r = 2r + 3r^2$, and $S_{r-1} = 2(r-1) + 3(r-1)^2 = 3r^2 - 4r + 1$.
Substituting them into (10, we get: $a_r = 6r - 1$.

Method 2:
Let the rth term be a_r and let the first term be a_1.
By formula (2.4), we have $a_1 = S_1 = 2 \cdot 1 + 3 \cdot 1^2 = 5$.
By formula (3.1), we have $S_r = \frac{r}{2}(a_1 + a_r) = 2r + 3r^2$, $\therefore a_1 + a_r = 4 + 6r$
$\therefore a_r = 4 + 6r - 5 = 6r - 1$.

Method 3:
$a_1 = S_1 = 5$, $S_2 = 16$. $\therefore a_2 = S_2 - S_1 = 11$, but $a_2 = a_1 + d$; $\therefore d = 6$.

$\therefore a_r = a + (r-1)d = 5 + (r-1)(6) = 6r - 1$.

Problem 20. Solution: (B).
The formula for the sum s of the first n terms may be written as
$S_n = \frac{n}{2}[2a + (n-1)d]$

In our cases, we have: $S_1 = \frac{n}{2}(12 + 4n) = 2n^2 + 6n$ and $S_2 = \frac{n}{2}(32 + 2n) = n^2 + 16n$.
Since $S_1 = S_2$, $2n^2 + 6n = n^2 + 16n$.
Or $n^2 - 10n = 0$.
Since $n \neq 0$, $n - 10 = 0$ $\Rightarrow$ $n = 10$.

Problem 21. Solution: (A).
Let a_1, a_2 denote the first terms, d_1 and d_2 the common differences of the arithmetic series with nth sums S_n and T_n, respectively.

Then $S_n = n[a_1 + \frac{n-1}{2}d_1]$, $T_n = n[a_2 + \frac{n-1}{2}d_2]$, and
$$\frac{S_n}{T_n} = \frac{2a_1 + (n-1)d_1}{2a_2 + (n-1)d_2} = \frac{7n+1}{4n+27} \text{ for all } n.$$
The eleventh terms of these series are $u_{11} = a_1 + 10d_1$ and $v_{11} = a_2 + 10d_2$, respectively, and their ratio is
$$\frac{u_{11}}{v_{11}} = \frac{a_1 + 10d_1}{a_2 + 10d_2} = \frac{2a_1 + 20d_1}{2a_2 + 20d_2}.$$
We note that the last expression is precisely $\frac{S_n}{T_n}$ for $n = 21$, so that
$$\frac{u_{11}}{v_{11}} = \frac{7(21)+1}{4(21)+27} = \frac{148}{111} = \frac{4}{3}.$$

Problem 22. Solution: (A).
Method 1:
Let S_m denote the sum of the first m positive integers. The formula for S_m is
$S_m = \frac{1}{2}m(m+1)$ so that $S_{3n} - S_n = \frac{1}{2}3n(3n+1) - \frac{1}{2}n(n+1) = 4n^2 + n = 150$.
Thus $4n^2 + n - 150 = (n-6)(4n+25) = 0$, $n = 6$ or $-\frac{25}{4}$.
Since n must be a positive integer, $n = 6$, $4n = 24$, and
$S_{4n} = S_{24} = \frac{1}{2}24(24+1) = 12 \cdot 25 = 300$.

Method 2:
$S_{3n} - S_n = \frac{1}{2} \cdot 3n(3n+1) - \frac{1}{2}n(n+1) = 4n^2 + n = 150$.
$S_{4n} = \frac{1}{2} \cdot 4n(4n+1) = 2 \cdot n(4n+1) = 2 \cdot (4n^2 + n) = 300$.

Problem 23. Solution: (C).
Let d denote the common difference of the progression $a_1 + b_1, a_2 + b_2, \ldots$
Then $99d = (a_{100} + b_{100}) - (a_1 + b_1) = 0$.
Thus $d = 0$, and $100(a_1 + b_1) = 10,000$ is the desired sum.

Problem 24. Solution: (B).

Since $a_4 + a_7 + a_{10} = 17$, $a_7 = \dfrac{17}{3}$.

Similarly, $a_9 = \dfrac{77}{11} = 7$.

Since $a_9 - a_7 = 2d$, $d = \dfrac{2}{3}$.

Since $a_7 = a_1 + 6d$, $a_1 = \dfrac{5}{3}$.

Therefore $a_k = a_1 + (k-1)d = \dfrac{5}{3} + (k-1)\dfrac{2}{3} = 13 \quad \Rightarrow \quad k = 18$.

Problem 25. Solution: (B).
The difference between the second and fourth terms is x; thus the difference between successive terms is $\dfrac{x}{2}$. Therefore $a = \dfrac{x}{2}$, $b = \dfrac{3x}{2}$ and $\dfrac{a}{b} = \dfrac{\frac{x}{2}}{\frac{3x}{2}} = \dfrac{1}{3}$.

Problem 26. Solution: (D).
The formula for the sum S_n of n terms of an arithmetic progression, whose first term is a and whose common difference is d, is $2S_n = n(2a + (n-1)d)$. Therefore,
$$200 = 10(2a + 9d),$$
$$20 = 100(2a + 99d),$$
$$2S_{110} = 110(2a + 109d).$$
Subtracting the first equation from the second and dividing by 90 yields $2a + 109d = -2$. Hence $2 S_{110} = 110(-2)$, so $S_{110} = -110$.

Problem 27. Solution: 1472.
The first arithmetic sequence has the first term of 2 and the common difference of 4. The second arithmetic sequence has the first term of 2 and the common difference of 6. The terms common to both sequences actually form a new arithmetic sequence with the first term of 2 and the common difference of $LCM(4, 6) = 12$.

We know that the last term of the new arithmetic sequence is not greater than 190, so if we let n be the number of terms in the new arithmetic sequence, then $a_n \le 190$.
$2 + 12(n - 1) = 12n - 10 \le 190 \quad \Rightarrow \quad n \le 16.6 \quad \Rightarrow \quad n = 16$.
The sum of the terms equals $16 \times 2 + \dfrac{16 \times 15}{2} \times 12 = 1472$.

Problem 28. Solution: 50.
The two sequences can be expressed as
$a_n = 2 + (n-1) \times 3$
$b_m = 5 + (m-1) \times 4$
We want to find the number of common terms so we set
$a_n = b_m \quad \Rightarrow 2 + (n-1) \times 3 = 5 + (m-1) \times 4 \quad \Rightarrow 4m + 2 = 3n$
Solve for m:
$4m + 2 \equiv 0 \pmod{3}$
$m \equiv 1 \pmod{3}$
Sequence m: 1, 4, 7, 10,..
Sequence n: 2, 6, 10, 14,..
Sequence n has a bigger common difference, so we calculate the greatest value for n:
$200 = 2 + (k-1) \times 4$, where k is the number of n's.

Solve for k, $k = \left\lfloor \dfrac{200-2}{4} + 1 \right\rfloor = 50$. This is the number of common terms in two sequences.

Note if we calculate the number of m's, we obtain $k = 67$, which would not be the answer.

Problem 29. Solution: 48.
The two sequences can be expressed as
$a_n = 1 + (n-1) \times 6$
$b_m = 4 + (m-1) \times 7$
$2009 = 1 + (n-1) \times 6$

$n = \left\lfloor \dfrac{2009-1}{6} + 1 \right\rfloor = 335$. The greatest value for n is 335.

$2009 = 4 + (m-1) \times 7$.
$m = \left\lfloor \dfrac{2009-4}{7} + 1 \right\rfloor = 287$. The greatest value for m is 287.

We want to find the number of common terms so we set
$a_n = b_m$
$1 + (n-1) \times 6 = 4 + (m-1) \times 7$
or $7m + 2 = 6n$

Solve for m,
$7m + 2 \equiv 0 \pmod{6}$
$m \equiv 4 \pmod{6}$
m can then be 4, 10, 16, ...

Calculate the number of m's:
$287 = 4 + (k-1) \times 6$
so $k = \left\lfloor \dfrac{287-4}{6} + 1 \right\rfloor = 48$.

Problem 30. Solution: 200.
These two sequences can be expressed as
$a_n = 1 + (n-1) \times 2$
$b_m = 1 + (m-1) \times 5$
$1991 = 1 + (n-1) \times 2$, so the greatest value for n is 996.
$1991 = 1 + (m-1) \times 5$, so the greatest value for m is 399.

We want to find common terms so we set
$a_n = 1 + (n-1) \times 2 = b_m = 1 + (m-1) \times 5$
We have $2m = 5n - 1$
Now solving for n, we get
$5n - 1 \equiv 0 \pmod{2}$
$n \equiv 1 \pmod{2}$

Since we know that the upper bound for n is 399, we must find the total number of numbers in the sequence: 1, 3, 5, 7, 9,..., 399.

$399 = 1 + (k-1) \times 2$ where k is the number of n's.
Solve for k, $k = 200$. There are 200 common terms in the two sequences.

Problem 31. Solution:
We know that $a_1 = 1$, $S_{n+1} = 4a_n + 2$, and $S_2 = 4a_1 + 2 = 6$.
Therefore $a_2 = 5$, $a_{n+1} = S_{n+1} - S_n = 4(a_n - a_{n-1})$.
$a_{n+1} - 2a_n = 2(a_n - 2a_{n-1})$, $(n \geq 2)$.
$a_n - 2a_{n-1} = 2(a_{n-1} - 2a_{n-2}) = 2^2(a_{n-2} - 2a_{n-3}) = \cdots =$
$2^{n-2}(a_2 - 2a_1) = 2^{n-2}(5-2) = 3 \times 2^{n-2} = \dfrac{3}{4} \times 2^n$.

Hence $\dfrac{a_n}{2^n} - \dfrac{a_{n-1}}{2^{n-1}} = \dfrac{3}{4}$.

So $\dfrac{a_n}{2^n}$ is an arithmetic sequence with common difference $d = \dfrac{3}{4}$ and first term $\dfrac{a_1}{2} = \dfrac{1}{2}$.

$\dfrac{a_n}{2^n} = \dfrac{1}{2} + (n-1) \times \dfrac{3}{4} = \dfrac{1}{4}(3n-1)$.

Or $a_n = 2^{n-2}(3n-1)$.

Problem 32. Solution:
Let d be the common difference and a be the first term.
$na + \dfrac{n(n-1)}{2} d = 97^2$

Or $[2a + (n-1)d]n = 2 \times 97^2$ \hfill (1)

Since $n > 2$, n can only be one of the factors of 2×97^2: $97, 2 \times 97, 97^2, 2 \times 97^2$.

Case I: If $d > 0$, n can only be 97 because $2 \times 97^2 \geq n(n-1)d \geq n(n-1)$.

Therefore (1) becomes $a + 48d = 97$ \hfill (2)

There are two sets of solutions for (2): $\begin{cases} n = 97, \\ d = 1, \\ a = 49; \end{cases}$ and $\begin{cases} n = 97, \\ d = 2, \\ a = 1. \end{cases}$

Case II: If $d = 0$, (1) becomes $a_n = 97^2$. \hfill (3)

(3) also has two sets of solutions: $\begin{cases} n = 97, \\ d = 0, \\ a = 97; \end{cases}$ and $\begin{cases} n = 97^2, \\ d = 0, \\ a = 1. \end{cases}$

Therefore there are 4 such progressions.

Problem 33. Solution:
Let k be the page number that was added twice. $0 < k < n + 1$.
Therefore $1 + 2 + \cdots + n = k$ will be between $1 + 2 + \cdots + n$ and $1 + 2 + \cdots + n + (n+1)$.

Therefore $\dfrac{n(n+1)}{2} < 1986 < \dfrac{(n+1)(n+2)}{2}$.

Or $n(n+1) < 3972 < (n+1)(n+2)$.
n should be greater than 60. $n = 62$.

$k = 1986 - \dfrac{62 \times 63}{2} = 1986 - 1953 = 33$.

Problem 34. Solution: 129.

Let a, $a + d$, $a + 2d$, and $\dfrac{(a+2d)^2}{a+d}$ be the terms of the sequence, with a and d positive integers. Then $(a + 30)(a + d) = (a + 2d)2$, which yields $3a(10 - d) = 2d(2d-15)$. It follows that either $10 - d > 0$ and $2d - 15 > 0$ or $10 - d < 0$ and $2d - 15 < 0$. In the first case, d is 8 or 9, and the second case has no solutions. When $d = 8$, $a = 8 = 3$, and when $d = 9$, $a = 18$. Thus, the only acceptable sequence is 18, 27, 36, 48, and the sum is 129.

Problem 35. Solution: 201.
Method 1:
Let the smallest elements of A and B be $(n+1)$ and $(k+1)$, respectively. Then
$2m = (n + 1) + (n + 2) + \ldots + (n + m) = mn + 1/2\ m(m + 1)$; and
$m = (k + 1) + (k + 2) + \ldots + (k + 2m) = 2km + 1/2\ 2m(2m + 1)$.
The second equation implies that $k + m = 0$. Substitute this into $|k + 2m - (n + m)| = 99$ to obtain $n = \pm 99$. Now simplify the first equation to obtain
$2 = n + (m + 1)/2$, and substitute $n = \pm 99$. This yields $m = -195$ or $m = 201$.
Because $m > 0$, $m = 201$.

Method 2:
The mean of the elements in A is 2, and the mean of the elements in B is 1/2. Because the mean of each of these sets equals its median, and the median of A is an integer, m is odd.
Thus $A = \{2 - \dfrac{m-1}{2}, \ldots, 2, \ldots, 2 + \dfrac{m-1}{2}\}$, and $B = \{m + 1; \because; 0; 1; \because; m\}$.
Therefore $\left|2 + \dfrac{m-1}{2} - m\right| = 99$, which yields $\left|\dfrac{3-m}{2}\right| = 99$, so $|3 - m| = 198$.
Because $m > 0$, $m = 201$.

PROBLEMS

Problem 1: Find a relationship of a, b, and c if the following equation has double roots. $(b-c)x^2 + (c-a)x + (a-b) = 0$.

Problem 2: The vertex of the parabola C: $y = -x^2 + 2ax + b$ is moving along the line L: $mx - y - 2m + 1 = 0$. Find the smallest positive integer value of m such that C intersects the parabola C: $y = x^2$.

Problem 3: Factor: $3x^2 - 7xy - 6y^2 - 10x + 8y + 8$.

Problem 4: Find the smallest possible value of $5x^2 - 4xy + y^2 - 10x + 6y + 5$.

Problem 5: Find the smallest integer of $y = 2x + \sqrt{2x-1}$.

Problem 6: Find the greatest real number of $x^2 + y^2$ if $x + 2y = 1$.

Problem 7: Find a if the equation $ax^2 - 12x + 9 = 0$ has two identical real roots.

Problem 8: Find k if the equation $4x^2 - 8x + k = 0$ has two distinct real roots.

Problem 9: Find b if a, b, and c are real numbers with $a^2 + b^2 + c^2 = 1$ and $a + b + c = \sqrt{3}$

Problem 10: Find the maximum and minimum values of if $\dfrac{y}{x}$ if $(x-3)^2 + (y-3)^2 = 6$. x and y are real numbers.

155

Problem 11: Find k if m is rational such that $x^2 - 4mx + 6x + 3m^2 - 2m + 4k = 0$ has rational roots.

Problem 12: Find the greatest value of m such that $x^2 - 2(2m-3)x + 4m^2 - 14m + 8 = 0$ has integer roots. $3 < m < 40$.

Problem 13: (1974 AMC) What is the smallest integral value of k such that $2x(kx-4) - x^2 + 6 = 0$ has no real roosts?
(A) -1 (B) 2   (C) 3   (D) 4   (E) 5

Problem 14: What is the real value of k such that $x^2 + 2kx = 4 - k$ has two distinct real roots?

Problem 15: Find real positive value of k if $x^2 + k(k+1)x + 9$ can be expressed as a square of a linear expression of x.

Problem 16: Find the positive real value for m such that $y^2 + 2xy + 2x + my - 3$ can be written as the product of two linear expression of x or y.

SOLUTIONS

Problem 1: Solution:
Since the equation has double roots, $\Delta = (c-a)^2 - 4(b-c)(a-b) = 0$.
So $2b = a+c$.

Problem 2: Solution:
$$\begin{cases} y = x^2 \\ y = -x^2 + 2ax + b \end{cases}$$
Since C and C^1 intersect, we have $2x^2 - 2ax - b = 0$ and
$\Delta = 4(a^2 + 2b) \geq 0$ \hfill (1)
The vertex of C is $(a, a^2 + b)$. Substitute into L gives $ma - (a^2 + b) - 2m + 1 = 0$.
or $b = ma - a^2 - 2m + 1$ \hfill (2)
Substituting (2) into (1): $a^2 - 2ma + 4m - 2 \leq 0$ \hfill (3)
In order to get the solutions of (3), we have $\Delta' = 4[m^2 - (4m-2)] \geq 0$.
$m \leq 2 - \sqrt{2}$ and $m \geq 2 + \sqrt{2}$.
The smallest positive integer value of m is 4.

Problem 3: Solution:
Let $3x^2 - (7y + 10)x - (6y^2 - 8y - 8) = 0$.
Solving for x: $x_1 = 3y + 2$ and $x_1 = -\dfrac{2y-4}{3}$.

$3(x - 3y - 2)(x + \dfrac{2y-4}{3}) = (x - 3y - 2)(3x + 2y - 4)$

$3x^2 - 7xy - 6y^2 - 10x + 8y + 8 = (x - 3y - 2)(3x + 2y - 4)$

Problem 4: Solution:
Let $S = 5x^2 - 4xy + y^2 - 10x + 6y + 5$.
$5x^2 - (10 + 4y)x + y^2 + 6y + 5 - S = 0$
Since x is real, $\Delta = (10 + 4y)^2 - 20(y^2 + 6y + 5 - S) \geq 0$.
$y^2 + 10y - 5S \leq 0$
$5S \geq y^2 + 10y = (y+5)^2 - 25$
Since $(y+5)^2 - 25 \geq -25$, $5S \geq -25 \Rightarrow S \geq -5$.
So $S_{\min} = -5$. The smallest value can be achieved when $x = -1$ and $y = -5$.

Problem 5: Solution:

Let $\sqrt{2x-1} = t, (t \geq 0)$.

$2x = t^2 + 1$

$t^2 + t + 1 - y = 0$

$\Delta = 1^2 - 4(1-y) \geq 0$

$y \geq \dfrac{3}{4}$.

The smallest integer for y is 1. This value can be achieved when $x = \frac{1}{2}$.

Problem 6: Solution:

Method 1:

Since $x = 1 - 2y$, $S = x^2 + y^2 = (1-2y)^2 + y^2 = 5y^2 - 4y + 1$.

Or $5y^2 - 4y + 1 - S = 0$

Since y is real, $\Delta = 16 - 20(1-S) \geq 0$.

$S \geq \dfrac{1}{5}$.

The smallest value is $S = \dfrac{1}{5}$.

Substituting $S = \dfrac{1}{5}$ into $5y^2 - 4y + 1 - S = 0$ gives $y = \dfrac{2}{5}$

Substituting $y = \dfrac{2}{5}$ into $x = 1 - 2y$ gives $x = \dfrac{1}{5}$.

The smallest value 1/5 can be achieved when $x = \dfrac{1}{5}$ and $y = \dfrac{2}{5}$.

Method 2:

By Cauchy inequality:

$x^2 + y^2 = \dfrac{x^2}{1} + \dfrac{(2y)^2}{4} \geq \dfrac{(x+2y)^2}{1+4} = \dfrac{1}{5}$ $\Rightarrow$ $x^2 + y^2 \geq \dfrac{1}{5}$

The smallest value of $x^2 + y^2 = \dfrac{1}{5}$.

This smallest value can be achieved when $x = \dfrac{1}{5}$ and $y = \dfrac{2}{5}$.

Problem 7: Solution:

If the given equation has two identical real roots, $\Delta=0$.

Or $\Delta = (-12)^2 - 4 \cdot a \cdot 9 = 0$
Solve for a: $a = 4$.

Problem 8: Solution:
Since the equation has two distinct real roots, $\Delta > 0$.
$\Delta = (-8)^2 - 4 \cdot 4 \cdot k > 0 \quad \Rightarrow \quad k < 4$.

Problem 9: Solution:
$a^2 + b^2 + c^2 = 1$ \hfill (1)
$a + b + c = \sqrt{3}$ \hfill (2)
From (2), we have $c = \sqrt{3} - a - b$ \hfill (3)
Substituting (3) into (1):
$a^2 + b^2 + (\sqrt{3} - a - b)^2 = 1$
$a^2 + b^2 + 3 + a^2 + b^2 - 2\sqrt{3}a - 2\sqrt{3}b + 2ab = 1$.
$a^2 + (b - \sqrt{3})a + (b^2 - \sqrt{3}b + 1) = 0$
Since a is real, $\Delta = (b - \sqrt{3})^2 - 4(b^2 - \sqrt{3}b + 1) \geq 0 \quad \Rightarrow \quad (\sqrt{3} \cdot b - 1)^2 \leq 0$.
$b = \dfrac{\sqrt{3}}{3}$.

Problem 10: Solution:

Let $\dfrac{y}{x} = k$, so $y = kx$.

Substituting $y = kx$ into $(x-3)^2 + (y-3)^2 = 6$: $(x-3)^2 + (kx-3)^2 = 6$.
$(k^2 + 1)x^2 - 6(k+1)x + 12 = 0$
$\Delta = 36(k+1)^2 - 48(k+1) \geq 0$
$k^2 - 6k + 1 \leq 0$
$[k - (3 - 2\sqrt{2})] \cdot [k - (3 + 2\sqrt{2})] \leq 0$
$3 - 2\sqrt{2} \leq k \leq 3 + 2\sqrt{2}$
When $k = 3 - 2\sqrt{2}$, $x = \dfrac{6(k+1)}{2(k^2+1)} = 2 + \sqrt{2}$. So $k_{\min} = 3 - 2\sqrt{2}$

When $k = 3 + 2\sqrt{2}$, $x = \dfrac{6(k+1)}{2(k^2+1)} = 2 - \sqrt{2}$. So $k_{\max} = 3 + 2\sqrt{2}$.

Problem 11: Solution:
The given equation can be written as:
$x^2 - 2(2m-3)x + (3m^2 - 2m + 4k) = 0$.
The discriminant is
$\Delta = 4(2m-3)^2 - 4(3m^2 - 2m + 4k) = 4m^2 - 24m + 4(4-4k) = 4(m^2 - 6m + 4 - 4k)$.
Since the original equation has rational roots, Δ should be a square number.
The discriminant of $m^2 - 6m + 4 - 4k$ should be zero.
Or $36 - 4(4-4k) = 0 \Rightarrow k = -\dfrac{5}{4}$.

Problem 12: Solution:
Since the equation has integer roots, the discriminant should be a square number.
$\Delta = [-2(2m-3)]^2 - 4(4m^2 - 14m + 8) = 4(2m+1)$
That is, $2m + 1$ is a square number.
Since $3 < m < 40$, $m = 4, 12,$ or 24. The greatest value is 24.

Problem 13: Solution: (B).
Putting the quadratic in its standard form: $(2k-1)x^2 - 8x + 6 = 0$.
We see that the discriminant D is $64 - 4(2k-1)6 = 88 - 48k = 8(11 - 6k)$. A quadratic has no real roots if and only if its discriminant is negative. D is negative if $11 - 6k < 0$, that is when $k > \dfrac{11}{6}$; the smallest integral value of k for which the equation has no real root is 2.

Problem 14: Solution:
Rewrite the given equation as $x^2 + 2kx + (k-4) = 0$.
The discriminant is
$\Delta = 4k^2 - 4(k-4) = 4k^2 - 4k + 16 = 4k^2 - 4k + 1 + 15 = (2k-1)^2 + 15$
Since $(2k-1)^2 \geq 0$, $(2k-1)^2 + 15 > 0$.
Since $\Delta > 0$, k can be any real value.

Problem 15: Solution:
If $x^2 + k(k+1)x + 9$ can be expressed as a square of a linear expression of x, we must have:
$\Delta_x = (k^2 + k)^2 - 36 = 0$.
$k^2 + k - 6 = 0$ or $k^2 + k + 6 = 0$.

For, $k^2 + k + 6 = 0$ we have no real solutions.
For $k^2 + k - 6 = 0$, we have $k_1 = -3$ or $k_2 = 2$
So $k = 2$.

Problem 16: Find the positive real value for m such that $y^2 + 2xy + 2x + my - 3$ can be written as the product of two linear expression of x or y.

Solution: 2.

The problem is equivalent to find two rational roots of the equation
$y^2 + 2xy + 2x + my - 3 = 0$ or $y^2 + (2x + m)y + 2x - 3 = 0$.
By the Theorem 2, we know that the quadratic equation $y^2 + (2x+m)y + 2x - 3 = 0$ has rational roots only if only Δ is a square of a ratioanl number.
$\Delta = (2x+m)^2 - 4 \cdot 1 \cdot (2x-3) = 0 \implies 4x^2 + m^2 + 4xm - 8x + 12 = 0 \implies$
$4x^2 + 4x(m-2) + m^2 + 12 = 0$.
Similarly, we have $\Delta_1 = [4(m-2)]^2 - 4 \cdot 4 \cdot (m^2 + 12) = 0 \implies (m-2)^2 - (m^2 + 12) = 0$.
$\implies m = -2$.

50 AMC Lectures Problems Book 1   (16) Method of Completing the Square

PROBLEMS

Problem 1: Is $4x^2 + 12 - 9$ the square of an expression linear in x?

Problem 2: Is $ax^2 - 4axy + 4ay^2 + 2ax - 4ay + a$ the square of an expression linear in x and y?

Problem 3: Simplify: $\sqrt{8 - 2\sqrt{6 + 2\sqrt{5}}}$.

Problem 4: Simplifying $\sqrt[4]{97 - 56\sqrt{3}}$.

Problem 5: Find $\sqrt{11 + 6\sqrt{2}} + \sqrt{11 - 6\sqrt{2}}$.

Problem 6: (1984 AMC) $\dfrac{2\sqrt{6}}{\sqrt{2} + \sqrt{3} + \sqrt{5}}$ equals
(A) $\sqrt{2} + \sqrt{3} - \sqrt{5}$ (B) $4 - \sqrt{2} - \sqrt{3}$ (C) $\sqrt{2} + \sqrt{3} + \sqrt{6} - 5$
(D) $\dfrac{1}{2}(\sqrt{2} + \sqrt{5} - \sqrt{3})$ (E) $\dfrac{1}{3}(\sqrt{3} + \sqrt{5} - \sqrt{2})$.

Problem 7: Find positive integer k such that $3x^2 + kx - 10$ can be expressed as the product of two linear terms in x. x is rational.

Problem 8: Solve for real numbers x and y: $\sqrt{x} + \sqrt{y-1} + \sqrt{z-2} = \dfrac{1}{2}(x + y + z)$.

Problem 9: (1967 AMC) Let $D = a^2 + c^2 + c^2$, where a, b are consecutive integers and $c = ab$. Then $\sqrt{D}$ is:
(A) always an even integer   (B) sometimes an odd integer, sometimes not
(C) always an odd integer   (D) sometimes rational, sometimes not
(E) always irrational

Problem 10: Find $a^2 + b^2 + c^2 + ab + bc - ac$ if $a = -2013$, $b = 2012$, and $c = -2010$.

Problem 11: Find a and b such that $x^2 + 2(1+a)x + (3a^2 + 4ab + 4b^2 + 2) = 0$ has real solutions.

Problem 12: (1983 AMC) Let f be a polynomial function such that, for all real x,
$$f(x^2 + 1) = x^4 + 5x^2 + 3.$$
For all real x, $f(x^2 - 1)$ is
(A) $x^4 + 5x^2 + 1$ (B) $x^4 + x^2 - 3$ (C) $x^4 - 5x^2 + 1$
(D) $x^4 + x^2 + 3$ (E) none of these

Problem 13: Find $\dfrac{x^2 + 1}{x}$ if $\sqrt{x} + \dfrac{1}{\sqrt{x}} = 8$

Problem 14: Show that $x^2 + y^2 + z^2 \geq \dfrac{1}{3}$ if $x + y + z = 1$.

Problem 15: Find the maximum and minimum values of $u = x^2 + 4xy + y^2 - 2x + 2y - 3$ if x and y are real numbers.

Problem 16: Find the smallest value of $x^2 - 2xy + 2y^2 + 2x - 6y$ if x and y are real.

Problem 17: Find real numbers x, y, and z such that $x^2 + y^2 + z^2$ has the smallest value with $x + 2y - z = 6$ and $x - y + 2z = 3$.

Problem 18: Find the smallest integer value of $M = 4x^2 - 12xy + 10y^2 + 4x + 1$. Both x and y are real numbers.

Problem 19: Find the greatest and smallest values $x^2 + 2y^2$ if x and y are real numbers satisfying $x^2 - xy + 2y^2 = 1$.

Problem 20: Find the greatest value $x^2 + y^2 + 2x$ if x and y are real and satisfying: $2x^2 - 6x + y^2 = 0$

Problem 21: Find the greatest value of $x^2 - xy + y^2$ if x and y are real satisfying $x^2 + xy + y - 2 = 0$.

Problem 22: Find the smallest value $x^2 - xy + y^2$ if x and y are real satisfying $x^2 + xy + y - 2 = 0$.

Problem 23: Find real values of a and b such that $-a^2 + 8a - b^2 - 10b - 40$ has the greatest possible value.

Problem 24: Find the smallest value of $a^2 + ab + b^2 - a - 2b$ for real numbers a and b.

SOLUTIONS

Problem 1: Solutions:
Since $\Delta = 12^2 - 4 \times 4 \times (-9) = 288 \neq 0$, $4x^2 + 12x - 9$ is not the square of an expression linear in x.

Problem 2: Solutions:
Since
$\Delta_{xy} = (-4a)^2 - 4 \times a \times (2a) = 0$,
$\Delta_x = (2a)^2 - 4 \times a \times a = 0$,
$\Delta_\lambda = (-4a) \times (2a) - 2 \times a \times (-4a) = 0$
$ax^2 - 4axy + 4ay^2 + 2ax - 4ay + a$ is the square of an expression linear in x and y for rational x and y if a is rational.
$ax^2 - 4axt + 4ay^2 + 2ax - 4ay + a$ is the square of an expression linear in x and y for real x and y if a is real.

Problem 3: Solution:

$= \sqrt{8 - 2\sqrt{5} + 2\sqrt{5+1}} = \sqrt{8 - 2(\sqrt{5}+1)} = \sqrt{6 - 2\sqrt{5}} = \sqrt{5 - 2\sqrt{5} + 1} = \sqrt{5} - 1$

Problem 4: $\sqrt[4]{97 - 56\sqrt{3}} = \sqrt[4]{7^2 - 2 \cdot 7 \cdot 4\sqrt{3} + (4\sqrt{3})^2}$
$= \sqrt[4]{(7 - 4\sqrt{3})^2} = \sqrt{7 - 4\sqrt{3}} = \sqrt{2^2 - 2 \cdot 2 \cdot \sqrt{3} + (\sqrt{3})^2} = \sqrt{(2 - \sqrt{3})^2} = 2 - \sqrt{3}.$

Problem 5: Solution:

$= \sqrt{9 + 2 \cdot 3 \cdot \sqrt{2} + 2} + \sqrt{9 - 2 \cdot 3 \cdot \sqrt{2} + 2} = \sqrt{(3+\sqrt{2})^2} + \sqrt{(3-\sqrt{2})^2} = (3+\sqrt{2}) + (3-\sqrt{2}) = 6.$

Problem 6: Solution: (A).
We have $2\sqrt{6} = 2\sqrt{2} \cdot \sqrt{3} = (\sqrt{2} + \sqrt{3})^2 - (\sqrt{5})^2$.

So $\dfrac{2\sqrt{6}}{\sqrt{2} + \sqrt{3} + \sqrt{5}} = \dfrac{(\sqrt{2} + \sqrt{3})^2 - 5}{\sqrt{2} + \sqrt{3} + \sqrt{5}} = \dfrac{(\sqrt{2} + \sqrt{3} + \sqrt{5})(\sqrt{2} + \sqrt{3} - \sqrt{5})}{\sqrt{2} + \sqrt{3} + \sqrt{5}} = \sqrt{2} + \sqrt{3} - \sqrt{5}.$

Problem 7: Solution:

Since x is rational, $\Delta = k^2 - 4\times 3\times(-10) = k^2 + 120$ must be a square number.
Let $k^2 + 120 = m^2$ $(m > 0)$
$\therefore \quad m^2 - k^2 = 120$
$(m-k)(m+k) = 2\times 3\times 4\times 5$.
Since $m + k$ and $m - k$ have the same parity, we have:

$$\begin{cases} m+k=60 \\ m-k=2 \end{cases} \quad \begin{cases} m+k=30 \\ m-k=4 \end{cases} \quad \begin{cases} m+k=12 \\ m-k=10 \end{cases} \quad \begin{cases} m+k=20 \\ m-k=6 \end{cases}$$

There are four values 29, 13, 7, 1 such that k is a positive integer.

Problem 8: Solution:
The given equation can be written as $x + y + z - 2\sqrt{x} - 2\sqrt{y-1} - 2\sqrt{z-2} = 0$
Completing the square:

$$(\sqrt{x}-1)^2 + (\sqrt{y-1}-1)^2 + (\sqrt{z-2}-1)^2 = 0$$
$\therefore x = 1, y = 2, z = 3$.
We checked and $x = 1$, $y = 2$, $z = 3$ indeed are solutions.

Problem 9: Solution: (C).
Since a and b are consecutive integers, one of them is even, the other odd; hence their product is even. We may let $b = a + 1$. Then $c = ab = a(a+1) = a^2 + a$ is an even integer and

$$\sqrt{D} = a^2 + b^2 + c^2 = a^2 + (a+1)^2 + a^2(a+1)^2$$
$$= a^4 + 2a^3 + 3a^2 + 2a + 1 = (a^2 + a + 1)^2$$

is the square of the positive odd integer $a^2 + a + 1 = c + 1$. We conclude that $\sqrt{D} = a^2 + a + 1$ is always an odd positive integer.

Problem 10: Solution:
$$a^2 + b^2 + c^2 + ab + bc - ac = \frac{1}{2}(2a^2 + 2b^2 + 2c^2 + 2ab + 2bc - 2ac)$$
$$= \frac{1}{2}[(a+b)^2 + (b+c)^2 + (a-c)^2] = \frac{1}{2}[(-1)^2 + (2)^2 + (-3)^2] = 7$$

Problem 11: Solution:
Multiplying both sides of the equation by 2:
$2x^2 + 4x + 4ax + 6a^2 + 8ab + 8b^2 + 4 = 0$.

Completing the square:

$(x+2)^2 + (x+2a)^2 + 2(a+2b)^2 = 0$.

$x = -2, a = 1, b = -\dfrac{1}{2}$.

$\therefore a = 1, b = -\dfrac{1}{2}$.

Problem 12: Solution:
$x^4 + 5x^2 + 3 = (x^4 + 2x^2 + 1) + (3x^2 + 3) - 1 = (x^2+1)^2 + 3(x^2+1) - 1$.
So $f(w) = w^2 + 3w - 1$
$f(x^2 - 1) = (x^2 - 1)^2 + 3(x^2 - 1) - 1 = x^4 + x^2 - 3$

Problem 13: Solution:
$\dfrac{x^2+1}{x} = x + \dfrac{1}{x} = \left(\sqrt{x} + \dfrac{1}{\sqrt{x}}\right)^2 - 2 = 62$.

Problem 14: Solution:
We rewrite the inequality as $3(x^2 + y^2 + z^2) \geq 1$ or $3(x^2 + y^2 + z^2) - 1 \geq 0$.
We have:

$3(x^2 + y^2 + z^2) - 1 = 3(x^2 + y^2 + z^2) - (x+y+z)^2$
$= 2x^2 + 2y^2 + 2z^2 - 2xy - 2yz - 2xz = (x-y)^2 + (y-z)^2 + (x-z)^2 \geq 0$.
$\therefore x^2 + y^2 + z^2 \geq \dfrac{1}{3}$

Problem 15: Solution:
Step one:
$u = x^2 + 4xy + y^2 - 2x + 2y - 3 = x^2 + 2(2y-1)x + (2y-1)^2 - (2y-1)^2 + y^2 + 2y - 3$
$= (x + 2y - 1)^2 - 3y^2 + 6y - 4$.

When $x = -2y + 1$, $\overline{u}_{\min} = -3y^2 + 6y - 4$. $\overline{u}_{\min} = -3y^2 + 6y - 4$.

Step 2:

$\overline{u}_{\min} = -3y^2 + 6y - 4 = -3(y^2 - 2y + 1) - 1 = -3(y-1)^2 - 1$.

When $y = 1$, $(\bar{u}_{min})_{max} = -4$.
So the given function does not have greatest or smallest value.

Problem 16: Solution:
$$M = x^2 - 2xy + 2y^2 + 2x - 6y + 8 = x^2 - 2(y-1)x + 2y^2 - 6y + 8$$
$$= [x - (y-1)]^2 + y^2 - 4y + 7 = (x - y + 1)^2 + (y - 2)^2 + 3.$$
Since $(x - y + 1)^2 \geq 0$, $(y - 2)^2 \geq 0$.
When $x - y + 1 = 0$, $y - 2 = 0$, or $x = 1$, $y = 2$, M has the smallest value 3.

Problem 17: Solution:
Considering the system of equations:

$$\begin{cases} x + 2y - z = 6 \\ x - y + 2z = 3 \end{cases}$$

Solve for x and y:

$x = 4 - z$, $y = z + 1$.

$x^2 + y^2 + z^2 = 3(z - 1)^2 + 14 \geq 14$
The smallest value of $x^2 + y^2 + z^2$ is 14 when $x = 1$, $y = 2$, $z = 3$

Problem 18: Solution:
$M = 4x^2 + 4(1 - 3y)x + 10y^2 + 11 = (2x - 3y + 1)^2 + (y + 3)^2 + 1.$
When, $\begin{cases} 2x - 3y + 1 = 0 \\ y + 3 = 0, \end{cases}$
When $x = -5$ and $y = -3$, $M_{min} = 1$.

Problem 19: Solution:
$2\sqrt{2} \cdot 1 = 2\sqrt{2}(x^2 - xy + 2y^2) = (x^2 - 2\sqrt{2}xy + 2y^2) + (2\sqrt{2} - 1)(x^2 + 2y^2)$
$= (x - \sqrt{2}y)^2 + (2\sqrt{2} - 1)(x^2 + 2y^2) \geq (2\sqrt{2} - 1)(x^2 + 2y^2).$
$x^2 + 2y^2 \leq \dfrac{2\sqrt{2}}{2\sqrt{2} - 1}$

$$(x^2 + 2y^2)_{max} = \frac{2\sqrt{2}}{2\sqrt{2} - 1}$$

$$2\sqrt{2} \cdot 1 = 2\sqrt{2}(x^2 - xy + 2y^2) = -(x^2 + 2\sqrt{2}xy + 2y^2) + (2\sqrt{2} + 1)(x^2 + 2y^2)$$
$$= -(x + \sqrt{2}y)^2 + (2\sqrt{2} + 1)(x^2 + 2y^2) \leq (2\sqrt{2} + 1)(x^2 + 2y^2)$$

$$x^2 + 2y^2 \geq \frac{2\sqrt{2}}{2\sqrt{2} + 1}$$

$$(x^2 + 2y^2)_{min} = \frac{2\sqrt{2}}{2\sqrt{2} + 1}$$

Problem 20: Solution:
Since, $2x^2 - 6x + y^2 = 0$, $2x(x - 3) = -y^2 \leq 0$.
Solve for x: $0 \leq x \leq 3$.
$x^2 + y^2 + 2x = (2x^2 - 6x + y^2) - (x^2 - 8x) = 0 - (x - 4)^2 + 16$
Since $0 \leq x \leq 3$, the greatest value for x is 3.
Therefore, the greatest value of $x^2 + y^2 + 2x$ is $16 - 1 = 15$ when $x = 3$.

Problem 21: Solution:
$x^2 - xy + y^2 = 3(x^2 + xy + y) - 2(x + y)^2 \leq 3 \cdot 2 = 6$

Problem 22: Solution:
$x^2 - xy + y^2 = \frac{1}{3}(x^2 + xy + y^2) + \frac{2}{3}(x - y)^2 \geq \frac{1}{2} \cdot 2 = \frac{2}{3}$.

Problem 23: Solution:
$-a^2 + 8a - b^2 - 10b - 40 = 1 - (a - 4)^2 - (b + 5)^2$
Since $(a - 4)^2$ and $(b + 5)^2$ are nonnegative, the original expression has the greatest possible value when $(a - 4)^2 = 0$ and $(b + 5)^2 = 0$.
So the greatest value is 1 when $a = 4$ and $b = -5$.

Problem 24: Solution:
$a^2 + ab + b^2 - a - 2b = a^2 + (b - 1)a + b^2 - 2b = (a + \frac{b-1}{2})^2 + \frac{3}{4}b^2 - \frac{3}{2}b - \frac{1}{4}$
$= (a + \frac{b-1}{2})^2 + \frac{3}{4}(b - 1)^2 - 1 \geq -1$. The smallest value is -1 when $a = 0$, $b = 1$.

50 AMC Lectures Problems Book 1   (17) Analytic Geometry Distance and Lines

PROBLEMS

Problem 1: What is the closest that the line $y = \dfrac{3}{5}x + \dfrac{2}{7}$ comes to a lattice point?

Problem 2: (1982 AMC) A vertical line divides the triangle with vertices (0, 0), (1,1) and (9,1) in the xy-plane into two regions of equal area. The equation of the line is $x =$
(A) 2.5   (B) 3.0   (C) 3.5   (D) 4.0   (E) 4.5

Problem 3: (2001 NC Math Contest) Find the slope of the line with a positive rational slope, which passes throug the point (6, 0) and at a distance of 5 from (1, 3). Write the slope in the form $\dfrac{a}{b}$, where a and b are relatively prime. What is the sum of a and b?
a. 24   b. 23   c. 22   d. 21   e. none of these.

Problem 4: Find $a + b$ if the line $ax + y + 1 = 0$ is parallel to the line $(a + 1)x + by + 2 = 0$ and two lines have the same distance to the origin.
(A) $-\dfrac{7}{3}$.   (B) 3.   (C) $-\dfrac{7}{3}$ or 3.   (D) any value except 3, $-\dfrac{7}{3}$.

Problem 5: Find the image of $P(-2, -1)$ under the reflection in line $x + 2y - 2 = 0$.

Problem 6: Find the image of the line $3x - y - 4 = 0$ under the reflection in (1, 1).

Problem 7: Find the equation of the line passing through point $P(-5, 4)$. It is known that P divides the segment $A(x, 0)$ and $B(0, y)$ of the line between the x and y axis into the ratio of 1:2.

Problem 8: Find the equation of the angle bisector of the angle formed by lines $x + y - 2 = 0$ and $7x - y + 4 = 0$.

Problem 9: Find the equation of the line passing through point $P(2, -1)$ and having a distance 2 from the origin.

Problem 10: (2003 AMC 12 A) A set S of points in the xy-plane is symmetric about the origin, both coordinate axes, and the line $y = x$. If $(2, 3)$ is in S, what is the smallest possible number of points in S?

(A) 1 (B) 2 (C) 4 (D) 8 (E) 16

Problem 11: (2004 AMC 12 B) The point $(3, 2)$ is rotated $90°$ clockwise around the origin to point B. Point B is then reflected in the line $y = x$ to point C. What are the coordinates of C?

(A) $(3, 2)$ (B) $(2, 3)$ (C) $(2, 3)$ (D) $(2, 3)$ (E) $(3, 2)$

Problem 12: (1981 AMC 12) The lines L and K are symmetric to each other with respect to the line $y = x$. If the equation of line L is $y = ax + b$ with $a \neq 0$ and $b \neq 0$, then the equation of K is $y =$

(A) $\dfrac{1}{a}x + b$ (B) $-\dfrac{1}{a}x + b$ (C) $-\dfrac{1}{a}x - \dfrac{b}{a}$ (D) $\dfrac{1}{a}x + \dfrac{b}{a}$ (E) $\dfrac{1}{a}x - \dfrac{b}{a}$

Problem 13: (2001 NC Math Contest Algebra II) Given $A(1, -2)$, $B(5, 1)$, and $C(-2, 2)$, find the equation of the angle bisector at A.

a. $5x - y = 7$ b. $7x - y = 2$ c. $7y - x = 2$ d. $y = x + 3$ e. none of the above

Problem 14: (1980 AMC 12) The equations of L_1 and L_2 are $y = mx$ and $y = nx$, respectively. Suppose L_1 makes twice as large an angle with the horizontal (measured counterclockwise from the positive x-axis) as does L_2, and that L_1 has 4 times the slope of L_2. If L_1 is not horizontal, then mn is

(A) $\dfrac{\sqrt{2}}{2}$ (B) $-\dfrac{\sqrt{2}}{2}$ (C) 2 (D) -2
(E) not uniquely determined by the given information

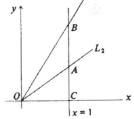

171

50 AMC Lectures Problems Book 1   (17) Analytic Geometry Distance and Lines

SOLUTIONS TO PROBLEMS

Problem 1: Solution:
Let m and n are the coordinates of a lattice point. The distance from this lattice point (m, n) to the given line is

$$d = \frac{\left|\frac{3}{5}m - n + \frac{2}{7}\right|}{\sqrt{\frac{9}{25}+1}} = \frac{\left|3m - 5n + \frac{10}{7}\right|}{\sqrt{34}} = \frac{|7(3m-5n)+10|}{7\sqrt{34}}$$

We know that $7(3m - 5n)$ is a multiple of 7. We also know that 3 and 5 are relatively prime. Since we want to get the smallest value for d, or the smallest value for the numerator, so $7(3m - 5n) = -7$ is the best value we could get ($m = -2$ and $n = -1$).

$$d_{min} = \frac{3}{7\sqrt{34}} = \frac{3\sqrt{34}}{238}$$

Problem 2: Solution: (B).

Method 1 (official solution): In the adjoining figure, ABC is the given triangle and $x = a$ is the dividing line.
Since area $\triangle ABC = \frac{1}{2}(1)(8) = 4$, the two regions must each have area 2. Since the portion of $\triangle ABC$ to the left of the vertical line through vertex A has area less than area $\triangle ABF = \frac{1}{2}$, the line $x = a$ is indeed right of A as shown. Since the equation of line BC is $y = \frac{x}{9}$, the vertical line $x = a$ intersects BC at a point E: $(a, \frac{a}{9})$.

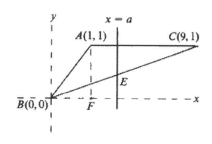

Thus area $\triangle DEC = 2 = \frac{1}{2}\left(1 - \frac{a}{9}\right)(9 - a)$, or $(9 - a)^2 = 36$.
Then $9 - a = \pm 6$, and $a = 15$ or 3. Since the line $x = a$ must intersect $\triangle ABC$, $x = 3$.

Method 2 (our solution):

Extend CA to meet y-axes at D. We see that $\triangle CDA \sim \triangle CGE$. Therefore, we get:
$\frac{DB}{GE} = \frac{CD}{CG}$ $\Rightarrow$ $\frac{1}{GE} = \frac{9}{CG}$ $\Rightarrow$ $GE = \frac{CG}{9}$

172

We also see that the area of $\triangle CDA$ = the area of $\triangle CAB$ + the area of at $\triangle DAB$ = the area of $\triangle CGE \times 2$ + the area of at $\triangle DAB$.

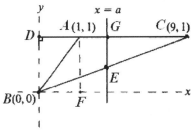

$$\frac{CD \times DB}{2} = \frac{CG \times GE}{2} \times 2 + \frac{AD \times DB}{2} \quad \Rightarrow$$

$$\frac{9 \times 1}{2} = \frac{CG \times GE}{2} \times 2 + \frac{1 \times 1}{2} \quad \Rightarrow$$

$$CG \times GE = 4 \quad \Rightarrow \quad CG \times \frac{CG}{9} = 4 \quad \Rightarrow$$

$$CG^2 = 36 \quad \Rightarrow \quad CG = 6.$$

$DG = DC - CG = 9 - 6 = 3$.
Therefore $x = 3$.

Problem 3: Solution: b.

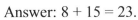 $\overline{DE} = 5$, $\overline{BE} = \sqrt{34}$, $\overline{OC} = \frac{18}{5}$.

$\angle DBE = z \quad \angle DBO = x$

$\tan z = \tan(x+y) = \frac{5}{3}$.

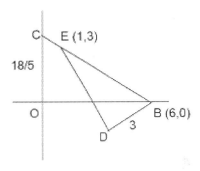

$\tan y = \frac{\frac{18}{5}}{6} = \frac{3}{5}$. $\qquad \tan x = \frac{\tan z - \tan y}{1 + \tan z \tan y} = \frac{8}{15}$.

Answer: $8 + 15 = 23$.

Problem 4: Solution: (A).
Since two lines are parallel, $ab = a + 1$ \hfill (1)
Since they have the same distance to the origin,

$$\frac{1}{\sqrt{a^2+1}} = \frac{2}{\sqrt{(a+1)^2+b^2}} \hfill (2)$$

Solving the system of equations (1) and (2) gives:

$$\begin{cases} a = 1 \\ b = 2 \end{cases} \text{ or } \begin{cases} a = -\frac{1}{3} \\ b = -2. \end{cases}$$

When $a = 1$, $b = 2$, these two lines are overlapped.

Therefore $a = -\frac{1}{3}$, $b = -2 \quad \Rightarrow \quad a + b = -\frac{7}{3}$.

Problem 5: Solution:
Let the image be $P'(x, y)$.
$$\begin{cases} \dfrac{x-2}{2} + 2 \cdot \dfrac{y-2}{2} - 2 = 0 \\ \dfrac{y+1}{x+2} \times (-\dfrac{1}{2}) = -1 \end{cases} \Rightarrow \begin{cases} x + 2y - 8 = 0 \\ 2x - y + 3 = 0 \end{cases}$$

Solve for x and y: $\begin{cases} x = \dfrac{2}{5} \\ y = \dfrac{19}{5} \end{cases} \Rightarrow P'(\dfrac{2}{5}, \dfrac{19}{5}).$

Problem 6: Solution:
Let the equation we want to find be $y = 3x + b$
We know that d, the distances from (1, 1) to these two parallel lines are the same.
$$d = \left|\dfrac{3 - 1 - 4}{\sqrt{3^2 + 1}}\right| = \dfrac{2}{\sqrt{10}}.$$
Therefore $\dfrac{|b + 2|}{\sqrt{10}} = \dfrac{2}{\sqrt{10}}$

Solving for b: $b = 0$ or $b = -4$ (extraneous).
So the equation is $y = 3x$.

Problem 7: Solution:
Let the equation of the line be: $\dfrac{x}{a} + \dfrac{y}{b} = 1$. The coordinates of A and B are $A(a, 0)$, $B(0, b.)$.
Since $\dfrac{AP}{PB} = \dfrac{1}{2}$, considering $P(-5, 4)$, by formula (3), we obtain: $a = -\dfrac{15}{2}$, $b = 12$.
The equation is $8x - 5y + 60 = 0$.

Problem 8: Solution:
Let $P(x, y)$ be a point on the angle bisector. The distances from point P to two given lines are the same. So $\dfrac{|x + y - 2|}{\sqrt{2}} = \dfrac{|7x - y + 4|}{5\sqrt{2}}.$
The equations are: $6x + 2y - 3 = 0$ and $x - 3y + 7 = 0$.

Problem 9: Solution:
If the slope of the line does not exist, the equation of the line is $x = 2$.

If the slope of the equation exists, let it be k.

The equation is then written as $y + 1 = k(x - 2)$, or $kx - y - 2k - 1 = 0$.

By the point to line distance formula, we have $\dfrac{|2k+1|}{\sqrt{k^2+1}} = 2$.

Solve for k: $k = \dfrac{3}{4}$.

The equation of the line is: $y + 1 = \dfrac{3}{4}(x - 2)$ or $3x - 4y - 10 = 0$.

The equations are $x - 2 = 0$ or $3x - 4y - 10 = 0$.

Problem 10: Solution: (D).
The set S is symmetric about the line $y = x$ and contains $(2, 3)$, so it must also contain $(3, 2)$. Also S is symmetric about the x-axis, so it must contain $(2, -3)$ and $(3, -2)$. Finally, since S is symmetric about the y-axis, it must contain $(-2, 3)$, $(-3, 2)$, $(-2, -3)$, and $(-3, -2)$. Since the resulting set of 8 points is symmetric about both coordinate axes, it is also symmetric about the origin.

Problem 11: Solution: (E).
The rotation takes $(3, 2)$ into $B = (2, 3)$, and the reflection takes B into $C = (3, 2)$.

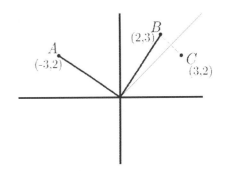

Problem 12: Solution: (E).
If (p, q) is point on line L, then by symmetry (q, p) must be a point on K. Therefore, the points on K satisfy $x = ay + b$.

Solving for y yields $y = \dfrac{x}{a} - \dfrac{b}{a}$.

Problem 13: Solution: (e).

We find that side AC and AB both have length 5, so the angle bisector is also the median, passing through $A(1, -2)$ and the midpoint $(3/2, 3/2)$, of side BC. This makes the slope 7 and the equation $y = 7(x - 1) - 2 = 7x - 9$.

Problem 14: Solution: (C).
In the adjoining figure, L_1 and L_2 intersect the line $x = 1$ at B and A, respectively; C is the intersection of the line $x = 1$ with the x-axis. Since $OC = 1$, AC is the slope of L_2 and BC is the slop of L_1. Therefore $AC = n$.

Since OA is an angle bisector, $\dfrac{OC}{OB} = \dfrac{AC}{AB}$.

This yields $\dfrac{1}{OB} = \dfrac{n}{3n}$ and $OB = 3$.

By the Pythagorean theorem $1 + (4n)^2 = 9$, so $n = \dfrac{\sqrt{2}}{2}$.

PROBLEMS:

Problem 1: Find $f(x)$ if $f(\frac{1+x}{x}) = \frac{x^2+1}{x^2} + \frac{1}{x}$.

Problem 2: Find $f(x)$ for any natural number $x \geq 3$ if
$(x-1)f(x-1) - (x-2)f(x) = 1$ with $f(1) = 3$ and $f(2) = 8$.

Problem 3: Find $f(n)$ for any natural number n if $f(n+1) = (n+1)f(n)$ with $f(1) = 1$.

Problem 4: Find f(x): $f(\frac{3x+1}{3x-2}) = \frac{3x+2}{4x-1}$.

Problem 5: Find f(x): $f(\frac{1-x}{x}) = \frac{1+2x}{x^2} + 4$.

Problem 6: Find f(x): $f(x) + f(\frac{x-1}{x}) = 1 + x$.

Problem 7: Find f(x): $3f(2x-1) + 2f(1-2x) = 2x + 3$.

Problem 8: Find f(x): $2f(x) + 3f(\frac{1}{x}) = 4x$.

Problem 9: Find f(x): $xf(x) + 2f(\frac{x-1}{x+1}) = 1$.

Problem 10: Find f(x): $f(x + \frac{1}{x}) = x^3 + \frac{1}{x^3}$.

Problem 11: Find $f(f(f(x)))$ if $f(x) = \frac{1}{1-x}$.

Problem 12: Find $f(x)$ if $f(\frac{x}{1+x}) - 2f(\frac{1}{1+x}) = \frac{x-2}{1+x}$.

Problem 13: Find f(2014) if for any real values of x and y, $f(x+y^2) = f(x) + 2f^2(y)$ and $f(1) \neq 0$.

Problem 14: Find $f(5)$ if for any integer x, $f(f(x)) = f(x+2) - 3$ with $f(1) = 4$ and $f(4) = 3$.

Problem 15: Find $f(x)$ if $3f(x) + 2f(\dfrac{1}{x}) = 4x$.

Problem 16: (1977 AMC #22) If $f(x)$ is a real valued function of the real variable x, and $f(x)$ is not identically zero, and for all a and b
$$f(a+b) + f(a-b) = 2f(a) + 2f(b),$$
then for all x and y
(A) $f(0) = 1$ (B) $f(-x) = -f(x)$ (C) $f(-x) = f(x)$ (D) $f(x+y) = f(x) + f(y)$
(E) there is a positive number T such the $f(x+T) = f(x)$

Problem 17: (1979 AMC 26) The function f satisfies the functional equation $f(x) + f(y) = f(x+y) - xy - 1$ for every pair x, y of real numbers. If $f(1) = 1$, then the number of integers $n \neq 1$ for which $f(n) = n$ is
(A) 0   (B) 1   (C) 2   (D) 3   (E) infinite

Problem 18: (1980 AMC 14) If the function f defined by $f(x) = \dfrac{cx}{2x+3}$, $x \neq -\dfrac{3}{2}$, c a constant, satisfies $f(f(x)) = x$ for all real numbers x except $-\dfrac{3}{2}$ then c is

(A) -3 (B) $-\dfrac{3}{2}$ (C) $\dfrac{3}{2}$ (D) 3   (E) not uniquely determined by the given information.

Problem 19: (1996 AMC #12) A function f from the integers to the integers is defined as follows: $f(n) = \begin{cases} n+3 & \text{if } n \text{ is odd} \\ \dfrac{n}{2} & \text{if } n \text{ is even} \end{cases}$

Suppose k is odd and $f(f(f(k))) = 27$. What is the sum of the digits of k?
(A) 3 (B) 6 (C) 9 (D) 12 (E) 15

Problem 20: (1998 AMC 17) Let $f(x)$ be a function with the two properties:
(a) for any two real numbers x and y, $f(x+y) = x + f(y)$, and (b) $f(0) = 2$.
What is the value of $f(1998)$?

(a) 0 (B) 2 (C) 1996 (D) 1998 (E) 2000

Problem 21: (1988 AIME) For any positive integer k, let $f_1(k)$ denote the square of the sum of the digits of k. For $n \geq 2$, let $f_n(k) = f_1(f_{n-1}(k))$. Find $f_{1988}(11)$.

Problem 22: Find $f(n)$ for any integer n if $f(n+1) = 2f(n) + 1$ and $f(1) = 1$.

SOLUTIONS

Problem 1: Solution:
$$f(\frac{1+x}{x}) = \frac{x^2+1}{x^2} + \frac{1}{x} = \frac{x^2+2x+1-2x}{x^2} + \frac{1}{x}$$
$$= (\frac{x+1}{x})^2 - \frac{1}{x} = (\frac{1+x}{x})^2 - \frac{1+x-x}{x} = (\frac{1+x}{x})^2 - (\frac{1+x}{x}) + 1$$

So $f(x) = x^2 - x + 1$.

Problem 2: Solution:
Since $(x-1)f(x-1) - (x-2)f(x) = 1$ (1)
so $(x-2)f(x-2) - (x-3)f(x-1) = 1$ (2)

From (1) and (2) we get:
$(x-2)f(x-2) - (x-3)f(x-1) = (x-1)f(x-1) - (x-2)f(x)$ (3)

Subtracting $f(x-1)$ from both sides of (3):
$(x-2)f(x-2) - (x-2)f(x-1) = (x-2)f(x-1) - (x-2)f(x)$

Since $x - 2 > 0$ ($x \geq 3$), we have
$f(x) - f(x-1) = f(x-1) - f(x-2)$ (4)

(4) representing a recursion relationship:
$f(x) - f(x-1) = f(x-1) - f(x-2) = \cdots = f(2) - f(1) = 5$

That is, $f(1), f(2), \cdots, f(x)$ is an arithmetic sequence with the common difference 5.

Therefore $f(x) = a_1 + (x-1)d = 3 + (x-1)5 = 5x - 2$.

Problem 3: Solution:
Let $n = 1, 2, 3, \cdots, k-1, \cdots$
$f(n+1) = (n+1)f(n)$
$f(2) = 2f(1)$
$f(3) = 3f(2)$
$f(4) = 4f(3)$
. . . .

$f(k) = kf(k-1)$

Multiplying all equations together: $f(k) = 1 \cdot 2 \cdot 3 \cdots\cdots k = k!$.

Therefore $f(n) = n!$.

Problem 4: Key: $f(x) = \dfrac{12x-1}{5x+6}$.

Problem 5: Key: $f(x) = x^2 + 4x + 7$.

Problem 6: Key: $f(x) = \dfrac{x^3 - x^2 - 1}{2x(x-1)}$.

Problem 7: Key: $f(x) = x + \dfrac{4}{5}$.

Problem 8: Key: $f(x) = \dfrac{12 - 8x^2}{5x}$.

Problem 9: Key: $f(x) = \dfrac{4x^2 - x + 1}{5x^2 - 5x}$, $x \neq -1, 0, 1$

Problem 10: Key: $f(x) = x^3 - 3x$.

Problem 11: Solution:

$$f(f(x)) = f(\dfrac{1}{1-x}) = \dfrac{1}{1 - \dfrac{1}{1-x}} = \dfrac{x-1}{x}$$

$$f(f(f(x))) = f(\dfrac{x-1}{x}) = \dfrac{1}{1 - \dfrac{x-1}{x}} = x.$$

Problem 12: Solution:

$$f(\dfrac{x}{1+x}) - 2f(\dfrac{1}{1+x}) = \dfrac{x-2}{1+x} \qquad (1)$$

Using $\dfrac{1}{x}$ to replace x in (1):

$$f(\frac{1}{1+x}) - 2f(\frac{x}{1+x}) = \frac{1-2x}{1+x} \qquad (2)$$

Solving system of equations (1) and (2):

$$f(\frac{1}{1+x}) = \frac{1}{1+x}$$

So $f(x) = x$

Method 2: Observing

$$\frac{x}{1+x} - 2 \cdot \frac{1}{1+x} = \frac{x-2}{1+x}$$

So $f(x) = x$.

Problem 13: Solution:

Let $x = y = 0$, we have $f(0) = f(0) + 2f^2(0)$.
So $f(0) = 0$.
Let $x = 0, y = 1$, we have $f(1) = f(0) + 2f^2(1) = 2f^2(1)$.
Since $f(1) \neq 0$, $f(1) = \frac{1}{2}$.

Let $x = n, y = 1$, $f(n+1) = f(n) + 2f^2(1) = f(n) + \frac{1}{2}$.

So $f(n) = \frac{n}{2}$ and $f(2014) = 1007$.

Problem 14: Solution:
$3 = f(4) = f(f(1)) = f(3) - 3 \Rightarrow f(3) = 6$
$6 = f(3) = f(f(4)) = f(6) - 3 \Rightarrow f(6) = 9$.
$9 = f(6) = f(f(3)) = f(5) - 3 \Rightarrow f(5) = 12$.

Problem 15: Key: $\dfrac{12x^2 - 8}{5x}$.

Problem 16: Solution: (C).
Choosing $a = b = 0$ yields $2f(0) = 4f(0)$, $f(0) = 0$.
Choosing $a = 0$ and $b = x$ yields $f(x) + f(-x) = 2f(0) + 2f(x)$, $f(-x) = f(x)$.

Problem 17: Solution: (B)

182

Substitute $x = 1$ into the functional equation and solve for the first term on the right side to obtain $f(y+1) = f(y) + y + 2$.

Since $f(1) = 1$, one sees by successively substituting $y = 2, 3, 4, \ldots$ that $f(y) > 0$ for every positive integer. Therefore, for y a positive integer, $f(y+1) > y+2 > y+1$, and $f(n) = n$ has no solutions for integers $n > 1$. Solving the above equation for $f(y)$ yields
$f(y) = f(y+1) - (y+2)$

Successively substituting $y = 0, -1, -2, \ldots$ into this equation yields $f(0) = -1, f(-1) = -2, f(-2) = -2, f(-3) = -1, f(-4) = 1$. Now $f(-4) > 0$ and, for $y < -4$, $-(y+2) > 0$. Thus, for $y < -4$, $f(y) > 0$. Therefore, $f(n) \neq n$ for $n < -4$; and the solutions $n = 1, -2$ are the only ones.

Problem 18: Solution: (A).

For all $x \neq -\dfrac{3}{2}$, $x = f(f(x)) = \dfrac{c\left(\dfrac{cx}{2x+3}\right)}{2\left(\dfrac{cx}{2x+3}\right)+3} = \dfrac{c^2 x}{2cx + 6x + 9}$, which implies

$(2c+6)x + (9 - c^2) = 0$. Therefore, $2c + 6 = 0$ and $9 - c^2 = 0$. Thus, $c = -3$.

Problem 19: Solution: (B).

Since k is odd, $f(k) = k + 3$. Since $k + 3$ is even, $f(f(k)) = f(k+3) = \dfrac{(k+3)}{2}$.

If $\dfrac{(k+3)}{2}$ is odd, then $27 = f(f(f(k))) = f\left(\dfrac{k+3}{2}\right) = \dfrac{k+3}{2} + 3$.

Which implies that $k = 45$. This is not possible because

$f(f(f(45))) = f(f(48)) = f(24) = 12$. Hence $\dfrac{k+3}{2}$ must be even, and

$27 = f(f(f(k))) = f\left(\dfrac{k+3}{2}\right) = \dfrac{k+3}{4}$,

Which implies that $k = 105$. Checking, we find that
$f(f(f(105))) = f(f(108)) = f(54) = 27$. Hence the sum of the digits of k is $1 + 0 + 5 = 6$.

Problem 20: Solution: (E).

Note that $f(x) = f(x + 0) = x + f(0) = x + 2$ for many real number x. Hence $f(1998) = 2000$. The function defined by $f(x) = x + 2$ has both properties: $f(0) = 2$ and $f(x + y) = x + y + 2 = x + (y + 2) = x + f(y)$.
Or Note that $2 = f(0) = f(-1998 + 1998) = -1998 + f(1998)$.
Hence $f(1998) = 2000$.

Problem 21: Solution:

$f_1(11) = (1 + 1)^2 = 4$
$f_2(11) = f_1(f_1(11)) = f_1(4) = 4^2 = 16$
$f_3(11) = f_1(f_2(11)) = f_1(16) = (1 + 6)^2 = 49$
$f_4(11) = f_1(f_3(11)) = f_1(49) = (4 + 9)^2 = 169$
$f_5(11) = f_1(f_4(11)) = f_1(169) = (1 + 6 + 9)^2 = 256$
$f_6(11) = f_1(f_5(11)) = f_1(256) = (2 + 5 + 6)^2 = 169$

Since $f_n(11)$ only depends on $f_{n-1}(11)$, 256 and 169 will appear in turns. That is, when $n \geq 4$, we have
$$f_n(11) = \begin{cases} 169, & n \text{ is even} \\ 256, & n \text{ is odd} \end{cases}$$
Since 1988 is even so $f_{1988}(11) = 169$.

Problem 22: Solution:

$$\begin{cases} f(1) = 1 & (1) \\ f(n+1) = 2f(n) + 1 & (2) \end{cases}$$

Adding 1 to each side of both (1) and (2):
$$\begin{cases} f(1) + 1 = 2 \\ f(n+1) + 1 = 2[f(n) + 1] \end{cases} \Rightarrow \begin{cases} f(1) + 1 = 2 \\ \dfrac{f(n+1) + 1}{f(n) + 1} = 2 \end{cases}$$

We see that $\{f(n) + 1\}$ is a geometric sequence with the first term 2 and the common ratio 2.
$f(n) + 1 = 2 \cdot 2^{n-1} = 2^n$
So $f(n) = 2^n - 1$.

PROBLEMS

Problem 1. In the following listed numbers, the one which must not be a perfect square is
(A) $3n^2 - 3n + 3$, (B) $4n^2 + 4n + 4$, (C) $5n^2 - 5n - 5$, (D) $7n^2 - 7n + 7$,
(E) $11n^2 + 11n - 11$.

Problem 2. Find the smallest integer greater than $(\sqrt{7} + \sqrt{5})^6$.

Problem 3. What is n if $n^2 - 71$ is divisible by $7n + 55$? n is a positive integer.

Problem 4. Find all possible values for n if $4n^2 + 17n - 15 = 2m(2m+1)$. m and n are positive integers.

Problem 5. Find the sum of all possible positive values of m such that $m^2 + m + 7$ is a square number.

Problem 6. Prove that it is not possible that the product of four consecutive positive integers is a cubic number of a positive integer.

Problem 7. Find all positive integer solutions for the equation $m^2 - 2mn + 14n^2 = 217$.

Problem 8. Find all positive integer solutions to the equation: $xy + yz + zx = xyz + 2$.

Problem 9. (1990 China Middle School Math Contest) Find the triples of positive integers x, y, and z satisfying $\frac{1}{x} + \frac{1}{y} + \frac{1}{z} = \frac{5}{6}$.

Problem 10. (2002 China Middle School Math Contest) Five-digit number $\overline{2x9y1}$ is a square number. Find $3x + 7y$.

SOLUTIONS

Problem 1. Solution
$3n^2 - 3n + 3 = 3(n^2 - n + 1)$ which is 32 when $n = 2$;
$5n^2 - 5n - 5 = 5(n^2 - n - 1) = 52$ when $n = 3$;
$7n^2 - 7n + 7 = 7(n^2 - n + 1) = 72$ when $n = 3$;
$11n^2 + 11n - 11 = 11(n^2 + n - 1) = 112$ when $n = 3$.

Therefore (A), (C), (D) and (E) are all not the answer.
On the other hand, $(2n+1)^2 = 4n^2 + 4n + 1 < 4n^2 + 4n + 4 < 4n^2 + 8n + 4 = (2n+2)^2$, implies that $4n^2 + 4n + 4$ is not a perfect square.
Thus, the answer is (B).

Problem 2. Solution:
Let
$x = \sqrt{7} + \sqrt{5}$ and $y = \sqrt{7} - \sqrt{5}$
$x + y = 2\sqrt{7}$
$xy = 2$
$x^2 + y^2 = (x+y)^2 - 2xy = 24$
$x^6 + y^6 = (x^2 + y^2)^3 - 3(xy)^2(x^2 + y^2) = 13536$
That is, $(\sqrt{7} + \sqrt{5})^6 + (\sqrt{7} - \sqrt{5})^6 = 13536$
Since $2 < \sqrt{5} < \sqrt{7} < 3 \quad \Rightarrow \quad 0 < \sqrt{7} - \sqrt{5} < 1 \quad \Rightarrow \quad 0 < (\sqrt{7} - \sqrt{5})^6 < 1$
$13535 < (\sqrt{7} + \sqrt{5})^6 < 13536$
The smallest integer greater than $(\sqrt{7} + \sqrt{5})^6$ is 13535.

Problem 3. Solution:
Let $\dfrac{n^2 - 71}{7n + 55} = k$
$n^2 - 7kn - (55k + 71) = 0$ \hfill (1)
$\Delta = 49k^2 + 4(55k + 71) = 49k^2 + 220k + 284$

Only when Δ is a perfect square, n is an integer.
$(7k + 15)^2 < \Delta = 49k^2 + 220k + 284 < (7k + 17)^2$

We have:

$\Delta = (7k+16)^2$
$(7k+16)^2 = 49k^2 + 220k + 284$

Solve for k: $k = 7$.

Substitute $k = 7$ into (1):
$n = 57$ or $n = -8$ (this one is not working).
So $n = 57$ is the desired solution.

Problem 4. Solution:
Since $2n(2n+1) - (4n^2 + 17n - 15) = -15(n-1) \leq 0$, we have:
$2n(2n+1) \leq (4n^2 + 17n - 15)$.

Since $(4n^2 + 17n - 15) - (2n+4)(2n+5) = -(n+35) < 0$, we have:
$(4n^2 + 17n - 15) < (2n+4)(2n+5)$.
So $2n(2n+1) \leq (4n^2 + 17n - 15) < (2n+4)(2n+5)$

Since $4n^2 + 17n - 15 = 2m(2m+1)$ is the product of two consecutive positive integers,
So $4n^2 + 17n - 15 = 2n(2n+1)$ $\Rightarrow$ $n = 1$
or $4n^2 + 17n - 15 = (2n+1)(2n+2)$ $\Rightarrow$ $n = \dfrac{17}{11}$ (not integer)
or $4n^2 + 17n - 15 = (2n+2)(2n+3)$ $\Rightarrow$ $n = 3$
or $4n^2 + 17n - 15 = (2n+3)(2n+4)$ $\Rightarrow$ $n = 9$

The solutions are $n = 1, 3,$ or 9.

Problem 5. Solution:
When $m \geq 7$, $m + 7 \leq 2m$
$m^2 < m^2 + m + 7 \leq m^2 + 2m$
$m^2 + 2m < m^2 + 2m + 1 = (m+1)^2$
$m^2 < m^2 + m + 7 \leq (m+1)^2$
$m^2 + m + 7$ is not a square number.

When $1 \leq m < 7$,
$m = 1$, $m^2 + m + 7 = 9 = 3^2$.
$m = 2$, $m^2 + m + 7 = 13$.

$m = 3$, $m^2 + m + 7 = 19$.
$m = 4$, $m^2 + m + 7 = 27$.
$m = 5$, $m^2 + m + 7 = 37$.
$m = 6$, $m^2 + m + 7 = 49 = 7^2$.
The desired solution is then $1 + 6 = 7$.

Problem 6. Solution:
We assume that there are integers $x \geq 2$ and y such that
$$(x-1)\, x\, (x+1)\, (x+2) = y^3 \tag{1}$$

When x is odd, $(x, x+2) = (x, 2) = 1$, which means that x is relatively prime to $(x+2)$. x is also relatively prime to $(x-1)$ and $(x+1)$ since they are consecutive numbers.

So x is relatively prime to $(x-1)(x+1)(x+2)$.

Therefore, from (1), we know that there exist positive integers u and v such that $(x-1)(x+1)(x+2) = u^3$ and $x = v^3$

In the other hand, $(x-1)(x+1)(x+2) = x^3 + 2x^2 - x - 2$,
and $x^3 < x^3 + 2x^2 - x - 2 < (x+1)^3$ (note that $x \geq 2$).

So $x^3 + 2x^2 - x - 2$ cannot be expressed as a cubic number u^3.

When x is even, $(x+1, x-1) = (x-1, 2) = 1$.

Similarly we can show that $(x+1)$ is relatively prime to $x\,(x-1)(x+2)$.

So $(x+1)$ is relatively prime to $x\,(x-1)(x+2)$.

Therefore, from (1), we know that both $(x+1)$ and $x\,(x-1)(x+2)$ are a cubic numbers.

However, $(x-1)\,x\,(x+2) = = x^3 + x^2 - 2x$,
and $x^3 < x^3 + x^2 - 2x < (x+1)^3$ if $x \neq 2$.

So $(x-1)\,x\,(x+2)$ is not a cubic number when $x \neq 2$.
When $x = 2$, $(x-1)\,x\,(x+1)\,(x+2) = 24$ and 24 is not a cubic number.
We are done.

Problem 7. Solution:
The given equation can be written as $(m-n)^2 + 13n^2 = 217$.

Since $217 = (m-n)^2 + 13n^2 \geq 13n^2$, so $n^2 \leq \dfrac{217}{13} < 17$.

For positive integer values, n can be 1, 2, 3 and 4.

When $n = 1$, $(m-1)^2 = 204$ (no integer solution)

When $n = 2$, $(m-2)^2 = 165$ (no integer solution)

When $n = 3$, $(m-3)^2 = 100 \quad \Rightarrow \quad m = 13$.

When $n = 4$, $(m-4)^2 = 9 \quad \Rightarrow \quad m = 1$ or 7.

The positive solutions are $(m, n) = (13, 1), (1, 4)$, and $(7, 4)$.

Problem 8. Solution:
WLOG, we assume that $x \leq y \leq z$. We have:
$$\frac{1}{x} + \frac{1}{y} + \frac{1}{z} = \frac{2}{xyz} + 1.$$
$$1 < \frac{2}{xyz} + 1 = \frac{1}{x} + \frac{1}{y} + \frac{1}{z} \leq \frac{3}{x}.$$
So $x \leq 2$.

When $x = 1$, $y + z = 2 \quad \Rightarrow \quad y = 1$ and $z = 1$.

When $x = 2$,
$$\frac{1}{y} + \frac{1}{z} = \frac{1}{yz} + \frac{1}{2}.$$
$$\frac{2}{y} > \frac{1}{y} + \frac{1}{z} = \frac{1}{yz} + \frac{1}{2} > \frac{1}{2} \qquad \Rightarrow \qquad \frac{1}{y} > \frac{1}{4}.$$
So $y \leq 3$.

In other hand, $\dfrac{1}{y} + \dfrac{1}{yz} < \dfrac{1}{y} + \dfrac{1}{z} = \dfrac{1}{yz} + \dfrac{1}{2} \quad \Rightarrow \quad \dfrac{1}{y} < \dfrac{1}{2}$

So $y \geq 3$.

Therefore, we must have $y = 3 \quad \Rightarrow \quad z = 4$.

All the solutions are: $(x, y, z) = (1, 1, 1), (2, 3, 4), (2, 4, 3), (3, 2, 4), (3, 4, 2), (4, 3, 2)$, and $(4, 2, 3)$.

Problem 9. Solution:

We know that x, y, and z are positive integers with $\frac{1}{x}+\frac{1}{y}+\frac{1}{z}=\frac{5}{6}<1$. WLOG, we assume that $1 < x \leq y \leq z$.

We have: $\frac{1}{x} \geq \frac{1}{y} \geq \frac{1}{z}$.

Therefore $\frac{1}{x} < \frac{1}{x}+\frac{1}{y}+\frac{1}{z} \leq \frac{3}{x}$ or $\frac{1}{x} < \frac{5}{6} \leq \frac{3}{x}$.

Solving we get $\frac{6}{5} < x \leq \frac{18}{5}$. So we are sure that $x = 2$ or $x = 3$.

When $x = 2$, y can be 4, 5, and 6.
When $x = 3$, y can be 3, and 6.
So z can be 12, 6, 6, and 4.
Therefore when $1 < x \leq y \leq z$, the triples are (2, 4, 12), (2, 6, 6), 3, 3, 6), and (3, 4, 4).

Problem 10. Solution:

Five-digit number $\overline{2x9y1}$ is a square number. Find $3x + 7y$.

We know that $\overline{2x9y1}$ is a five-digit square number with the ten thousands digit 2. Since $141^2 = 19881$ and $175^2 = 30625$, $141^2 \leq \overline{2x9y1} \leq 175^2$.

We also know that the units digit of $\overline{2x9y1}$ is 1, so the the square root of $\overline{2x9y1}$ can only be 149, 151, 159, 161, 169, and 171.

Only $161^2 = 25921$ satisfies the condition.

Therefore $x = 5$ and $y = 2$. $3x + 7y = 29$.

50 AMC Lectures Problems Book 1   (20) Nonnegative Integers

PROBLEMS

Problem 1: (1962 AMC) For what real values of K does $x = K^2(x-1)(x-2)$ have real roots?

(A) none   (B) $-2 < K < 1$ (C) $-2\sqrt{2} < K < 2\sqrt{2}$ (D) $K > 1$ or $K < -2$ (E) all

Problem 2: If the equation $x^2 + 2(1+a)x + (3a^2 + 4ab + 4b^2 + 2) = 0$ about x has real solutions, find the values of both a and b.

Problem 3: Comparing $\sqrt{a-1} + \sqrt{a-4}$ and $\sqrt{a-2} + \sqrt{a-3}$ $(a \geq 4)$.

Problem 4: Find $(x-y)^2$ for real numbers x and y if
$|2x - y| + \sqrt{y + 2z} + z^2 - 4z + 4 = 0$.

Problem 5: (1977 AMC) For every triple (a, b, c) of non-zero real numbers, form the number

$$\frac{a}{|a|} + \frac{b}{|b|} + \frac{c}{|c|} + \frac{abc}{|abc|}.$$

The set of all numbers formed is

(A) $\{0\}$ (B) $\{-4, 0, 4\}$ (C) $\{-4, -2, 0, 2, 4\}$
(D) $\{-4, -2, 2, 4\}$ (E) none of these

Problem 6: Find $x + y$ if $2x^2 - xy - 5x + y + 4 = 0$, $x \geq y \geq 1$.

Problem 7: Find $\dfrac{a+b}{a-b}$ if $a^2 + b^2 = 4ab$ with $a < b < 0$.

Problem 8: Find $a + b + x + y$ if $y + |\sqrt{x} - 2| = 1 - a^2$ and $|x - 4| = 3y - 3 - b^2$ for real numbers $a, b, x,$ and y.

Problem 9: Find real numbers x and y such that $\dfrac{x^2}{5} - 2x + 5 + \sqrt{y^2 - 4y + 3} = 0$.

Problem 10: Find the product of xyz for real numbers x, y and z such that.

$(x-3)^2 + |2y+1| + \sqrt{z+2} = 0$.

Problem 11: Find real numbers x and y such that
$$\begin{cases} (x+2y-8)^2 + (2-x)^2 = 0 \\ x \cdot z^2 + y \cdot z - 5\sqrt{xz^2 + yz + 9} + 3 = 0. \end{cases}$$

Problem 12: Find a and b such that the following equation has real roots:
$x^2 + 2(1+a)x + (3a^2 + 4ab + 4b^2 + 2) = 0$.

Problem 13: The sides of a quadrilateral are a, b, c, and d. Show that the quadrilateral is a parallelogram if $a^2 + b^2 + c^2 + d^2 = 2ac + 2bd$.

Problem 14: Find $a^{-6} + b^{-2013}$ If a and b are real numbers and $\sqrt{3a-1} + b^2 + 2b + 1 = 0$.

Problem 15: Solve for real x and y: $9x^2 + y^2 - 6x + 18y + 82 = 0$

Problem 16: Solve for real x and y: $\sqrt{x^2 - 1} + \sqrt{y^2 - 3x - 4} = 0$

Problem 17: Show that $2y = x + z$ if $(z-x)^2 - 4(x-y)(y-z) = 0$. x, y, and z are real numbers.

Problem 18: Find real numbers x and y if $|x - 16y| + (8y - 1)^2 = 0$.

Problem 10: Find real numbers x and y if $\dfrac{|16 - x^2| + 4(x - 2y)^2}{\sqrt{x+4}} = 0$.

Problem 20: How many integer vaues of a such that x is a negative integer and $|2y - 24| + \sqrt{ax - y - x} = 0$?

50 AMC Lectures Problems Book 1   (20) Nonnegative Integers

SOLUTIONS TO THE PROBLEMS

Problem 1: Solution: (E).
If $k = 0$, $x = 0$.
If $k \neq 0$, $x = K^2(x^2 - 3x + 2) \quad \Rightarrow \quad K^2 x^2 - x(3K^2 + 1) + 2K^2 = 0$.

For x to be a real number the discriminant must be greater than or equal to zero, i. e. $K^4 + 6K^2 + 1 \geq 0$. This is true for all values of K.

Problem 2: Solution: $a = 1$ and $b = -\dfrac{1}{2}$.

Since the equation has real solutions, the discriminant must be greater than or equal to zero.
$\Delta = 4(a+1)^2 - 4 \times (3a^2 + 4ab + 2) \geq 0 \quad \Rightarrow \quad a^2 + 2a + 1 - 3a^2 - 4ab - 4b^2 - 2 \geq 0$
Or $-2a^2 + 2a - 1 - 4ab - 4b^2 \geq 0 \quad \Rightarrow \quad (a-1)^2 + (a+2b)^2 \leq 0$.

Since $(a-1)^2 \geq 0$ and $(a+2b)^2 \geq 0$, so $a - 1 = 0$ and $a + 2b = 0$

Solve: $a = 1$ and $b = -\dfrac{1}{2}$.

Problem 3: Solution:
$(\sqrt{a-1} + \sqrt{a-4})^2 = 2a - 5 + 2\sqrt{a^2 - 5a + 4}$
$(\sqrt{a-2} + \sqrt{a-3})^2 = 2a - 5 + 2\sqrt{a^2 - 5a + 6}$

Hence $\sqrt{a-1} + \sqrt{a-4} < \sqrt{a-2} + \sqrt{a-3}$

Problem 4: Solution: $x = -2$, $y = -4$ and $z = 2$.

$|2x - y| + \sqrt{y + 2z} + z^2 - 4z + 4 = 0$ can be written as $|2x - y| + \sqrt{y + 2z} + (z-2)^2 = 0$.
Since $|2x - y| + \sqrt{y + 2z} + (z-2)^2 = 0$, we have:

$$\begin{cases} |2x-y|=0 \\ \sqrt{y+2z}=0 \\ (z-2)^2=0 \end{cases}$$

Solving the system of equations gives: $x = -2$, $y = -4$ and $z = 2$.

Problem 5: Solution: (B).

If a, b and c are all positive (negative), then 4 (respectively, -4) is formed; otherwise 0 is formed.

Problem 6: **Solution**: 4.

$(x^2 - 4x + 4) + (x^2 - xy - x + y) = 0 \quad \Rightarrow \quad (x-2)^2 + (x-y)(x-1) = 0$

Since, $x \geq y \geq 1$, $(x-y)(x-1) \geq 0$.

We also know that $(x-2)^2 \geq 0$, so $(x-2)^2 = 0$ and $(x-y)(x-1) = 0$.

Therefore $x = y = 2$ and $x + y = 4$.

Problem 7. Solution:

$a^2 + b^2 = 4ab \quad \Rightarrow \quad (a+b)^2 = 6ab \quad \Rightarrow \quad (a-b)^2 = 2ab$.

Since $a < b < 0$, we have $a + b = -\sqrt{6ab}$ and $a - b = -\sqrt{2ab}$.

Hence $\dfrac{a+b}{a-b} = \sqrt{3}$.

Problem 8: **Solution**: 5.

$$\begin{cases} y + |\sqrt{x}-2| = 1 - a^2 \\ |x-4| = 3y - 3 - b^2 \end{cases}$$

Eliminating y from the system of equations above:

$3|\sqrt{x}-2| + |x-4| = -(3a^2 + b^2)$.

Since $3|\sqrt{x}-2| \geq 0$ and $|x-4| \geq 0$, $-(3a^2 + b^2) \geq 0$.

Or $3|\sqrt{x}-2| = 0 \quad \Rightarrow \quad x = 4$.

$-(3a^2 + b^2) = 0 \quad \Rightarrow \quad a = b = 0$.

$|x-4|=0 \implies x=4$.
and $y=1$.

$a+b+x+y=5$.

Problem 9:
Solution: $\begin{cases} x=5 \\ y=1 \end{cases}$ or $\begin{cases} x=5 \\ y=3 \end{cases}$.

Problem 10: $xyz=3$.

Problem 11: Solution:

$\begin{cases} x_1=2; \\ y_1=3; \\ z_1=3; \end{cases}$ or $\begin{cases} x_2=2; \\ y_2=3; \\ z_2=-\dfrac{9}{2} \end{cases}$

Problem 12: Solution: $a=1$ and $b=-\dfrac{1}{2}$.

If the equation has real roots, $\Delta \geq 0$.

$\Delta = [2(1+a)]^2 - 4(3a^2+4ab+4b^2+2) \geq 0$
$= 4(1+2a+a^2-3a^2-4ab-4b^2-2) = 4(-1+2a-2a^2-4ab-4b^2)$
$= -4(1-2a+a^2+a^2+4ab+4b^2) = -4[(1-a)^2+(a+2b^2)] \geq 0$

So $(1-a)^2 + (a+2b^2) \leq 0$.

Since $(1-a)^2 \geq 0$ and $(a+2b^2) \geq 0$, so $(1-a)^2 = 0$ and $(a+2b^2)=0$.

$1-a=0$ and $a+2b=0$.
$a=1$ and $b=-\dfrac{1}{2}$.

Problem 13: Solution:

Since $a^2 + b^2 + c^2 + d^2 = 2ac + 2bd$, $(a^2 - 2ac + c^2) + (b^2 - 2cd + d^2) = 0$.

Or $(a-c)^2 + (b-d)^2 = 0$ $\Rightarrow$ $a - c = 0$ and $b - d = 0$.
$a = c$ and $b = d$.

The quadrilateral is a parallelogram.

Problem 14: Solution: 728.
We rewrite the given equation as $\sqrt{3a-1} + (b+1)^2 = 0$.

We know that $\sqrt{3a-1} \geq 0$ and $(b+1)^2 \geq 0$. Since $\sqrt{3a-1} + (b+1)^2 = 0$, $\sqrt{3a-1} = 0$ and $b + 1 = 0$.

So $a = \frac{1}{3}$ and $b = -1$.

$a^{-6} + b^{-2013} = (\frac{1}{3})^{-6} + (-1)^{-2013} = 3^6 - 1 = 729 - 1 = 728$.

Problem 15: Solution: $x = \frac{1}{3}$ and $y = -9$.

Problem 16: Solution:

$x = 1, y = 4$; $x = 1$; $y = -1$; $x = -1, y = 4$; $x = -1$; $y = -1$.

Problem 17: Solution:
Since $(z-x)^2 - 4(x-y)(y-z) = 0$, $z^2 - 2xz + x^2 - 4xy + 4xz + 4y^2 - 4yz = 0$.

Or $z^2 + x^2 + 4y^2 + 2xz - 4xy - 4yz = 0$ $\rightarrow$ $(x + z - 2y)^2 = 0$

Therefore $x + y - 2y = 0$ $\Rightarrow$ $2y = x + z$

Problem 18: Solution: $y = 1/8$ and $x = 2$.
We know that $|x - 16y| \geq 0$ and $(8y - 1)^2 \geq 0$.
Since $|x - 16y| + (8y - 1)^2 = 0$, $|x - 16y| = 0$, and $(8y - 1)^2 = 0$.
$y = 1/8$ and $x = 2$.

Problem 19: Solution:

$$\begin{cases} 16 - x^2 = 0, \\ x - 2y = 0, \\ x + 4 > 0. \end{cases}$$

$x = 4, y = 2.$

Problem 20: Solution:
$$\begin{cases} 2y - 24 = 0, \\ ax - y - x = 0. \end{cases}$$

$$\begin{cases} x = \dfrac{12}{a-1}, \\ y = 12. \end{cases}$$

When $a = 0, -1, -2, -3, -5, -11$, x is negative integer.

There are 6 integer values.

50 AMC Lectures Problems Book 1   (21) Similar Triangles

PROBLEMS

Problem 1: In triangle ABC, if $\angle A = 2\angle B$, then $a^2 = b^2 + bc$.

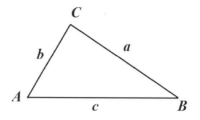

Problem 2: (2009 AMC 12 A #20) Convex quadrilateral $ABCD$ has $AB = 9$ and $CD = 12$. Diagonals AC and BD intersect at E, $AC = 14$, and $\triangle AED$ and $\triangle BEC$ have equal areas. What is AE?

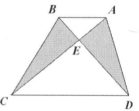

Problem 3: (2005 AMC 12 A) Let AB be a diameter of a circle and C be a point on AB with $2 \times AC = BC$. Let D and E be points on the circle such that $DC \perp AB$ and DE is a second diameter. What is the ratio of the area of $\triangle DCE$ to the area of $\triangle ABD$?

(A) $\dfrac{1}{6}$ (B) $\dfrac{1}{4}$ (C) $\dfrac{1}{3}$ (D) $\dfrac{1}{2}$ (E) $\dfrac{2}{3}$

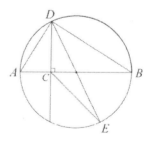

Problem 4: (2002 AMC12 B) Let $\triangle XOY$ be a right-angled triangle with m$\angle XOY = 90°$. Let M and N be the midpoints of legs OX and OY, respectively. Given that $XN = 19$ and $YM = 22$, find XY.

(A) 24   (B) 26   (C) 28   (D) 30   (E) 32

Problem 5: (1984 AMC) In $\triangle ABC$, D is on AC and F is on BC. Also $AB \perp AC$, $AF \perp BC$, and $BD = DC = FC = 1$. Find AC.

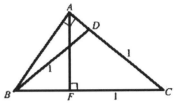

Problem 6: Take a point D on the side BC of the equilateral triangle ABC such that $\dfrac{BD}{CD} = \dfrac{1}{2}$. Draw $CH \perp AD$ at H. Connect BH. Prove: $\angle DBH = \angle DAB$.

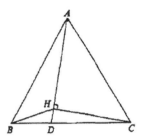

Problem 7: As shown in the figure, P is a point inside $\triangle ABC$. Connect AP, BP, and CP and extend them to meet the sides at D, E, and F, respectively.

Prove: (1) $\dfrac{PD}{AD} + \dfrac{PE}{BE} + \dfrac{PF}{CF} = 1$.

(2) At least one of $\dfrac{AP}{PD}, \dfrac{BP}{PE}, \dfrac{CP}{PF}$ not greater than 2, and at least one of them not less than 2.

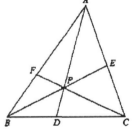

Problem 8: In $\triangle ABC$, $\angle BAC = 120°$. AD is the angle bisector of $\angle BAC$ and meets BC at D. Prove: $\dfrac{1}{AD} = \dfrac{1}{AB} + \dfrac{1}{AC}$.

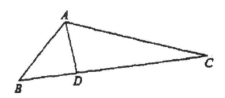

Problem 9: In rectangle ABCD, M is the middle point of AD. N is the middle point of BC. P is any point on the extension of CD. PM meets AC at Q. Prove: $\angle QNM = \angle MNP$.

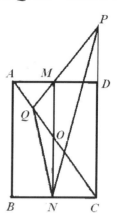

Problem 10: ABCD is an isosceles trapezoid with AB//DC, AB = 2CD, and $\angle DAB = 60°$. E is a point on AB. FE = FB = AC. FA = AB. Find AE : EB.

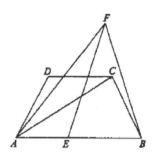

Problem 11: P and Q are two points on AD and BC of quadrilateral ABCD. $\dfrac{AP}{PD} = \dfrac{QB}{QC} = \dfrac{AB}{CD}$. Prove: the angle formed by PQ and AB is the same as the angle formed by PQ and CD.

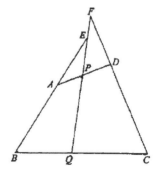

Problem 12: In $\triangle ABC$, $\angle A : \angle B : \angle C = 4:2:1$. AD and AE are the angle bisectors of $\angle BAC$ and $\angle ABC$, respectively. Prove: $AB^2 = AD \times BE$.

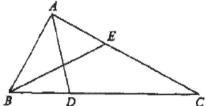

Problem 13: In right $\triangle ABC$, $\angle A = 90°$. $AD \perp BC$ at D. P is the middle point of AD. Extend BP to meet CA at E. Passing through E to construct $EF \perp BC$ at F. Prove: $EF^2 = AE \times EC$.

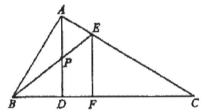

Problem 14: In $\triangle ABC$, $\angle BCA = 90°$. D is any point on AB. Prove: $(AB \times CD)^2 = (AC \times BD)^2 + (BC \times AD)^2$.

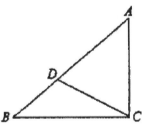

Problem 15: In a regular 7-gons $ABCDEFG$, a is the longest diagonal. b is the shortest diagonal. c is the length of the side. Prove: $\dfrac{1}{c} = \dfrac{1}{a} + \dfrac{1}{b}$.

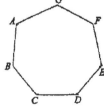

Problem 16: (2002 AIME I 13) In triangle *ABC*, the medians *AD* and *CE* have lengths 18 and 27, respectively, and *AB* = 24. Extend *CE* to intersect the circumcircle of *ABC* at *F*. The area of triangle *AFB* is $m\sqrt{n}$, where m and n are positive integers and n is not divisible by the square of any prime. Find $m + n$.

SOLUTIONS

Problem 1: Proof:
Extend CA to D such that $AD = AB$.
Since $AD = AB$, $\angle D = \angle ABD$.
Since $\angle A = \angle D + \angle ABD = 2\angle D$, and $\angle A = 2\angle CBA$, $\angle D = \angle CBA$.

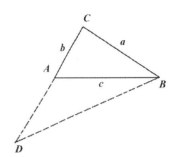

We conclude that $\triangle ABC \sim \triangle BDC$ ($\angle D = \angle CBA$, and $\angle C = \angle C$).

We have the following equation:
$$\frac{CD}{CB} = \frac{BC}{AC} \quad \Rightarrow \quad \frac{b+c}{a} = \frac{a}{b} \quad \Rightarrow \quad a^2 = b^2 + bc$$

Problem 2: Solution: 6.
Since $\triangle AED$ and $\triangle BEC$ have equal areas, $AB // CD$. $ABCD$ is a trapezoid. $\triangle ABE \sim \triangle CDE$.

$$\frac{AB}{CD} = \frac{AE}{CE} = \frac{AE}{AC - AE} \quad \Rightarrow \quad \frac{9}{12} = \frac{AE}{14 - AE} \quad \Rightarrow \quad AE = 6.$$

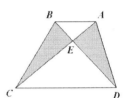

Problem 3: Solution: (C).
Let O be the center of the circle. Each of $\triangle DCE$ and $\triangle ABD$ has a diameter of the circle as a side. Thus the ratio of their areas is the ratio of the two altitudes to the diameters. These altitudes are DC and the altitude from C to DO in $\triangle DCE$. Let F be the foot of this second altitude. Since $\triangle CFO$ is similar to $\triangle DCO$,

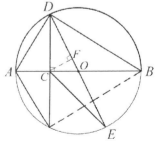

$$\frac{CF}{DC} = \frac{CO}{DO} = \frac{AO - AC}{DO} = \frac{\frac{1}{2}AB - \frac{1}{3}AB}{\frac{1}{2}AB} = \frac{1}{3}$$

$$\frac{CF}{DC} = \frac{CO}{DO} = \frac{AO - AC}{DO} = \frac{\frac{1}{2}AB - \frac{1}{3}AB}{\frac{1}{2}AB} = \frac{1}{3}$$

which is the desired ratio.

Problem 4: Solution: (B).

Let $OM = a$ and $ON = b$. Then $19^2 = (2a)^2 + b^2$ and $22^2 = a^2 + (2b)^2$.

Hence $5(a^2 + b^2) = 19^2 + 22^2 = 845$.

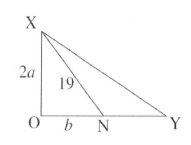
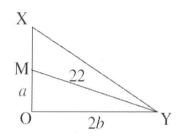

It follows that
$MN = \sqrt{a^2 + b^2} = \sqrt{169} = 13$.
Since $\triangle XOY$ is similar to $\triangle MON$ and $XO = 2 \cdot MO$, we have $XY = 2 \cdot MN = 26$.

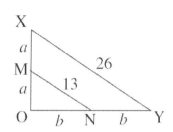

Problem 5: Solution: $\sqrt[3]{2}$.
Drop $DG \perp BC$. Let $AC = x$, $GC = y$.
Note that $BC = 2y$, for $\triangle BDC$ is isosceles.
Since $\triangle DCG \sim \triangle ACF \sim \triangle BCA$, we obtain $\frac{1}{y} = \frac{x}{1} = \frac{2y}{x}$.

thus $y = \frac{1}{x}$ and $y = \frac{x^2}{2}$, implying $x^3 = 2$, or $x = \sqrt[3]{2}$.

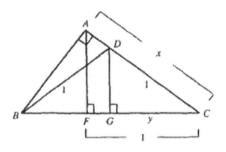

Problem 6: Solution:
Passing through A to draw $AE \perp BC$ at E. Since $\angle ADE = \angle CDH$, $\angle AED = 90° = \angle CHD$
so $\triangle ADE \sim \triangle CDH$. $\frac{AD}{DE} = \frac{CD}{DH}$.

We also know that $\frac{DE}{DB} = \frac{\frac{1}{2}BC - \frac{1}{3}BC}{\frac{1}{3}BC} = \frac{1}{2}$, and $\frac{BD}{CD} = \frac{1}{2}$.

So $\frac{DE}{DB} = \frac{BD}{CD}$.

Multiplying the above equation by $\frac{AD}{DE} = \frac{CD}{DH}$, we get:

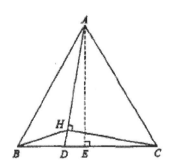

204

$\dfrac{AD}{DB} = \dfrac{BD}{DH}$.

Since $\angle ADB = \angle BDH$, so $\triangle ADB \sim \triangle BDH$. $\angle DAB = \angle DBH$.

Problem 7: Proof:
(1): Draw $GH // BC$ through P to meet AB at G, and to meet AC at H.

Then $\dfrac{PE}{BE} = \dfrac{PH}{BC}$, $\dfrac{PF}{CF} = \dfrac{PG}{BC}$, $\dfrac{AP}{AD} = \dfrac{GH}{BC}$.

So $\dfrac{PE}{BE} + \dfrac{PF}{CF} = \dfrac{PH + PE}{BC} = \dfrac{GH}{BC} = \dfrac{AP}{AD}$.

$\dfrac{PD}{AD} + \dfrac{PE}{BE} + \dfrac{PF}{CF} = \dfrac{PD}{AD} + \dfrac{AP}{AD} = 1$.

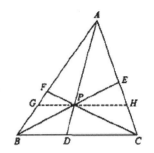

(2) From (1) we know that at least one of $\dfrac{PD}{AD}, \dfrac{PE}{BE}$, or $\dfrac{PF}{CF}$ is not greater than $\dfrac{1}{3}$, and at least one of them is not less than $\dfrac{1}{3}$. WLOG, we assume that $\dfrac{PD}{AD} \le \dfrac{1}{3}, \dfrac{PE}{BE} \ge \dfrac{1}{3}$. Then

$\dfrac{AP}{PD} = \dfrac{AD}{PD} - 1 = \dfrac{1}{\frac{PD}{AD}} - 1 \ge 2$. $\dfrac{BP}{PE} = \dfrac{BE}{PE} - 1 = \dfrac{1}{\frac{PE}{BE}} - 1 \le 2$.

Problem 8: Proof:
Passing through D we draw $DE // AB$ and meets AC at E.

Since $\angle ADE = \angle BAD = 60°$, $\angle DAE = 60°$, so $\triangle ADE$ is an equilateral triangle.

$\dfrac{AD}{AB} = \dfrac{DE}{AB} = \dfrac{CE}{AC}$. $\dfrac{AD}{AC} = \dfrac{AE}{AC}$.

$\dfrac{AD}{AB} + \dfrac{AD}{AC} = \dfrac{CE + AE}{AC} = 1$. $\dfrac{1}{AD} = \dfrac{1}{AB} + \dfrac{1}{AC}$.

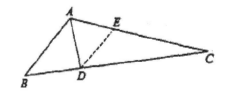

Problem 9: Proof:
Passing through M to draw $ME // PN$ and ME meets QN at E. Connect EO.

Since $\dfrac{QM}{MP} = \dfrac{QO}{OC}$, $\dfrac{QM}{MP} = \dfrac{QE}{EN}$, so $\dfrac{QO}{OC} = \dfrac{QE}{EN}$ and $EO // NC$.

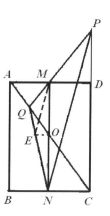

That is $EO \perp MN$.

Since $MO = ON$, $\triangle EMN$ is an equilateral triangle. $EM = EN$.

$\angle ENM = \angle EMN = \angle MNP$. $\angle QNM = \angle MNP$.

Problem 10: Solution:
Take the midpoint C of AB, connect CG, then $CD = AG$ and $CD // AG$, $AGCD$ is a parallelogram. So $AD = CG$.

Since $AD = BC$, $BC = CG$.
Since $CG = CB$, and $\angle CBG = 60°$, $\triangle BCG$ is an equilateral triangle.

Therefore we have $CG = BG = AG$.
$\triangle ACB$ is a right triangle with $\angle ABC = 60°$.

Let $CD = 1$, then $AB = 2$.
Let $BE = x$.

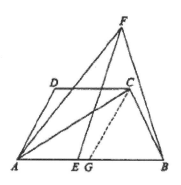

Since $AF = AB$, $\angle FAB = 180° - 2\angle ABF$.
Since $FE = FB$, $\angle EFB = 180° - 2\angle EBF$.
In $\triangle AFB$ and $\triangle FBE$, $\angle ABF = \angle FBE$, $\angle BAF = \angle BFE$.
$\triangle AFB \sim \triangle FEB$.

Then we have $\dfrac{BE}{BF} = \dfrac{BF}{AB}$ or $\dfrac{BE}{AC} = \dfrac{AC}{AB}$.

We have $AC = \sqrt{3}$, so $\dfrac{x}{\sqrt{3}} = \dfrac{\sqrt{3}}{2}$.

Solving for x, we have $x = \dfrac{3}{2}$.

Thus $BE = \dfrac{3}{2}$, $AE = AB - BE = \dfrac{1}{2}$.
$AE : BE = 1 : 3$.

Problem 11: Proof:

Passing through P, B, and C we draw $PG//AB$, $BG//AD$, and $CH//AD$, respectively. Connect PH. The extension of GQ meets PH and CH at H.
Then $BG//HC$, $BG = AP$. $\dfrac{BQ}{QC} = \dfrac{BG}{HC}$.

We have $\dfrac{AP}{PD} = \dfrac{BQ}{QC}$, $AP = BG$, and then $PD = HC$.

Since $PD//HC$, $PHCD$ is a parallelogram. So $PH = DC$, $PH//DC$. $\dfrac{AB}{CD} = \dfrac{PG}{PH}$.

However, $\dfrac{AB}{CD} = \dfrac{QB}{QC} = \dfrac{GQ}{QH}$. So $\dfrac{PG}{PH} = \dfrac{GQ}{QH}$.

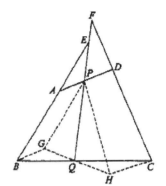

PQ is the angle bisector of $\angle GPH$, that is, $\angle GPQ = \angle HPQ$.
Since $\angle BEQ = \angle GPQ$, and $\angle CFQ = \angle HPQ$, $\angle BEQ = \angle CFQ$, that is, the angle formed by PQ and AB is the same as the angle formed by PQ and CD.

Problem 12: Proof:

Construct $\angle ABF = \dfrac{\pi}{7}$ outside $\triangle ABC$.

Line BF meets the extension of CA at F.
Then $\angle FBE = \dfrac{2\pi}{7}$. $\angle FEB = \angle EBC + \angle ECB = \dfrac{2\pi}{7}$.

Since $\angle DAB = \angle ABD = \dfrac{2\pi}{7}$, $\triangle ADB \sim \triangle BFE$ and
$\dfrac{AB}{AD} = \dfrac{BE}{BF}$.

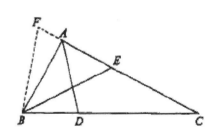

Since $\angle F = \pi - \angle FBE - \angle FEB = \dfrac{3\pi}{7}$, $\angle FAB = \pi - \angle BAC = \dfrac{3\pi}{7}$.

Therefore $\angle F = \angle FAB$. Thus $FB = AB$. So $\dfrac{AB}{AD} = \dfrac{BE}{AB}$. $AB^2 = AD \cdot BE$.

Problem 13: Proof:

Passing through P we draw $PG \perp AB$ at G. Then we have $\angle GAP = \angle DCA$, $\angle PGA = 90°$
$= \angle ADC$. So $\triangle AGP \sim \triangle CDA$. $\dfrac{AP}{GP} = \dfrac{AC}{AD}$.

Since $PA = PD$, $\dfrac{AC}{AD} = \dfrac{PD}{GP}$.

We also have $\dfrac{GP}{AE} = \dfrac{BP}{BE} = \dfrac{PD}{EF}$. So $\dfrac{PD}{GP} = \dfrac{EF}{AE}$.

$\dfrac{AC}{AD} = \dfrac{EF}{AE}$.

We also know that $EF//AD$, Which means
$\dfrac{EC}{EF} = \dfrac{AC}{AD}$. So $\dfrac{EC}{EF} = \dfrac{EF}{AE}$. $EF^2 = AE \cdot EC$.

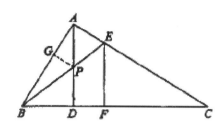

Problem 14: Proof:
Passing through B we draw $BE//DC$ to meet the extension of AC at E. Then
$\dfrac{AB}{AD} = \dfrac{BE}{CD}$, and $\dfrac{AC}{CE} = \dfrac{AD}{BD}$.

So $\dfrac{AB \cdot CD}{AD} = BE$, and $\dfrac{AC \cdot BD}{AD} = CE$.

In Rt$\triangle BCE$: $BC^2 + CE^2 = BE^2$.

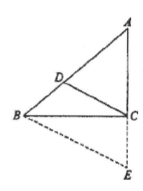

So $(\dfrac{AB \cdot CD}{AD})^2 = BC^2 + (\dfrac{AC \cdot BD}{AD})^2$.

$(AB \cdot CD)^2 = (AC \cdot BD)^2 + (BC \cdot AD)^2$.

Problem 15: Proof:
Connect AE and extend it to meet the extension of CD at H. Connect AD and CE.

Then each inscribed angle faced by each side of the 7-gons is
$\dfrac{\pi}{7}$.

So $\angle DAE = \dfrac{\pi}{7}$, $\angle ADC = \dfrac{2\pi}{7}$. $\angle H = \angle ADC - \angle DAE = \dfrac{\pi}{7}$.

Since $\angle ECD = \dfrac{\pi}{7} = \angle H$, $CE = EH$. That is, $AH = a + b$

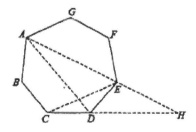

Note in $\triangle ADH$, $\angle DAH = \angle H = \dfrac{\pi}{7}$.

In $\triangle CDE$, $\angle ECD = \angle CED = \dfrac{\pi}{7}$. So $\triangle ADH \sim \triangle CDE$. $\dfrac{AH}{AD} = \dfrac{CE}{CD}$. That is $\dfrac{a+b}{a} = \dfrac{b}{c}$ or $\dfrac{1}{a} + \dfrac{1}{b} = \dfrac{1}{c}$.

Problem 16: Solution: 63
Let P be the intersection of AD and CE. Since angles ABF and ACF intercept the same arc, they are congruent, and therefore triangles ACE and FBE are similar. Thus $EF/12 = 12/27$, yielding $EF = 16/3$. The area of triangle AFB is twice that of triangle AEF, and the ratio of the area of triangle AEF to that of triangle AEP is $(16/3)/9$, since the medians of a triangle trisect each other. Triangle AEP is isosceles, so the altitude to base PE has length

$$\sqrt{12^2 - \left(\dfrac{9}{2}\right)^2} = \dfrac{1}{2}\sqrt{24^2 - 9^2} = \dfrac{3}{2}\sqrt{8^2 - 3^2} = \dfrac{3}{2}\sqrt{55},$$

and the area of triangle AEP is $(27/4)\sqrt{55}$.

Therefore, $[AFB] = 2[AFE] = 2(16/27) \times [AEP] = 2(16/27) \times (27/4)\sqrt{55} = 8\sqrt{55}$,
and $m + n = 63$.

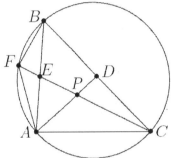

PROBLEMS

Problem 1. (1972 AMC) Inside square *ABCD* (see figure) with sides of length 12 inches, segment *AE* is drawn, where *E* is the point on *DC* which is 5 inches from *D*. The perpendicular bisector of *AE* is drawn and intersects *AE*, *AD*, and *BC* at points *M*, *P*, and *Q* respectively. Find the ratio of segment *PM* to *MQ*.

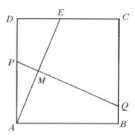

Problem 2. (1973 AMC) In △*ABC* with right angle at *C*, altitude *CH* and median *CM* trisect the right angle. If the area of △*CHM* is *K*, find the area of △ *ABC*.

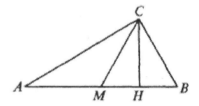

Problem 3. (1976 AMC) In triangle *ABC*, *D* is the midpoint of *AB*; *E* is the midpoint of *DB*; and *F* is the midpoint of *BC*. If the area of △ *ABC* is 96, what is the area of *AEF*?

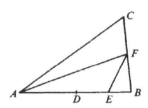

Problem 4. (2002 AMC12 A Problem #23) In triangle *ABC*, side *AC* and the perpendicular bisector of *BC* meet in point *D*, and *BD* bisects ∠*ABC*. If *AD* = 9 and *DC* = 7, what is the area of triangle *ABD*.

Problem 5. (2009 AMC 10 B #20) Triangle *ABC* has a right angle at *B*, *AB* = 1, and *BC* = 2. The bisector of ∠*BAC* meets *BC* at *D*. What is *BD*?

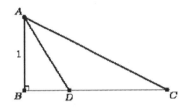

Problem 6. (1959 AMC) In triangle *ABC*, *AL* bisects angle *A* and *CM* bisects angle *C*. Points *L* and *M* are on *BC* and *AB*, respectively. The sides of triangle *ABC* are *a*, *b*, and *c*. Then $\dfrac{\overline{AM}}{\overline{MB}} = k \dfrac{\overline{CL}}{\overline{LB}}$ where *k* is:

(A) 1   (B) $\dfrac{bc}{a^2}$ (C) $\dfrac{a^2}{bc}$ (D) $\dfrac{c}{b}$ (E) $\dfrac{c}{a}$

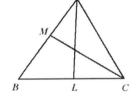

Problem 7. (1959 AMC) In triangle *ABC*, *BD* is a median. *CF* intersects *BD* at *E* so that $\overline{BE} = \overline{ED}$. Point *F* is on *AB*. Then, if $\overline{BF} = 5$, $\overline{BA}$ equals:

(A) 10   (B) 12   (C) 15   (D) 20   (E) none of these

Problem 8. (1952) Angle *B* of triangle *ABC* is trisected by *BD* and *BE* which meet *AC* at *D* and *E* respectively. Then:

(A) $\dfrac{\overline{AD}}{\overline{EC}} = \dfrac{\overline{AE}}{\overline{DC}}$ (B) $\dfrac{\overline{AD}}{\overline{EC}} = \dfrac{\overline{AB}}{\overline{BC}}$ (C) $\dfrac{\overline{AD}}{\overline{EC}} = \dfrac{\overline{BD}}{\overline{BE}}$

(D) $\dfrac{\overline{AD}}{\overline{EC}} = \dfrac{(\overline{AB})(\overline{BD})}{(\overline{BE})(\overline{BC})}$ (E) $\dfrac{\overline{AD}}{\overline{EC}} = \dfrac{(\overline{AE})(\overline{BD})}{(\overline{DC})(\overline{BE})}$

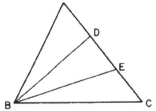

Problem 9. In isosceles $\triangle ABC$ ($AB = AC$), the angle bisector BE divides the perimeter into two parts: 168 cm and 112 cm. Find the length AB.

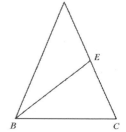

(A) 80.   (B) 105 or 80.   (C) 105.   (D) None of them

Problem 10. (1964 AMC) The sides PQ and PR of triangle PQR are respectively of lengths 4 inches, and 7 inches. The median PM is $3\frac{1}{2}$ inches. Then QR, in inches, is:

(A) 6   (B) 7   (C) 8   (D) 9   (E) 10.

Problem 11. (1967 AMC) In right triangle ABC the hypotenuse $AB = 5$ and leg $AC = 3$. The bisector of angle A meets the opposite side in A_1. A second right triangle PQR is then constructed with hypotenuse $PQ = A_1B$ and leg $PR = A_1C$. If the bisector of angle P meets the opposite side in P_1, the length of PP_1 is :

(A) $\dfrac{3\sqrt{6}}{4}$ (B) $\dfrac{3\sqrt{5}}{4}$ (C) $\dfrac{3\sqrt{3}}{4}$ (D) $\dfrac{3\sqrt{2}}{2}$ (E) $\dfrac{15\sqrt{2}}{16}$

Problem 12. If G is the centroid of triangle ABC, show that
$3AG^2 + BC^2 = 3BG^2 + AC^2 = 3CG^2 + AB^2$.

Problem 13. (1962 AMC) The medians AN and BP of a triangle with unequal sides are, respectively, 3 inches and 6 inches long. Its area is $3\sqrt{15}$ square inches. The length of the third median, in inches, is:

(A) 4   (B) $3\sqrt{3}$ (C) $3\sqrt{6}$ (D) $6\sqrt{3}$ (E) $6\sqrt{6}$

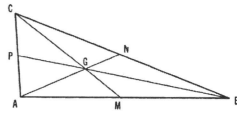

Problem 14. (2002 AMC 12 A) In triangle *ABC*, side *AC* and the perpendicular bisector of *BC* meet in point *D*, and *BD* bisects $\angle ABC$. If *AD* = 9 and *DC* = 7, what is the area of triangle *ABD*?

(A) 14 (B) 21 (C) 28 (D) $14\sqrt{5}$ (E) $28\sqrt{5}$

Problem 15. (2000 AMC12) In triangle *ABC*, *AB* = 13, *BC* = 14, and *AC* = 15. Let *D* denote the midpoint of $\overline{BC}$ and let *E* denote the intersection of $\overline{BC}$ with the bisector of angle *BAC*. Which of the following is closest to the area of the triangle *ADE*?

(A) 2 (B) 2.5 (C) 3 (D) 3.5 (E) 4

Problem 16. (1995 AIME) Triangle *ABC* is isosceles, with *AB* = *AC* and altitude *AM* = 11. Suppose that there is a point *D* on $\overline{AM}$ with *AD* = 10 and $\angle BDC$ = $3\angle BAC$. Then the perimeter of $\triangle ABC$ may be written in the form $a + \sqrt{b}$, where a and b are integers. Find $a + b$.

Problem 17. (1996 AIME 13) In triangle *ABC*, $AB = \sqrt{30}$, $AC = \sqrt{6}$, and $BC = \sqrt{15}$. There is a point *D* for which $\overline{AD}$ bisects $\overline{BC}$ and $\angle ADB$ is a right angle. The ratio $\dfrac{\text{Area}(\triangle ADB)}{\text{Area}(\triangle ABC)}$ can be written in the form $\dfrac{m}{n}$, where *m* and *n* are relatively prime positive integers. Find $m + n$.

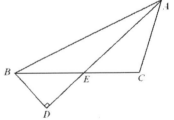

Problem 18. (2002 AIME I 10) In the diagram below, angle *ABC* is a right angle. Point *D* is on *BC*, and *AD* bisects angle *CAB*. Points *E* and *F* are on *AB* and *AC*, respectively, so that *AE* = 3 and *AF* = 10. Given that *EB* = 9 and *FC* = 27, find the integer closest to the area of quadrilateral *DCFG*.

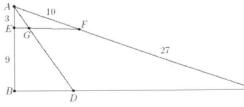

Problem 19. (1998 AMC 12) In triangle ABC, angle C is a right angle and $CB > CA$. Point D is located on $\overline{BC}$ so that angle CAD is twice angle DAB. If $\dfrac{AC}{AD} = \dfrac{2}{3}$, then $\dfrac{CD}{BD} = \dfrac{m}{n}$, where m and n are relatively prime positive integers. Find $m + n$.

Problem 20. The two shorter sides of a triangle measure 9 and 18. If the internal angle bisector drawn to the longest side measures 8, find the measure of the longest side of the triangle.

SOLUTIONS

Problem 1. 5:19.
Let the line through M parallel to side AB of the square intersect sides AD and BC in points R and S, respectively; see figure. Since M is the midpoint of AE, $RM = \frac{1}{2}DE = \frac{5}{2}$ inches, and hence $MS = 12 - \frac{5}{2} = \frac{19}{2}$ inches.
Since PMR and QMS are similar right triangles, the required ratio
$$PM : MQ = RM : MS = 5 : 19$$
because corresponding sides of similar triangles are proportional.

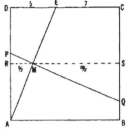

Problem 2. Solution: (E).
Right triangle CHM and CHB are congruent since their angles at C are equal. Therefore the base MH of △CMH is ¼ $\frac{1}{4}$ of the base AB of △ABC, while their altitudes are equal. Hence the area of △ABC is 4K.

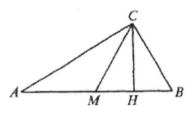

Problem 3. Solution:
Since F is the midpoint of BC, the altitude of △AEF from F to AE (extended if necessary) is one half the altitude of △ABC from C to AB (extended if necessary). Base AE of △AEF is $\frac{3}{4}$ of base AB of △ABC. Therefore, the area of △AEF is $(\frac{1}{2})(\frac{3}{4})(96) = 36$.

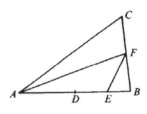

Problem 4. Solution: (C).

Method 1:

Let M be the midpoint of $\overline{BC}$, let $AM = 2a$, and let $\theta = \angle AMB$. Then $\cos \angle AMC = -\cos \theta$. Applying the Law of Cosines to △ABM and to △AMC yields, respectively,
$a^2 + 4a^2 - 4a^2 \cos \theta = 1$ and $a^2 + 4a^2 + 4a^2 \cos \theta = 4$.

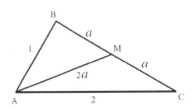

215

Adding, we obtain $10a^2 = 5$, so $a = \frac{\sqrt{2}}{2}$ and $BC = 2a = \sqrt{2}$.

Method 2:

As above, let M be the midpoint of BC and $AM = 2a$. Put a rectangular coordinate system in the plane of the triangle with the origin at M so that A has coordinates $(0, 2a)$. If the coordinates of B are (x, y), then the point C has coordinates $(-x, -y)$,
So $x^2 + (2a - y)^2 = 1$ and $x^2 + (2a + y)^2 = 4$.

Combining the last two equations gives $2(x^2 + y^2) + 8a^2 = 5$. But, $x^2 + y^2 = a^2$, so $10a^2 = 5$. Thus, $a = \frac{\sqrt{2}}{2}$ and $BC = \sqrt{2}$.

Problem 5. Solution: (B).

By the Pythagorean Theorem, $AC = \sqrt{5}$. By the Angle Bisector Theorem, $\frac{BD}{AB} = \frac{CD}{AC}$.

Therefore $CD = \sqrt{5}$ and $BD + CD = 2$.

$BD = \frac{2}{1 + \sqrt{5}} = \frac{\sqrt{5} - 1}{2}$.

Problem 6. Solution:

The bisector of an angle of a triangle divides the opposite sides into segments proportional to the other two sides.

$\therefore \frac{\overline{AM}}{\overline{MB}} = \frac{b}{a}$ and $\frac{\overline{CL}}{\overline{LB}} = \frac{b}{c}$. Since $\frac{c}{a} \cdot \frac{b}{c} = \frac{b}{a}$, $k = \frac{c}{a}$.

Problem 7. Solution: (C).

Let G be a point on EC so that $\overline{FE} = \overline{EG}$. Connect D with G. Then $FDGB$ is a parallelogram. $\therefore \overline{DG} = 5$, $\overline{AF} = 10$, $\overline{AB} = 15$.

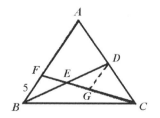

216

Problem 8. Solution: (D).

Since BD bisects angle ABE, we have $\dfrac{\overline{AD}}{\overline{DE}} = \dfrac{\overline{AB}}{\overline{BE}}$; since BE bisects angle DBC, we have $\dfrac{\overline{DE}}{\overline{EC}} = \dfrac{\overline{BD}}{\overline{BC}}$. Hence $\dfrac{\overline{AD}}{\overline{EC}} = \dfrac{\overline{DE}(\overline{AB}/\overline{BE})}{\overline{DE}(\overline{BC}/\overline{BD})} = \dfrac{(\overline{AB})(\overline{BD})}{(\overline{BE})(\overline{BC})}$.

Problem 9. Solution:

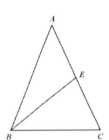

$\dfrac{BC}{AB} = \dfrac{CE}{EA} = \dfrac{BC+CE}{AB+EA} = \dfrac{112}{168}$ or

$\dfrac{BC}{AB} = \dfrac{CE}{EA} = \dfrac{BC+CE}{AB+EA} = \dfrac{168}{112}$.

Therefore we have either $BC = \dfrac{112}{168} AB$ or $BC = \dfrac{168}{112} AB$.

Since $112 + 168 = 2AB + BC$, $AB = 105$ or 80.

Problem 10. Solution: (D)

Method 1 (official solution):

Let y denote half the length of QR, and let x be the distance from M to the foot of the altitude from P. Then the square of the altitude may be written

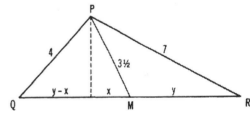

$16 - (y-x)^2 = (\dfrac{7}{2})^2 - x^2$,

$\therefore (y-x)^2 - x^2 = \dfrac{15}{4} = y^2 - 2xy$.

$16 - (y-x)^2 = 7^2 - (y+x)^2$,

Method 2 (our solution):

By the median length formula): $(PM^2) + (PM^2) = (PQ^2 - QM^2) + (PR^2 - MR^2)$

Problem 11. Solution: (B).

Leg $BC = 4$ of the 3, 4, 5 right triangle ABC is divided by the bisector of angle A at A_1 into segments A_1B and A_1C proportional to the adjacent sides AB and AC (see figure):
$\frac{A_1B}{A_1C} = \frac{A_1B}{4 - A_1B} = \frac{5}{3}$; so $A_1B = \frac{5}{2} = PQ$ and $A_1C = \frac{3}{2} = PR$
are the hypotenuse and leg, respectively, of the second right $\triangle PQR$. Its third side is $RQ = \frac{4}{2} = 2$.

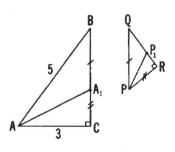

Each side of $\triangle PQR$ is one-half the corresponding side of the first right triangle ABC. Also bisector $PP_1 = \frac{1}{2} AA_1 = \frac{1}{2}\sqrt{AC^2 + CA_1^2} = \frac{1}{2}\sqrt{3^2 + \left(\frac{3}{2}\right)^2} = \frac{3\sqrt{5}}{4}$.

Problem 12. Proof:

Method 1:

Draw $AD \perp BC$, $GE \perp BC$.

Since $AM = 3GM$, $MD = 3ME$.

We have

$AB^2 - AC^2 = BD^2 - DC^2$

$= (BD + DC)(BD - DC)$

$= BC[(BM + MD) - (CM - MD)]$

$= BC \cdot 2MD = 2BC \cdot MD$.

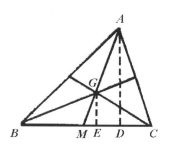

We also know that

$BG^2 - CG^2 = BE^2 - EC^2 = (BE + EC)(BE - EC) = BC \cdot 2ME = 2BC \cdot ME$,

$\therefore \frac{AB^2 - AC^2}{BG^2 - CG^2} = \frac{2BC \cdot MD}{2BC \cdot ME} = 3$. $\therefore AB^2 - AC^2 = 3BG^2 - 3CG^2$, or $AB^2 + 3CG^2 = AC^2 + 3BG^2$.

Similarly we can show that $AB^2 + 3CG^2 = BC^2 + 3AG^2$.

∴ $AB^2 + 3CG^2 = BC^2 + 3AG^2 = CA^2 + 3BG^2$.

Method 2:

Extend GM such that $MG' = MG$. Connect BG', $G'C$. $GBG'C$ is a parallelogram.

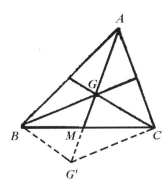

$2BG^2 + 2CG^2 = BC^2 + (2GM)^2$, or
$2BG^2 + 2CG^2 = BC^2 + AG^2$

∴ $2(BG^2 + CG^2 + AC^2) = BC^2 + 3AG^2$.

Similarly,

$2(CG^2 + AG^2 + BG^2) = CA^2 + 3BG^2 = AB^2 + 3CG^2$.

Problem 13. Solution: (C).
Since the diagonals of the quadrilateral $ADBG$ bisect each other, it is a parallelogram.

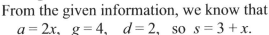

$\frac{1}{2}$ Area($ADBG$) = Area(ABG) = $\frac{1}{3}$ Area (ABC) = $(15)^{\frac{1}{2}}$,

$\frac{1}{2}$ Area($ADBG$) = Area(AGD) = $[s(s-a)(s-g)(s-d)]^{\frac{1}{2}}$,

where a, g, d are the lengths of the sides of $\triangle AGD$, and $2s = a + g + d$.

From the given information, we know that
$a = 2x$, $g = 4$, $d = 2$, so $s = 3 + x$.

If we substitute in the above formula, we obtain

$[(3+x)(3-x)(x-1)(x+1)]^{\frac{1}{2}} = (15)^{\frac{1}{2}}$ and, squaring both sides,

$(x^2-1)(9-x^2) = 15$ or $x^4 - 10x^2 + 24 = (x^2-4)(x^2-6) = 0$;

$x^2 = 4$ or 6, so $x = 2$ or $6^{\frac{1}{2}}$ and $CM = 6$ or $3(6)^{\frac{1}{2}}$. However, since the median $BP = 6$, and the triangle has unequal sides, we must reject this solution and retain $CM = 3(6)^{\frac{1}{2}}$.

Problem 14. Solution: (D).
By the angle-bisector theorem, $AB/BC = 9/7$. Let $AB = 9x$ and $BC = 7x$, let m$\angle ABD$ = m$\angle CBD = \theta$, and let M be the midpoint of BC. Since M is on the perpendicular bisector of BC, we have $BD = DC = 7$.

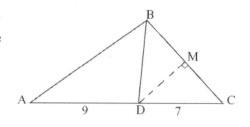

Then $\cos\theta = \dfrac{\frac{7x}{2}}{7} = \dfrac{x}{2}$.

Applying the Law of Cosines to $\triangle ABD$ yields
$9^2 = (9x)^2 + 7^2 - 2(9x)(7)(x/2)$
from which $x = 4/3$ and $AB = 12$. Apply Heron's formula to obtain the area of triangle ABD as $\sqrt{14 \cdot 2 \cdot 5 \cdot 7} = 14\sqrt{5}$.

Problem 15. Solution: (C).

By Heron's Formula the area of triangle ABC is $\sqrt{(21)(8)(7)(6)}$, which is 84, so the altitude from vertex A is $2(84)/14 = 12$. The midpoint D divides BC into two segments of length 7, and the bisector of angle BAC divides BC into segments of length $14(13/28) = 6.5$ and $14(15/28) = 7.5$ (since the angle bisector divides the opposite side into lengths proportional to the remaining two sides). Thus the triangle ADE has base $DE = 7 - 6.5 = 0.5$ and altitude 12, so its area is 3.

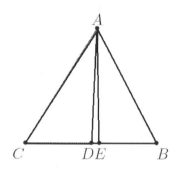

Problem 16. Solution:

Draw BE, the angle bisector of $\angle ABD$ to meet AD at E. Let $BE = AE = x$.

By Pythagorean Theorem,

$BM = \sqrt{BE^2 - EM^2} = \sqrt{x^2 - (11-x)^2} = \sqrt{22x - 121}$.

Applying Pythagorean Theorem twice:

$AB = \sqrt{BM^2 + AM^2} = \sqrt{22x}$, $BD = \sqrt{BM^2 + DM^2} = \sqrt{22x - 120}$.

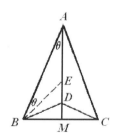

By the angle bisector theorem,

$$\frac{AB}{BD} = \frac{AE}{DE}$$

Therefore

$$\frac{\sqrt{22x}}{\sqrt{22x-120}} = \frac{x}{10-x}$$

Solving for x: $x = \frac{55}{8}$.

Then $BM = \frac{11}{2}$, $AB = \frac{11}{2}\sqrt{5}$

$a + \sqrt{b} = 2(AB + AM) = 11\sqrt{5} + 11 = 11 + \sqrt{605}$.
$a + b = 616$.

Problem 17. Solution:

Let E be the midpoint of BC and $AD = \frac{x}{2}$.

By the Theorem 2 (The angle bisector length formula), we calculate:

$$AE = \frac{\sqrt{57}}{2}.$$

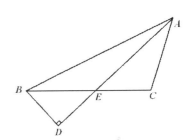

Applying Pythagorean Theorem,

$$(\sqrt{30})^2 - (\frac{x}{2})^2 = (\frac{\sqrt{15}}{2})^2 - (\frac{x}{2} - \frac{\sqrt{57}}{2})^2, \text{ or } 120 - 15 + 57 = 2\sqrt{57}\,x.$$

$$\frac{m}{n} = \frac{S_{\Delta ADB}}{2S_{\Delta AEB}} = \frac{AD}{2AE} = \frac{x}{2\sqrt{57}} = \frac{120-15+57}{4 \times 57} = \frac{27}{38}$$

$m + n = 27 + 38 = 65$.

Problem 18. Solution: 148.

By the Angle-Bisector Theorem, $BD : DC = AB : AC = 12 : 37$, and thus the area of triangle ADC is $37=49$ of the area of triangle ABC.
By the Angle-Bisector Theorem, $EG : GF = AE : AF = 3 : 10$, and thus the area of triangle AGF is $10=13$ of the area of triangle AEF. The area of triangle AEF is $3=12$ of the area of triangle AFB, which is in turn $10=37$ of the area of triangle ABC. Since $BC = p372$ $¡ 122 = 35$, the area of triangle ABC is 210. It follows

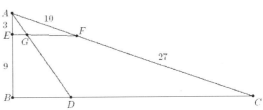

that the area of quadrilateral DCFG is
$(\frac{37}{49} - \frac{10}{13} \cdot \frac{3}{12} \cdot \frac{10}{37})210 = \frac{1110}{7} - \frac{5250}{481} = 158\frac{4}{7} - 10\frac{440}{481}$.

So the requested integer is 148.

Problem 19. Solution:

Let E denote the point on $\overline{BC}$ for which $\overline{AE}$ bisects $\angle CAD$. Because the answer is not changed by a similarity transformation, we may assume that $AC = 2\sqrt{5}$ and $AD = 3\sqrt{5}$. Apply the Pythagorean Theorem to triangle ACD to obtain $CD = 5$, then apply the Angle Bisector Theorem to triangle CAD to obtain $CE = 2$ and $ED = 3$. Let $x = DB$ Apply the Pythagorean Theorem to triangle ACE to obtain $AE = \sqrt{24}$, then apply the Angle Bisector Theorem to triangle EAB to obtain $AB = \frac{x}{3}\sqrt{24}$. Now apply the Pythagorean Theorem to triangle ABC to get $(2\sqrt{5})^2 + (x+5)^2 = (\frac{x}{3}\sqrt{24})^2$,

from which it follows that $x = 9$. Hence $\frac{BD}{DC} = \frac{9}{5}$, and $m + n = 14$.

Problem 20. Solution:
Let $AB = 9$, $AC = 18$, and angle bisector $AD = 8$.

Since $BD/DC = AB/AC = 1/2$, we can let $BD = m = x$, so that $DC = n = 2x$. By the angle bisector length formula, we know $(AD)^2 = (AB)(AC) - (BD)(DC)$.

Therefore, $(8)2 = (18)(9) - 2x^2$, and $x = 7$.

Thus, $BC = 3x = 21$.

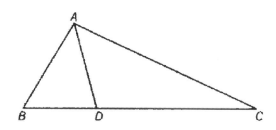

PROBLEMS

Problem 1. (1980 AMC) Sides *AB, BC, CD* and *DA* of convex quadrilateral *ABCD* have lengths 3, 4, 12, and 13, respectively; and ∠*CBA* is a right angle. The area of the quadrilateral is
(A) 32   (B) 36   (C) 39   (D) 42   (E) 48

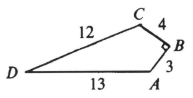

Problem 2. In △*ABC*, ∠*C*=90°. *D* is the middle point of *BC*. *DE*⊥*AB* at *E*. Prove $BC^2 = 2BE \times AB$

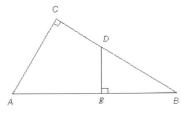

Problem 3: (1998 AMC) In quadrilateral *ABCD*, it is given that ∠*A* = 120°, angles *B* and *D* are right angles, *AB* = 13, and *AD* = 46. Then *AC* =
(A) 60   (B) 62   (C) 64   (D) 65   (E) 72

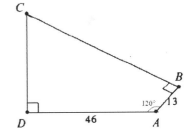

Problem 4: On sides *AB* and *DC* of rectangle *ABCD*, points F and E are chosen so that *AFCE* is a rhombus, as shown in the figure. If *AB* = 16 and *BC* = 12, find *EF*.

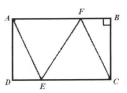

Problem 5. On sides *AB* and *DC* of rectangle *ABCD*, points F and E are chosen so that *AFCE* is a rhombus, as shown in the figure. If *AB* = *a* and *BC* = *b*, find *EF*.

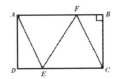

Problem 6: If the measures of two sides and the included angle of a triangle are 7, $\sqrt{50}$, and 135°, respectively, find the measure of the segment joining the midpoints of the two given sides.

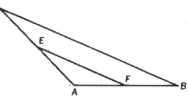

Problem 7: Two circles intersect in A and B, and the measure of the common chord AB = 10. The line joining the centers cuts the circles in P and Q. If PQ = 3 and the measure of the radius of one circle is 13, find the radius of the other circle. (Note that the illustration is not drawn to scale.)

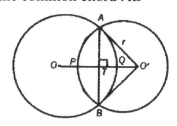

Problem 8: (1961 AMC) In triangle *ABC* the ratio *AC* : *CB* is 3:4. The bisector of the exterior angle at *C* intersects *BA* extended at *P* (*A* is between *P* and *B*). The ratio *PA*: *AB* is :
(A) 1:3   (B) 3:4   (C) 4:3   (D) 3:1   (E) 7:1

Problem 9: (1960 AMC) Given right triangle *ABC* with legs *BC* = 3, *AC* = 4. Find the length of the shorter angle trisector from *C* to the hypotenuse:
(A) $\dfrac{32\sqrt{3}-24}{13}$ (B) $\dfrac{12\sqrt{3}-9}{13}$ (C) $6\sqrt{3}-8$ (D) $\dfrac{5\sqrt{10}}{6}$ (E) $\dfrac{25}{12}$

Problem 10: (1985 AMC) In a circle with center *O*, *AD* is a diameter, *ABC* is a chord, *BO* = 5 and $\angle ABO = \overparen{CD} = 60°$. The length of *BC* is
(A) 3   (B) $3+\sqrt{3}$ (C) $5-\dfrac{\sqrt{3}}{2}$ (D) 5   (E) none of the above

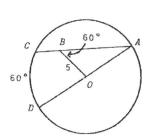

Problem 11. In the figure, *AC* = *BD*, *AD* ⊥*AC*, *BD*⊥ *BC*. Prove *AD* = *BC*.

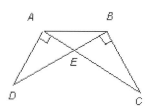

224

Problem 12: As shown in the figure, AC and BD are two diagonals of trapezoid $ABCD$ and $AC \perp BD$. Show that $AC^2 + BD^2 = (AB + DC)^2$.

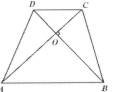

Problem 13: In quadrilateral $ABCD$, $\angle B = \angle D = 90°$, $\angle A = 60°$, $AB = 4$, and $AD = 5$. Find $BC : CD$.

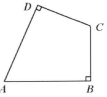

Problem 14: As shown in the figure, $ABCD$ is a trapezoid. Half circle O is inscribed into $ABCD$. Find BC if $AB = 2$ and $CD = 3$.

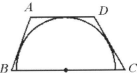

Problem 15: As shown in the figure, in equilateral triangle ABC, we extend BA to E and BC to D such that $AE = BD$. Connect CD. Show that $CE = DE$.

Problem 16: A convex octagon $ABCDEFG$ has eight equal interior angles. The lengths of the sides are 7, 4, 2, 5, 6, 2, x, and y, as shown in the figure. Find its perimeter.

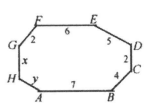

50 AMC Lectures Problems Book 1   (23) 8 more methods to draw auxiliary lines

SOLUTIONS:

Problem 1. Solution: (B).
By the Pythagorean Theorem, diagonal AC has length 5. Since $5^2 + 12^2 = 13^2$, ΔDAC is a right triangle by the converse of the Pythagorean theorem. The area of $ABCD$ is
$(\frac{1}{2})(3)(4) + (\frac{1}{2})(5)(12) = 36$.

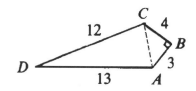

Problem 2.
Proof:
Method 1:
Since $DE \perp AB$, $\angle ACB = \angle DEB = 90°$.
$\angle B = \angle B$, so $\Delta ABC \sim \Delta DBE$.
So $\dfrac{BC}{BE} = \dfrac{AB}{BD}$,
Since D is the middle point of BC, so $BD = 1/2\ BC$.
So $\dfrac{BC}{BE} = \dfrac{2AB}{BC}$. That is $BC^2 = 2BE \times AB$

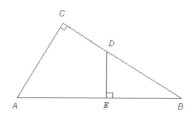

Method 2: (our method)
Draw $CG \perp AB$. Since $CG // DE$, and DE cuts BC into two equal parts, DE also cuts GE into two equal parts, that is $GE = EB$ and $GB = 2BE$
$AC^2 = AB \times AG$
$AB^2 - AC^2 = BC^2$ (Pythagorean Theorem)
Then
$BC^2 = AB^2 - AB \times AG = AB(AB - AG) = GB \times AB = 2BE \times AB$

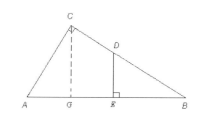

Problem 3: Solution: (B).
Extend DA through A and CB through B and denote the intersection by E. Triangle ABE is a 30°-60°-90° triangle with $AB = 13$, so $AE = 26$. Triangle CDE is also a 30°-60°-90° triangle, from which it follows that $CD = (46 + 26)/\sqrt{3} = 24\sqrt{3}$. Now apply the Pythagorean Theorem to triangle CDA to find that $AC = \sqrt{46^2 + (24\sqrt{3})^2} = 62$.

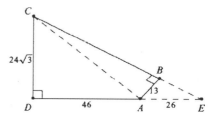

Problem 4:
Method 1
Let $AF = FC = EC = AE = x$.
Since $AF = x$ and $AB = 16$, $BF = 16 - x$.
Since $BC = 12$, in right $\triangle FBC$, $(FB)^2 + (BC)^2 = (FC)^2$ or $(16-x)^2 + (12)^2 = x^2$, and $x = \dfrac{25}{2}$.

Again by applying the Pythagorean Theorem to $\triangle ABC$, we get $AC = 20$.
Since the diagonals of a rhombus are perpendicular and bisect each other, $\triangle EGC$ is a right triangle, and $GC = 10$. Once more applying the Pythagorean Theorem in $\triangle EGC$, $(EG)^2 + (GC)^2 = (EC)^2$.
$(EG)^2 + 100 = \dfrac{625}{4}$, and $EG = \dfrac{15}{2}$ Thus, $FE = 2(EG) = 15$.

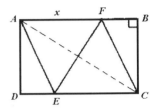

Method 2:
Since $x = \dfrac{25}{2}$ (see Method 1), $EC = \dfrac{25}{2}$.

Draw a line through B parallel to $\overline{EF}$ meeting $\overline{DC}$ at H.
Since quadrilateral $BFEH$ is a parallelogram and $FB = AB - AF = \dfrac{7}{2}$, $EH = \dfrac{7}{2}$. Therefore, $HC = 9$.
In right $\triangle BCH$, $(BH)^2 = (BC)^2 + (HC)^2$, so $BH = 15$. Therefore, $EF = BH = 15$.

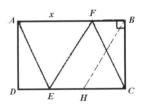

Problem 5. If you can figure out the solution to problem 4, I am sure you can get the answer: $EF = \dfrac{b}{a}\sqrt{a^2 + b^2}$.

Problem 6: Solution:
Draw altitude CD. Since $\angle CAB = 135$, $\angle DAC = 45$, therefore, $\triangle ADC$ is an isosceles right triangle. If $AC = \sqrt{50} = 5\sqrt{2}$, then $DA = DC = 5$.
In $\triangle DBC$, since $DB = 12$ and $DC = 5$, $BC = 13$.
Therefore, $EF = \dfrac{1}{2}BC = \dfrac{13}{2}$.

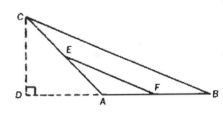

Problem 7: Solution:
Since $O'A = O'B$ and $OA = OB$, OO' is the perpendicular bisector of AB. Therefore, in right $\triangle ATO$, since $AO = 13$ and $AT = 5$, we find $OT = 12$. Since $OQ = 13$ (also a radius of

circle O), and $OT = 12$, $TQ = 1$. We Know that $PQ = 3$. $PT = PQ - TQ$; therefore, $PT = 2$. Let $O'A = O'P = r$, and $PT = 2$, $TO' = r - 2$. Applying the Pythagorean Theorem in tight $\triangle ATO'$, $(AT)^2 + (TO')^2 = (AO')^2$.

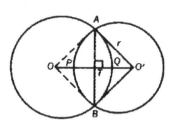

Substituting, $5^2 + (r - 2)^2 = r^2$, and $r = \dfrac{29}{4}$. $PT = PQ + TQ$;

therefore, $PT = 4$. Again, let $O'A = O'P = r$ then $TO' = r - 4$. Applying the Pythagorean Theorem in right $\triangle ATO'$, $(AT)^2 + (TO')^2 = (AO')^2$.

Substituting, $5^2 + (r - 4)^2 = r^2$, and $r = \dfrac{41}{8}$.

Problem 8: Solution: (D).
Draw PA' so that $\angle BPC = \angle A'PC$; then $\triangle ACP \cong \triangle A'CP$ (asa) and $AC = A'C$, $PA = PA'$. Since PC bisects $\angle BPA'$ in $\triangle BPA'$,

$$\dfrac{BC}{CA'} = \dfrac{PB}{PA'} \quad \text{or} \quad \dfrac{BC}{CA} = \dfrac{PB}{PA} = \dfrac{4}{3}.$$

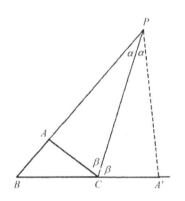

$AB = PB - PA$ since A is between P and B.
$\dfrac{AB}{PA} = \dfrac{PB}{PA} - \dfrac{PA}{PA} = \dfrac{4}{3} - 1 = \dfrac{1}{3}$, so $\dfrac{PA}{AB} = 3$.

Problem 9: Solution: (A).
Since CD trisects right angle C, $\angle BCD = 30°$ and $\angle DCA = 60°$ and $\angle CDE = 30°$, so that $\triangle DEC$ is a $30° - 60° - 90°$ triangle.
Let $EC = x$. $\therefore DE = x\sqrt{3}$ and $DC = 2x$.

$\dfrac{AE}{DE} = \dfrac{AC}{BC} \Rightarrow \dfrac{4 - x}{x\sqrt{3}} = \dfrac{4}{3} \Rightarrow x = \dfrac{12}{3 + 4\sqrt{3}}$

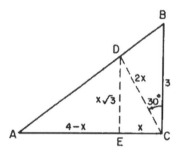

Therefore $2x = \dfrac{24}{3 + 4\sqrt{3}} = \dfrac{32\sqrt{3} - 24}{13}$.

Problem 10: Solution: (D).

Since $\overset{\frown}{CD} = 60°$, $\angle BAO = 30°$. Therefore, $\triangle ABO$ is a $30° - 60° - 90°$ right triangle.
Since $BO = 5$, $AO = 5\sqrt{3}$, $AB = 10$.

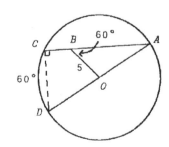

Connect CD. Since AD is the diameter, $\triangle ADC$ is a 30° – 60° – 90° right triangle.
$AD = 2AO = 10\sqrt{3}$. $AC = \frac{\sqrt{3}}{2} \cdot 10\sqrt{3} = 15$, $BC = AC - AB = 15 - 10 = 5$.

Problem 11. Proof :
Extend DA and CB to meet at F.
For right triangles $\triangle DBF \cong \triangle CAF$ (AAS, $\angle F = \angle F$,
$\angle DBF = \angle CAF$ (right angles), AC = BD (given)).
Then AF = FB, DF = FC.
AD = DF – AF, BC = CF – FB. We already proved that AF = FB, so
AD = BC.

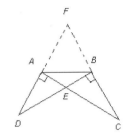

Problem 12: Solution:
Draw $DA' // CA$ and meets the extension of BA at A.
$A'ACD$ is a parallelogram with $A'D // AC$ and $A'D = AC$.
Therefore, we know that $\angle A'DB$ is a right angle.
$A'D^2 + DB^2 = A'B^2 \Rightarrow$
$AC^2 + BD^2 = (A'A + AB)^2 = (DC + AB)^2$

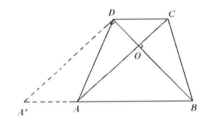

Problem 13: Solution
Extend AD through D and BC through C and denote the intersection by E.
Since $\angle B = \angle D = 90°$, $\triangle ABE$ and $\triangle CDE$ are right triangles. $\angle E = 30°$.
Therefore $AE = 2AB = 8$, $DE = 3$.
In right triangle ABE, we have: $CD = \sqrt{3}$, $CE = 2\sqrt{3}$.
In right triangle ABE, we have: $BE = 4\sqrt{3}$, $BC = 2\sqrt{3}$.
Hence $BC : CD = 2\sqrt{3} : \sqrt{3} = 2$.

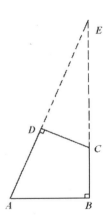

Problem 14: Solution:
Draw whole circle and extend AB to E and DC to F to meet EF, the tangent of the circle, at E and F, respectively. M is the tangent point.
$AE = 2AB = 4$, $DF = 2DC = 6$.
Since the trapezoid is circumscribed the circle,
$AD + EF = AE + DF = 10$
$BC = \frac{1}{2}(AD + EF) = 5$

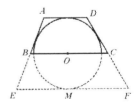

Problem 15: Solution:

Since triangle ABC is equilateral and $\angle B = 60°$, we construct an equilateral triangle BEF by extending BD to F such that $BF = BE$ and connecting EF.

$BE = AE + AB = BD + BC$ (1)
$BF = BD + DF$ (2)

Since $BE = BF$, $BC = DF$.
Therefore $\triangle EBC \cong \triangle EFD$ ($EB = EF$, $\angle B = \angle F = 60°$, $BC = DF$).
Hence $CE = DE$.

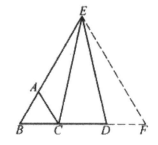

Problem 16: Solution:

We can image that the original figure is a rectangle. The perimeter is then $32 + \sqrt{2}$.

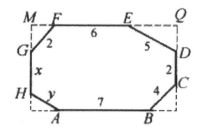

PROBLEMS

Problem 1. Calculate: $\dfrac{1+\tan 75°}{1-\tan 75°}$.

Problem 2. Simplify: $\sin 50°(1 + \sqrt{3}\tan 10°)$.

Problem 3. Find the value of $\cos 20° \cdot \cos 40° \cdot \cos 80°$.

Problem 4. Find the value $4\sin 18° \cos 36°$.

Problem 5. Find the value of $\cos \dfrac{2\pi}{7} + \cos \dfrac{4\pi}{7} + \cos \dfrac{6\pi}{7}$.

Problem 6. Find $\sin 18°$.

Problem 7. Find $\cos \dfrac{\pi}{7} + \cos \dfrac{3\pi}{7} + \cos \dfrac{5\pi}{7}$.

Problem 8. Show that $\sqrt{1-\sin 20°} = \cos 10° - \sin 10°$.

Problem 9. α is an acute angle and $\alpha \neq 45°$. If $2\sin\alpha\cos\alpha + \dfrac{1}{3}\sin\alpha - \dfrac{1}{3}\cos\alpha = 1$, what is the quadratic equation with the two toots $\tan\alpha$ and $\cot\alpha$?

Problem 10. (2003 AMC I) Square $ABCD$ has sides of length 4, and M is the midpoint of $\overline{CD}$. A circle with radius 2 and center M intersects a circle with radius 4 and center A at points P and D. What is the distance from P to $\overline{AD}$?
(A) 3   (B) $\dfrac{16}{5}$ (D) $\dfrac{13}{4}$ (D) $2\sqrt{3}$ (E) $\dfrac{7}{2}$.

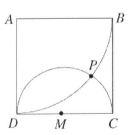

Problem 11. (2007 AMC 17) Suppose that $\sin a + \sin b = \sqrt{\dfrac{5}{3}}$ and $\cos a + \cos b = 1$. What is $\cos(a-b)$?

231

(A) $\sqrt{\dfrac{5}{3}} - 1$ (B) $\dfrac{1}{3}$ (C) $\dfrac{1}{2}$ (D) $\dfrac{2}{3}$ (E) 1

Problem 12. (1999 NC Math Contest) Define the function $f(x) = \dfrac{5\sin^3(x)\cos(x)}{\tan^2(x)+1}$.
Which of the following numbers is the maximum value of the function?
(a) $\dfrac{1}{2}$ (b) $\dfrac{5}{8}$ (c) $\dfrac{3}{4}$ (d) 1   (e) $\dfrac{5}{2}$

Problem 13. Solve $x^2 + x \cot A \cos A - 1 = 0$ for x given $0 < A < \dfrac{\pi}{2}$. Find the sum of the roots.
a) $\sin A - \tan A$ b) $\sin A - \csc A$ c) 1   d) $\cos A - \sec A$ e) none of these

Problem 14. (2004 NC Math Contest) How long is the side of the largest equilateral triangle that can be inscribed in a square whose side has length 1?
a. 1   b. $\dfrac{\sqrt{5}}{2}$ c. $\dfrac{3\sqrt{5}}{4}$ d. $2 - \sqrt{3}$ e. $\sqrt{8 - 4\sqrt{3}}$

Problem 15. (1978 AMC 15) If $\sin x + \cos x = \dfrac{1}{5}$ and $0 \le x < \pi$, then $\tan x$ is
(A) $-\dfrac{4}{3}$ (B) $-\dfrac{3}{4}$ (C) $\dfrac{3}{4}$ (D) $\dfrac{4}{3}$ (E) undetermined.

Problem 16. (1985 AMC 16) If $A = 20°$ and $B = 25°$, then the value of $(1 + \tan A)(1 + \tan B)$ is
(A) $\sqrt{3}$ (B) 2   (C) $1 + \sqrt{2}$ (D) $2(\tan A + \tan B)$.

Problem 17. (1990 AMC) Consider a pyramid P-$ABCD$ whose base $ABCD$ is square and whose vertex P is equidistant from A, B, C and D. If $AB = 1$ and $\angle APB = 2\theta$ then the volume of the pyramid is
(A) $\dfrac{\sin\theta}{6}$ (B) $\dfrac{\cot\theta}{n}$ (C) $\dfrac{1}{6\sin\theta}$ (E) $\dfrac{\sqrt{\cos 2\theta}}{6\sin\theta}$.

SOLUTIONS

Problem 1. Solution:
$$\tan 45° = 1$$
$$\frac{1+\tan 75°}{1-\tan 75°} = \frac{\tan 45° + \tan 75°}{1-\tan 45° \tan 75°} = \tan(45° + 75°) = \tan 120° = -\sqrt{3}.$$

Problem 2. Solution:
$$\sin 50°(1+\sqrt{3}\tan 10°) = \sin 50°\left(1+\frac{\sqrt{3}\sin 10°}{\cos 10°}\right) = \sin 50° \cdot \frac{2\left(\frac{1}{2}\cos 10° + \frac{\sqrt{3}}{2}\sin 10°\right)}{\cos 10°}$$
$$= 2\sin 50° \frac{\sin 30°\cos 10° + \cos 30°\sin 10°}{\cos 10°} = 2\cos 40° \cdot \frac{\sin 40°}{\cos 10°} = \frac{\sin 80°}{\cos 10°} = \frac{\cos 10°}{\cos 10°} = 1.$$

Problem 3. Solution:
$c = \cos 20°\cos 40°\cos 80°$
$s = \sin 20° \sin 40° \sin 80°$
$cs = \frac{1}{2}\sin 40° \cdot \frac{1}{2}\sin 80° \cdot \frac{1}{2}\sin 160° = \frac{1}{8}\sin 40° \sin 80° \sin 20° = \frac{1}{8}s.$
Since $s \neq 0$, $c = \frac{1}{8}$, $\cos 20°\cos 40°\cos 80° = \frac{1}{8}$.

Problem 4. Solution:
$c = 4\sin 18° \cos 36°,$
$s = \cos 18° \sin 36°.$
$cs = \sin 36° \sin 72° = \sin 36° \cos 18° = s$
We know that $s \neq 0$, $c = 1$. Therefore $4\sin 18° \cos 36° = 1$.

Problem 5. Solution:
$$\cos\frac{2\pi}{7} + \cos\frac{4\pi}{7} + \cos\frac{6\pi}{7} = 2\cos\frac{3\pi}{7}\cos\frac{\pi}{7} + 2\cos\frac{3\pi}{7} - 1$$
$$= 2\cos\frac{3\pi}{7}\left(\cos\frac{\pi}{7} + \cos\frac{3\pi}{7}\right) - 1 = 4\cos\frac{3\pi}{7}\cos\frac{2\pi}{7}\cos\frac{\pi}{7} - 1.$$
$c = 4\cos\frac{3\pi}{7}\cos\frac{2\pi}{7}\cos\frac{\pi}{7},$
$s = \sin\frac{3\pi}{7}\sin\frac{2\pi}{7}\sin\frac{\pi}{7}.$ So

$cs = \frac{1}{2} \sin \frac{6\pi}{7} \sin \frac{4\pi}{7} \sin \frac{2\pi}{7} = \frac{1}{2} \sin \frac{\pi}{7} \sin \frac{3\pi}{7} \sin \frac{2\pi}{7} = \frac{1}{2} s$

We know that $s \neq 0$, so $c = \frac{1}{2}$.

Therefore $\cos \frac{2\pi}{7} + \cos \frac{4\pi}{7} + \cos \frac{6\pi}{7} = -\frac{1}{2}$.

Problem 6. Solution:
$\sin 36° = \cos 54°$
$\sin 36° = 2 \sin 18° \cos 18°$
$\cos 54° = \cos(18° + 36°) = \cos 18° \cos 36° - \sin 18° \sin 36°$
$\quad\quad = \cos 18°(1 - 2\sin^2 18°) - 2\sin^2 18° \cos 18°$
We know that $\cos 18° \neq 0$, $\therefore\ 2\sin 18° = 1 - 2\sin^2 18° - 2\sin^2 18°$
Or $4\sin^2 18° + 2\sin 18° - 1 = 0$.

Solving: $\sin 18° = \frac{-2 \pm \sqrt{4+16}}{8} = \frac{-2 \pm 2\sqrt{5}}{8} = \frac{-1 \pm \sqrt{5}}{4}$.

Since $\sin 18° > 0$, $\sin 18° = \frac{\sqrt{5}-1}{4}$.

Problem 7. Solution:
$= \frac{1}{2\sin \frac{\pi}{7}} (2 \sin \frac{\pi}{7} \cos \frac{\pi}{7} + 2 \sin \frac{\pi}{7} \cos \frac{3\pi}{7} + 2 \sin \frac{\pi}{7} \cos \frac{5\pi}{7})$

$= \frac{1}{2\sin \frac{\pi}{7}} [\sin \frac{2\pi}{7} + (\sin \frac{4\pi}{7} - \sin \frac{2\pi}{7}) + (\sin \frac{6\pi}{7} - \sin \frac{4\pi}{7})]$

$= \frac{1}{2\sin \frac{\pi}{7}} \cdot \sin \frac{6\pi}{7} = \frac{\sin \frac{\pi}{7}}{2\sin \frac{\pi}{7}} = \frac{1}{2}$.

Problem 8. Solution:

$\sqrt{1 - \sin 20°} = \sqrt{1 - 2\sin 10° \cos 10°} = \sqrt{\sin^2 10° + \cos^2 10° - 2\sin 10° \cos 10°}$
$= \sqrt{(\sin 10° - \cos 10°)^2} = -(\sin 10° - \cos 10°) = \cos 10° - \sin 10°$.

Problem 9. Solution:

$\frac{1}{3}\sin\alpha - \frac{1}{3}\cos\alpha = 1 - 2\sin\alpha\cos\alpha$.

$\frac{1}{3}(\sin\alpha - \cos\alpha) = (\sin\alpha - \cos\alpha)^2$.

α is an acute angle and $\alpha \neq 45°$ $\Rightarrow$ $\sin\alpha \neq \cos\alpha$ $\rightarrow$ $\sin\alpha - \cos\alpha = \frac{1}{3}$.

Squaring both sides: $\sin\alpha\cos\alpha = \frac{4}{9}$.

$\tan\alpha + \cot\alpha = \frac{\sin\alpha}{\cos\alpha} + \frac{\cos\alpha}{\sin\alpha} = \frac{1}{\sin\alpha\cos\alpha} = \frac{9}{4}$.

Since $\tan\alpha \cdot \cot\alpha = 1$, so $x^2 - \frac{9}{4}x + 1 = 0$ or $4x^2 - 9x + 4 = 0$.

Problem 10. Solution: (B).
Let $\angle MAD = \alpha$. Then $PQ = (PA)\sin(\angle PAQ) = 4\sin(2\alpha) = 8\sin\alpha\cos\alpha = 8(\frac{2}{\sqrt{20}})(\frac{4}{\sqrt{20}}) = \frac{16}{5}$.

Problem 11. Solution: (B).
Square both sides of both given equations to obtain $\sin^2 a + 2\sin a \sin b + \sin^2 b = \frac{5}{3}$ and $\cos^2 a + 2\cos a \cos b + \cos^2 b = 1$.
Then add corresponding sides of the resulting equations to obtain
$(\sin^2 a + \cos^2 a) + (\sin^2 b + \cos^2 b) + 2(\sin a \sin b + \cos a \cos b) = \frac{8}{3}$.
Because $\sin^2 a + \cos^2 a = \sin^2 b + \cos^2 b = 1$, it follows that it follows that
$\cos(a - b) = \sin a \sin b + \cos a \cos b = \frac{1}{3}$.
One ordered pair (a, b) that satisfies the given condition is approximately $(0.296, 1.527)$.

Problem 12. Solution: (b).
$\tan^2(x) + 1 = \sec^2(x)$
$f(x) = 5\sin^3(x)\cos^3(x) = \frac{5}{2}\sin(2x)\sin^2(x)\cos^2(x) = \frac{5}{8}\sin^3(2x)$

Therefore the maximum value is $\frac{5}{8}$.

Problem 13. Solution: (b).
Method 1:

$$x^2 + (\cot A \cos A) x - 1 = 0 \quad \text{with } 0 < A < \frac{\pi}{2}.$$

$$x^2 + \frac{\cos^2 A}{\sin A} x - 1 = 0 \quad \Rightarrow \quad (\sin A) \cdot x^2 + (\cos^2 A) \cdot x - \sin A = 0.$$

Solving this quadratic equation we get:

$$x = \frac{-\cos^2 A \pm \sqrt{\cos^4 A + 4\sin^2 A}}{2\sin A}.$$

Or

$$x = \frac{-\cos^2 A \pm \sqrt{\cos^4 A + 4(1 - \cos^2 A)}}{2\sin A} = \frac{-\cos^2 A \pm \sqrt{\cos^4 A - 4\cos^2 A + 1}}{2\sin A}$$

$$= \frac{-\cos^2 A \pm \sqrt{(\cos^2 A - 2)^2}}{2\sin A} = \frac{-\cos^2 A \pm (\cos^2 A - 2)}{2\sin A}.$$

So

$$x_1 = \frac{-\cos^2 A + (\cos^2 A - 2)}{2\sin A} = \frac{-2}{2\sin A} = -\csc A.$$

$$x_2 = \frac{-\cos^2 A - (\cos^2 A - 2)}{2\sin A} = \frac{-2\cos^2 A + 2}{2\sin A} = \sin A$$

Thus $x_1 + x_2 = \sin A - \csc A$.

Method 2:
A quicker answer may be found by using the following way:
For the equation $x^2 + (\cot A \cos A) x - 1 = 0$, by Vieta formula, the sum of the roots is

$$x_1 + x_2 = -\frac{\cot A \cos A}{1} = -\frac{\cos^2 A}{\sin A} = -\frac{1 - \sin^2 A}{\sin A} = -\frac{1}{\sin A} - \sin A = \sin A - \csc A.$$

Problem 14. Solution: (e).
By symmetry, the largest inscribed equilateral triangle has one vertex at a vertex of the square and adjacent sides making angle of $\frac{1}{2}(90° - 60°) = 15°$. So the length of

triangle's side $= \dfrac{1}{\cos 15°} = \dfrac{1}{\sqrt{\dfrac{1 + \cos 30°}{2}}} = \sqrt{\dfrac{2}{1 + \dfrac{\sqrt{3}}{2}}} = 2\sqrt{2 - \sqrt{3}} = \sqrt{8 - 4\sqrt{3}}$.

Problem 15. Solution: (A).

If $\sin x + \cos x = \frac{1}{5}$, then $\cos x = \frac{1}{5} - \sin x$ and $\cos^2 x = 1 - \sin^2 x = (\frac{1}{5} - \sin x)^2$; so $25 \sin^2 x - 5\sin x - 12 = 0$.

The solutions of $25s^2 - 5s - 12 = 0$. $s = \frac{4}{5}$ and $s = -\frac{3}{5}$. Since $0 \le x < \pi$, $\sin x \ge 0$, so $x = \frac{4}{5}$ and $\cos x = \frac{1}{5} - \sin x = -\frac{3}{5}$. Hence $\tan x = -\frac{4}{3}$.

Problem 16. Solution: (B).
$\tan(20° + 25°) = \tan 45° = 1$
$\tan(20° + 25°) = \dfrac{\tan 20° + \tan 25°}{1 - \tan 20° \tan 25°}$,
$\tan 20° + \tan 25° = 1 - \tan 20° \tan 25°$,
$1 - \tan 20° \tan 25° - \tan 20° - \tan 25° = 0$.
$(1 + \tan 20°)(1 + \tan 25°) = 1 + \tan 20° + \tan 25° + \tan 20° \tan 25°$
$\therefore 2 - (1 - \tan 20° \tan 25° - \tan 20° - \tan 25°) = 2$
$1 + \tan 20° \tan 25° + \tan 20° + \tan 25° = 2$

Problem 17. Solution: (E).
Let M be the midpoint of B and O be the center of the square. Thus $AM = OM = 1/2$ and slant heigh $PM = \frac{1}{2} \cot \theta$. Hence

$$PO^2 = PM^2 - OM^2 = \frac{1}{2}\cot^2 \theta - \frac{1}{4} = \frac{\cos^2 \theta - \sin^2 \theta}{4\sin^2 \theta} = \frac{\cos 2\theta}{4\sin^2 \theta}.$$

Since $0 < \theta < 45°$, th volume is $\frac{1}{3} \cdot 1^2 \cdot PO = \dfrac{\sqrt{\cos 2\theta}}{6\sin \theta}$

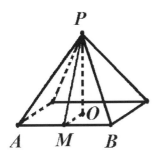
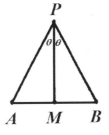

PROBLEMS

Problem 1: (1958 AMC) For values of x less than 1 but greater than -4, the expression $\frac{x^2 - 2x + 2}{2x - 2}$ has:
(A) no maximum or minimum value
(B) a minimum value of $+1$
(C) a maximum value of $+1$
(D) a minimum value of -1
(E) a maximum value of -1

Problem 2: If $xyz = 27$, x, y, and z are positive, find the minimum value of $x + y + z$.

Problem 3: x and y are real positive numbers with $x + 2y = 1$. Find the smallest value for $\frac{1}{x} + \frac{1}{y}$.

Problem 4: Let $a > 5$, find the smallest value of $a + \frac{4}{a - 5}$.

Problem 5: Show that $(x + y)(y + z) \geq 2$ if $xyz(x + y + z) = 1$, where x, y, z are positive numbers.

Problem 6: Find the smallest value of $a + \frac{1}{(a-b)b}$. $a > b > 0$.

Problem 7: Find the smallest value of $x + y$ if $\frac{a}{x} + \frac{b}{y} = 1$. $x, y, a,$ and b are positive real numbers.

Problem 8: Find the greatest possible value of $\sqrt{3a+1} + \sqrt{3b+1} + \sqrt{3c+1}$ if $a + b + c = 1$.

Problem 9: Find the smallest value for $\left(a+\dfrac{1}{a}\right)\left(b+\dfrac{1}{b}\right)$ if $a+b=1$, $a>0$, $b>0$.

(A) 6 (B) $\dfrac{25}{4}$ (C) $\dfrac{27}{4}$ (D) None of them.

Problem 10: (1979 AMC) For each positive number x, let
$$f(x) = \dfrac{\left(x+\dfrac{1}{x}\right)^6 - \left(x^6+\dfrac{1}{x^6}\right) - 2}{\left(x+\dfrac{1}{x}\right)^3 + \left(x^3+\dfrac{1}{x^3}\right)}.$$
The minimum value of $f(x)$ is

(A) 1 (B) 2 (C) 3 (D) 4 (E) 6

Problem 11: Show that $\sqrt{\dfrac{a}{b+c}} + \sqrt{\dfrac{b}{c+a}} + \sqrt{\dfrac{c}{a+b}} > 2$. $a, b, c > 0$,

Problem 12: Show that $a^4 + b^4 \geq \dfrac{1}{8}$ if $a+b=1$.

Problem 13: The smallest value of $a^2+b^2+c^2+d^2+ab+ac+ad+bc+bd+cd$ is 10 if $abcd=1$. Prove it for positive numbers a, b, c, and d.

Problem 14: Farmer Bob has 96 square inches of wrapping paper. Find the volume of the largest rectangular box he can wrap with the paper.

Problem 15: (1977 AMC) Find the smallest integer n such that
$(x^2+y^2+z^2)^2 \leq n(x^4+y^4+z^4)$ for all real numbers x, y, and z.

(A) 2 (B) 3 (C) 4 (D) 6 (E) There is no such integer n.

Problem 16: (1975 AMC) Which of the following inequalities are satisfied for all real numbers a, b, c, x, y, z which satisfy the conditions $x < a$, $y < b$, and $z < c$?
I. $xy + yz + zx < ab + bc + ca$
II. $x^2 + y^2 + z^2 < a^2 + b^2 + c^2$
III. $xyz < abc$

(A) None are satisfied. (B) I only (C) II only (D) III only (E) All are satisfied.

Problem 17: Show that $\dfrac{a^6}{b^2c^2} + \dfrac{b^6}{a^2c^2} + \dfrac{c^6}{a^2b^2} \geq ab + bc + ca$.

Problem 18: Show that $\dfrac{1}{A} + \dfrac{1}{B} + \dfrac{1}{C} \geq \dfrac{9}{\pi}$ if A, B, C are three interior angles of $\triangle ABC$.

Problem 19: Show that $\dfrac{a}{b+c-a} + \dfrac{b}{c+a-b} + \dfrac{c}{a+b-c} \geq 3$ if a, b, c are three sides of $\triangle ABC$.

Problem 20: Prove that $a^2 + b^2 + c^2 + 2\sqrt{3abc} \leq 1$ if $a + b + c = 1$. a, b, c are positive numbers.

Problem 21: If $a, b, c \in R$, show that: $\sqrt{a^2+b^2} + \sqrt{b^2+c^2} + \sqrt{c^2+a^2} \geq \sqrt{2}(a+b+c)$.

Problem 22: Show that $\left(1+\dfrac{1}{x}\right)\left(1+\dfrac{1}{y}\right) \geq 9$ if $x + y = 1$ and x and y are positive numbers.

Problem 23: If a, b, and c are positive numbers, show that:
$2\left(\dfrac{a+b}{2} - \sqrt{ab}\right) \leq 3\left(\dfrac{a+b+c}{3} - \sqrt[3]{abc}\right)$

Problem 24: $a, b, c \in (0, +\infty)$. $a+b+c=1$. Show that $\sqrt{a} + \sqrt{b} + \sqrt{c} \leq \sqrt{3}$.

Problem 25: For $a > b > c$, show that $\dfrac{1}{a-b} + \dfrac{1}{b-c} \geq \dfrac{4}{a-c}$.

Problem 26: If a, b, and c are positive integers less than 1, show that not all of $(1-a)b$, $(1-b)c$, and $(1-c)a$ greater than $1/4$.

SOLUTIONS:

Problem 1: Solution: (E).

$$y = \frac{1}{2} \cdot \frac{x^2 - 2x + 2}{x-1} = \frac{1}{2}[x - 1 + \frac{1}{x-1}] = -\frac{1}{2}[(1-x) + \frac{1}{1-x}]$$

Note that $-4 < x < 1$, so $1 - x > 0$.

By AM–GM: $(1-x) + \frac{1}{1-x} \geq 2\sqrt{(1-x)(\frac{1}{1-x})} = 2$.

Equality occurs when $(1-x) = \frac{1}{1-x}$. Solving we get $x = 0$. Since y is negative 1, y is a maximum when $x = 0$.

Problem 2: Solution: 9.

From the AM–GM inequality, we have:

$$\frac{x + y + z}{3} \geq \sqrt[3]{(xyz)} = \sqrt[3]{27} = 3. \text{ So } x + y + z \geq 9.$$

The minimum value of $x + y + z$ is 9. This is true when $x = y = z = 3$.

Problem 3: Solution: $3 + 2\sqrt{2}$.
Method 1:

$$\frac{1}{x} + \frac{1}{y} = \frac{x + 2y}{x} + \frac{x + 2y}{y} = 3 + \frac{2y}{x} + \frac{x}{y}.$$

Applying *AM-GM* yields
$\frac{2y}{x} + \frac{x}{y} \geq 2\sqrt{\frac{2y}{x} \times \frac{x}{y}} = 2\sqrt{2}$. Substituting this into the above equation yields
$\frac{1}{x} + \frac{1}{y} \geq 3 + 2\sqrt{2}$.

This value can be achieved when $\frac{2y}{x} = \frac{x}{y}$, which gives $x = 2 - \sqrt{2}$ and $y = \frac{\sqrt{2}-1}{2}$.

Method 2:
We are given that $x + 2y = 1$. Applying Cauchy's inequality yields:
$$\frac{1}{x} + \frac{1}{y} = \frac{1}{x} + \frac{2}{2y} \geq \frac{(1+\sqrt{2})^2}{x+2y} = 3 + 2\sqrt{2}.$$
So the smallest value for $\frac{1}{x} + \frac{1}{y}$ is $3 + 2\sqrt{2}$. This value can be achieved by letting $x = 2 - \sqrt{2}$ and $y = \frac{\sqrt{2}-1}{2}$.

Problem 4: Solution: 9.
Applying *AM-GM* yields
$$a + \frac{4}{a-5} = a - 5 + \frac{4}{a-5} + 5 \geq 2\sqrt{(a-5) \times \frac{4}{a-5}} + 5 = 4 + 5 = 9.$$

The smallest value is 9, which can be achieved when $a - 5 = \frac{4}{a-5}$ or $a = 7$.

Problem 5: Solution:
$(x+y)(y+z) = xz + y(x+y+z) \geq 2\sqrt{xyz(x+y+z)} = 2.$

Problem 6: Solution:
$$a + \frac{1}{(a-b)b} = (a-b) + b + \frac{1}{(a-b)b} \geq 3,$$
The smallest value 3 is achieved when $a = 2$, $b = 1$.

Problem 7: Solution:
From $a > 0$, $b > 0$, $x > 0$, $y > 0$ and $\frac{a}{x} + \frac{b}{y} = 1$, we get
$x > a$, $y > b$ (otherwise $\frac{a}{x} + \frac{b}{y}$ would be greater than 1) and $\frac{ay+bx}{xy} = 1$.
Therefore we can write $x - a > 0$, $y - b > 0$, and $xy - ay - bx = 0$ \hfill (1)
Add ab to both sides of (1): $xy - ay - bx + ab = ab$ \hfill (2)
Factoring (1): $(x-a)(y-b) = ab$.

By *AM – GM*:

$x + y = (x - a) + (y - b) + (a + b) \geq 2\sqrt{(x - a)(y - b)} + (a + b)$
$= 2\sqrt{ab} + a + b = (\sqrt{a} + \sqrt{b})^2$.
Thus $(x + y) \geq (\sqrt{a} + \sqrt{b})^2$ \hfill (3)

We know that x and y satisfy $\dfrac{a}{x} + \dfrac{b}{y} = 1$ and equality occurs in (3) when $x - a = y - b$.

Therefore we have $\begin{cases} (x - a)(y - b) = ab \\ x - a = y - b. \end{cases}$

Solving we get $x = a + \sqrt{ab}$ and $y = b + \sqrt{ab}$.

Then we have $(x + y)_{\min} = a + \sqrt{ab} + b + \sqrt{ab} = (\sqrt{a} + \sqrt{b})^2$.

Problem 8: Solution:
Let $x = \sqrt{3a + 1}$, $y = \sqrt{3b + 1}$, $z = \sqrt{3c + 1}$, $t = x + y + z$.
Then $t^2 = x^2 + y^2 + z^2 + 2xy + 2yz + 2zx$.

By $AM - GM$ (25.14), we have $t^2 \leq 3(x^2 + y^2 + z^2) = 18$.
Therefore $t \leq 3\sqrt{2}$. Equality occurs when $a = b = c = \dfrac{1}{3}$.

Problem 9: Solution:
$\left(a + \dfrac{1}{a}\right)\left(b + \dfrac{1}{b}\right) = \left(ab + \dfrac{1}{ab}\right) + \dfrac{b}{a} + \dfrac{a}{b} \geq ab + \dfrac{1}{ab} + 2 = ab + \dfrac{1}{16ab} + \dfrac{15}{16ab} + 2$

$\geq \dfrac{5}{2} + \dfrac{15}{16ab} \geq \dfrac{5}{2} + \dfrac{15}{16(\frac{a+b}{2})^2} = \dfrac{25}{4}$.

Note: The following method is not working: $\left(a + \dfrac{1}{a}\right)\left(b + \dfrac{1}{b}\right) = \left(\dfrac{ab}{1} + \dfrac{1}{ab}\right) + \dfrac{b}{a} + \dfrac{a}{b}$

$\geq 2 + 2 = 4$.

This is because the condition $\dfrac{ab}{1} = \dfrac{1}{ab}$ or $ab = 1$ will not be true. Considering $ab = 1$ and $a + b = 1$ we get $(a - b)^2 = -1$.

Problem 10: Solution: (E).
By observing that $\left[x^3 + \dfrac{1}{x^3}\right]^2 = x^6 + 2 + \dfrac{1}{x^6}$, one sees that

$f(x) = \left(x + \dfrac{1}{x}\right)^3 - \left(x^3 + \dfrac{1}{x^3}\right) = 3\left(x + \dfrac{1}{x}\right) \geq 3 \times 2 = 6$.

$f(x) = 3\left(x + \dfrac{1}{x}\right)$ has a minimum value of 6, which is taken on at $x = 1$.

Problem 11: Solution:

Since $\sqrt{a} \cdot \sqrt{b+c} \leq \dfrac{a+b+c}{2}$,

so $\sqrt{\dfrac{a}{b+c}} = \dfrac{a}{\sqrt{a} \cdot \sqrt{b+c}} \geq \dfrac{a}{\dfrac{a+b+c}{2}} = \dfrac{2a}{a+b+c}$,

similarly $\sqrt{\dfrac{b}{c+a}} \geq \dfrac{2b}{a+b+c}$,

$\sqrt{\dfrac{c}{a+b}} \geq \dfrac{2c}{a+b+c}$,

Add them together we are done.

Problem 12: Solution:

By $AM - GM$, $\dfrac{a^2 + b^2}{2} \geq \left(\dfrac{a+b}{2}\right)^2 = \left(\dfrac{1}{2}\right)^2 = \dfrac{1}{4}$.

$\dfrac{a^4 + b^4}{2} \geq \left(\dfrac{a^2 + b^2}{2}\right)^2 \geq \left[\left(\dfrac{a+b}{2}\right)^2\right]^2 = \left(\dfrac{1}{4}\right)^2 = \dfrac{1}{16}$.

Therefore $a^4 + b^4 \geq 2 \cdot \dfrac{1}{16} = \dfrac{1}{8}$.

Problem 13: Proof:

$a^2 + b^2 + c^2 + d^2 + ab + ac + ad + bc + bd + cd$
$= (a-b)^2 + (c-d)^2 + 3ab + ac + ad + bc + bd + 3cd$
$\geq 3ab + ac + ad + bc + bd + 3cd = 3(ab + cd) + (ac + bd) + (ad + bc)$
$= 3\left(ab + \dfrac{1}{ab}\right) + \left(ac + \dfrac{1}{ac}\right) + \left(ad + \dfrac{1}{ad}\right) \geq 3 \times 2 + 2 + 2 = 10$.

Problem 14: Solution: 64.

Let the box have dimensions x, y, and z. The amount of wrapping paper should equal the surface area of the box, or

$2(xy + yz + zx) = 96 \implies (xy + yz + zx) = 48$

From the *AM-GM* inequality, we have

$\dfrac{xy + yz + zx}{3} \geq \sqrt[3]{(xy)(yz)(zx)} = \sqrt[3]{(xyz)^2}$, that is $16 \geq \sqrt[3]{(xyz)^2}$.

So the maximum value of *xyz*, the volume of the box, is 64. This value can be achieved by letting $x = y = z = 4$.

Problem 15: Solution: (B).
Let $a = x^2$, $b = y^2$ and $c = z^2$. By AM–GM, $a^2 + b^2 \geq 2ab$, we see that
$(a + b + c)^2 = a^2 + b^2 + c^2 + 2ab + 2ac + 2bc$
$\quad \leq a^2 + b^2 + c^2 + (a^2 + b^2) + (a^2 + c^2) + (b^2 + c^2)$
$\quad = 3(a^2 + b^2 + c^2)$.
Therefore $n \leq 3$. Choosing $a = b = c > 0$ shows n is not less than three.

Problem 16: Solution: (A).
None of the inequalities are satisfied if a, b, c, x, y, z are chosen to be $1, 1, -1, 0, 0, -10$, respectively.

Problem 17: Solution:
We know that $x^2 + y^2 + z^2 \geq xy + xz + yz$.
Therefore we can have

$\left(\dfrac{a^3}{bc}\right)^2 + \left(\dfrac{b^3}{ac}\right)^2 + \left(\dfrac{a^3}{ab}\right)^2 \geq \dfrac{a^3 b^3}{abc^2} + \dfrac{b^3 c^3}{a^2 bc} + \dfrac{a^3 c^3}{ab^2 c}$

$= \left(\dfrac{ab}{c}\right)^2 + \left(\dfrac{bc}{a}\right)^2 + \left(\dfrac{ac}{b}\right)^2 \geq \dfrac{ab^2 c}{ca} + \dfrac{abc^2}{ab} + \dfrac{a^2 bc}{bc}$

$= a^2 + b^2 + c^2 \geq ab + bc + ac$

Therefore $\dfrac{a^6}{b^2 c^2} + \dfrac{b^6}{a^2 c^2} + \dfrac{c^6}{a^2 b^2} \geq ab + bc + ca$.

Problem 18: Solution:
Method 1:
We know that $A + B + C = \pi$ and $A > 0, B > 0, C > 0$.
Therefore

$\dfrac{1}{A} + \dfrac{1}{B} + \dfrac{1}{C} = \dfrac{1}{A+B+C}\left(\dfrac{A+B+C}{A} + \dfrac{A+B+C}{B} + \dfrac{A+B+C}{C}\right)$

$= \dfrac{1}{\pi}\left(\dfrac{A}{A} + \dfrac{B}{A} + \dfrac{C}{A} + \dfrac{A}{B} + \dfrac{B}{B} + \dfrac{C}{B} + \dfrac{A}{C} + \dfrac{B}{C} + \dfrac{C}{C}\right) = \dfrac{1}{\pi}\left[3 + \left(\dfrac{B}{A} + \dfrac{A}{B}\right) + \left(\dfrac{C}{B} + \dfrac{B}{C}\right) + \left(\dfrac{C}{A} + \dfrac{A}{C}\right)\right]$

$$\geq \frac{1}{\pi}(3+2+2+2) = \frac{9}{\pi}.$$

Method 2:

We know that $A + B + C = \pi$ and $A > 0, B > 0, C > 0$.

By $AM - GM$, $\frac{1}{A} + \frac{1}{B} + \frac{1}{C} \geq 3 \cdot \sqrt[3]{\frac{1}{ABC}} = \frac{3}{\sqrt[3]{ABC}}$

We have $\pi = A + B + C \geq 3 \cdot \sqrt[3]{ABC} \Rightarrow \frac{1}{\sqrt[3]{ABC}} \geq \frac{3}{\pi}$.

Therefore $\frac{1}{A} + \frac{1}{B} + \frac{1}{C} \geq \frac{9}{\pi}$.

Problem 19: Solution:
Method 1:

We have $x > 0, y > 0, z > 0$. By AM–GM (25.17), $(x + y + z)\left(\frac{1}{x} + \frac{1}{y} + \frac{1}{z}\right) \geq 9$.

We can write $a + b + c = b + c - a + c + a - b + a + b - c$

Therefore $(a + b + c)\left(\frac{1}{b+c-a} + \frac{1}{c+a-b} + \frac{1}{a+b-c}\right) \geq 9$.

Method 2:
Let $2x = b + c - a$, $2y = a + c - b$, $2z = a + b - c$ with $x, y, z > 0$.
Then $a = y + z, b = z + x, c = x + y$.

Therefore $\frac{a}{b+c-a} + \frac{b}{c+a-b} + \frac{c}{a+b-c} = \frac{y+z}{2x} + \frac{z+x}{2y} + \frac{x+y}{2z}$

$= \frac{1}{2}(\frac{y}{x} + \frac{x}{y} + \frac{z}{x} + \frac{x}{z} + \frac{z}{y} + \frac{y}{z}) \geq \frac{1}{2} \times (2+2+2) = 3$.

Problem 20: Solution:
Note that $a^2b^2 + b^2c^2 \geq 2ab^2c$,
$$b^2c^2 + c^2a^2 \geq 2abc^2,$$
$$c^2a^2 + a^2b^2 \geq 2a^2bc,$$
So we have
$a^2b^2 + b^2c^2 + c^2a^2 \geq ab^2c + abc^2 + a^2bc$,
so $(ab + bc + ca)^2 \geq 3(ab^2c + abc^2 + a^2bc) = 3(a + b + c) \cdot abc$.

So we have $a^2 + b^2 + c^2 + 2(ab + bc + ca) \geq a^2 + b^2 + c^2 + 2\sqrt{3(a+b+c)abc}$,

That is $(a+b+c)^2 \geq a^2 + b^2 + c^2 + 2\sqrt{3(a+b+c)abc}$.

Note that $a + b + c = 1$, we are done.

Problem 21: Solution:

Since $a^2 + b^2 \geq 2ab \therefore 2(a^2 + b^2) \geq a^2 + 2ab + b^2 \geq (a+b)^2$

That is, $a^2 + b^2 \geq \dfrac{(a+b)^2}{2}$.

Taking the square roots in both sides: $\sqrt{a^2 + b^2} \geq \dfrac{\sqrt{2}}{2}|a+b| \geq \dfrac{\sqrt{2}}{2}(a+b)$ \hfill (1)

Similarly we get: $\sqrt{b^2 + c^2} \geq \dfrac{\sqrt{2}}{2}(b+c)$ \hfill (2)

$\sqrt{c^2 + a^2} \geq \dfrac{\sqrt{2}}{2}(c+a)$ \hfill (3)

Adding (1), (2), and (3):
$$\sqrt{a^2 + b^2} + \sqrt{b^2 + c^2} + \sqrt{c^2 + a^2} \geq \sqrt{2}(a+b+c)$$

Problem 22: Solution:

Method 1:

$$(1+\dfrac{1}{x})(1+\dfrac{1}{y}) = (1+\dfrac{x+y}{x})(1+\dfrac{x+y}{y})$$
$$= (2+\dfrac{y}{x})(2+\dfrac{x}{y}) = 5 + 2(\dfrac{y}{x}+\dfrac{x}{y})$$
$$\geq 5 + 2 \cdot 2 = 9$$

Method 2:

We know that $x + y = 1 \therefore xy \leq \dfrac{1}{4}$.

$\left(1+\dfrac{1}{x}\right)\left(1+\dfrac{1}{y}\right) = 1 + \dfrac{1}{x} + \dfrac{1}{y} + \dfrac{1}{xy} = 1 + \dfrac{x+y}{xy} + \dfrac{1}{xy} = 1 + \dfrac{2}{xy} \geq 1 + 8 = 9$.

$\therefore \left(1+\dfrac{1}{x}\right)\left(1+\dfrac{1}{y}\right) \geq 9$.

Problem 23: Solution:

$$2(\frac{a+b}{2}-\sqrt{ab})\le 3(\frac{a+b+c}{3}-\sqrt[3]{abc}) \Leftrightarrow -2\sqrt{ab}\le c-3\sqrt[3]{abc}$$
$$\Leftrightarrow c+2\sqrt{ab}\ge 3\sqrt[3]{abc}.$$

We know that $c+\sqrt{ab}+\sqrt{ab}\ge 3\sqrt[3]{c\sqrt{ab}\sqrt{ab}}=3\sqrt[3]{abc}$ is true. Therefore, the original inequality is true.

Problem 24: Solution:
$$\sqrt{a}+\sqrt{b}+\sqrt{c}\le \sqrt{3} \Leftrightarrow (\sqrt{a}+\sqrt{b}+\sqrt{c})^2\le 3 \text{ or}: 2\sqrt{ab}+2\sqrt{bc}+2\sqrt{ac}\le 2$$
$$\because 2\sqrt{ab}\le a+b \quad 2\sqrt{bc}\le b+c \quad 2\sqrt{ac}\le a+c \text{ or}$$
$$2\sqrt{ab}+2\sqrt{bc}+2\sqrt{ac}\le (a+b)+(b+c)+(a+c)=2.$$

Therefore the original inequality is true.

Problem 25: Solution:
Since $a-b>0$, $b-c>0$, $a-c>0$, we assume that $a-b=x$, $b-c=y$ ($x,y>0$).
Thus $a-c=x+y$. The original inequality becomes: $\frac{1}{x}+\frac{1}{y}\ge \frac{4}{x+y}$ $\Rightarrow$
$$(x+y)(\frac{1}{x}+\frac{1}{y})\ge 4 \Rightarrow 2+\frac{x}{y}+\frac{y}{x}\ge 4.$$

We know that $\frac{x}{y}+\frac{y}{x}\ge 2$. Therefore the original inequality is true.

Equality occurs when $x=y$.

Problem 26: Solution:

We assume that $(1-a)b>\frac{1}{4}$, $(1-b)c>\frac{1}{4}$, and $(1-c)a>\frac{1}{4}$.

Since a is less than 1, $1-a>0$.
$$\frac{(1-a)+b}{2}\ge \sqrt{(1-a)b}>\sqrt{\frac{1}{4}}=\frac{1}{2} \Rightarrow \quad 1-a+b>1 \qquad (1)$$
Similarly, we get $\quad 1-b+c>1 \qquad (2)$
$\quad 1-c+a>1 \qquad (3)$

Adding (1), (2), and (3) we get: $3>3$ that is not possible.
Therefore not all of $(1-a)b$, $(1-b)c$, and $(1-c)a$ greater than 1/4.

A

absolute value, 40, 54, 143
acute angle, 125, 231, 235
acute triangle, 98
angle, 83, 84, 85, 86, 87, 88, 90, 91, 95, 111, 119, 123, 124, 125, 128, 129, 130, 131, 170, 171, 174, 176, 199, 200, 201, 207, 208, 210, 211, 212, 213, 214, 216, 217, 218, 220, 221, 222, 223, 224, 228, 229, 231, 235, 236
arc, 120, 209
area, 38, 45, 83, 85, 87, 88, 95, 96, 97, 98, 99, 100, 101, 102, 104, 106, 108, 109, 110, 114, 116, 125, 130, 170, 172, 173, 198, 202, 209, 210, 211, 212, 213, 215, 220, 221, 223, 226, 244
arithmetic sequence, 139, 140, 141, 142, 143, 144, 145, 150, 153, 180
average, 29, 30, 39, 47

B

base, 45, 102, 109, 114, 115, 128, 130, 209, 215, 220, 232
bisect, 219, 227

C

Cauchy inequality, 158
center, 100, 110, 112, 116, 124, 129, 203, 224, 231, 237
central angle, 124
chord, 224
circle, 95, 100, 110, 115, 116, 124, 128, 129, 198, 203, 224, 225, 228, 229, 231
circumference, 128
combination, 75
common factor, 81
common multiple, 77
composite number, 81
congruent, 83, 86, 110, 119, 120, 209, 215
constant, 37, 70, 123, 128, 178
Converse, 57
convex, 124, 223, 225
Convex, 198
cube, 12, 63, 68
cylinder, 122, 128

D

decimal, 12, 25
degree, 128
degree measure, 128
denominator, 7, 17
diagonal, 98, 201, 226
diameter, 95, 112, 116, 198, 203, 224, 229
difference, 54, 55, 62, 70, 76, 139, 140, 142, 143, 145, 146, 149, 150, 151, 153, 180
digit, 63, 64, 67, 68, 71, 73, 76, 77, 82, 185, 190
Divisibility, 76
divisible, 62, 64, 67, 70, 71, 73, 75, 76, 77, 79, 80, 81, 82, 185, 202
divisor, 74

E

equation, 4, 9, 15, 16, 19, 26, 27, 29, 30, 31, 32, 33, 34, 35, 37, 42, 43, 46, 48, 49, 50, 53, 54, 55, 56, 57, 59, 61, 64, 101, 122, 123, 124, 135, 136, 137, 148, 150, 154, 155, 157, 158, 159, 160, 161, 166, 170, 171, 172, 174, 175, 176, 178, 183, 185, 188, 191, 192, 193, 195, 196, 203, 204, 231, 236, 241
equidistant, 232
equilateral, 85, 86, 87, 92, 93, 94, 97, 199, 205, 206, 225, 230, 232, 236
equilateral triangle, 85, 86, 87, 92, 93, 94, 97, 199, 205, 206, 225, 230, 232, 236
exponent, 13
expression, 2, 7, 9, 10, 11, 12, 13, 15, 17, 23, 37, 42, 76, 77, 149, 156, 160, 161, 162, 165, 169, 238

F

factor, 31, 71, 74, 75, 78, 80, 81
finite, 142
formula, 13, 20, 148, 149, 150, 174, 175, 217, 219, 220, 221, 222, 236
fraction, 2, 12, 17
function, 123, 125, 128, 163, 168, 178, 179, 184, 232

G

GCF, 88
geometric sequence, 139, 144, 184
graph, 36, 38, 41, 42, 46, 47

H

hypotenuse, 121, 124, 125, 129, 212, 218, 224

I

inequality, 35, 57, 66, 158, 167, 241, 242, 245, 248
inscribed angle, 95, 208
integer, 2, 6, 8, 12, 16, 17, 25, 32, 48, 53, 55, 60, 61, 62, 63, 64, 65, 66, 67, 70, 71, 72, 73, 74, 77, 78, 80, 82, 131, 133, 134, 138, 149, 154, 155, 156, 157, 158, 160, 162, 163, 166, 178, 179, 183, 185, 186, 187, 189, 192, 197, 213, 222, 239
integers, 8, 11, 16, 26, 38, 39, 45, 53, 62, 63, 64, 65, 66, 69, 70, 71, 72, 73, 74, 76, 77, 78, 79, 80, 81, 110, 133, 134, 136, 139, 140, 141, 143, 144, 149, 154, 162, 166, 178, 179, 183, 185, 187, 188, 190, 202, 213, 214, 240
intercept, 209
intersection, 39, 41, 42, 46, 91, 109, 110, 129, 176, 209, 213, 226, 229
isosceles, 83, 87, 95, 100, 111, 118, 120, 200, 204, 209, 212, 213, 227
isosceles triangle, 111, 118, 120

L

Law of Cosines, 215, 220
LCM, 150
least common multiple, 77
line, 36, 39, 41, 42, 47, 92, 109, 113, 114, 115, 124, 129, 155, 170, 171, 172, 174, 175, 176, 215, 224, 227
line segment, 109, 114, 124
lowest terms, 125

M

mean, 23, 154
median, 109, 110, 121, 154, 176, 210, 211, 212, 217, 219
midpoint, 94, 96, 97, 100, 109, 110, 112, 113, 114, 115, 121, 176, 206, 210, 213, 215, 216, 220, 221, 231, 237
multiple, 64, 67, 69, 70, 72, 76, 79, 80, 128, 146, 172

N

natural number, 177
negative number, 12, 23
number line, 36

numerator, 172

O

octagon, 225
odd number, 67, 70, 72, 140
ordered pair, 235
origin, 170, 171, 173, 175, 216

P

parallel, 99, 103, 114, 115, 170, 173, 174, 215, 227
parallelogram, 45, 92, 98, 105, 130, 192, 196, 206, 207, 216, 219, 227, 229
pentagon, 85
perimeter, 96, 101, 110, 116, 212, 213, 225, 230
permutation, 39
perpendicular, 83, 90, 95, 98, 129, 210, 211, 213, 220, 227
plane, 38, 170, 171, 216
point, 39, 46, 47, 83, 85, 86, 87, 89, 90, 91, 97, 99, 109, 110, 111, 112, 116, 118, 120, 170, 171, 172, 174, 175, 198, 199, 200, 201, 210, 211, 213, 216, 222, 223, 226, 229
polynomial, 2, 54, 163
positive number, 2, 7, 12, 178, 238, 239, 240
power, 11
prime factorization, 32
prime number, 53, 57, 62, 71, 81
probability, 71, 77
product, 1, 53, 56, 60, 62, 74, 75, 76, 77, 78, 80, 81, 97, 123, 130, 156, 161, 162, 166, 185, 187, 191
proportion, 31
pyramid, 232
Pythagorean Theorem, 116, 216, 220, 221, 222, 226, 227, 228

Q

quadrant, 41, 123, 125, 131
quadrilateral, 84, 96, 97, 101, 109, 111, 119, 124, 192, 196, 198, 200, 213, 219, 222, 223, 225, 227
quotient, 70

R

radius, 95, 110, 116, 124, 128, 224, 227, 231
random, 71
range, 36, 142
ratio, 99, 104, 107, 108, 109, 114, 141, 142, 146, 149, 170, 184, 198, 203, 209, 210, 213, 215, 224

rational number, 8
real number, 2, 6, 48, 50, 51, 55, 124, 134, 140, 155, 162, 163, 164, 178, 179, 184, 191, 192, 193, 238, 239
real numbers, 2, 6, 48, 51, 55, 134, 140, 155, 162, 163, 164, 178, 179, 191, 192, 238, 239
rectangle, 97, 98, 105, 200, 223, 230
reflection, 170, 175
relatively prime, 39, 110, 170, 172, 188, 213, 214
remainder, 63, 67, 68, 70, 71, 72, 73, 77, 79, 80, 82, 134, 138
rhombus, 86, 96, 101, 128, 130, 223, 227
right angle, 129, 210, 211, 213, 214, 223, 228, 229
right triangle, 85, 87, 94, 95, 100, 116, 121, 124, 129, 130, 140, 206, 212, 215, 218, 224, 226, 227, 228, 229
root, 23, 27, 32, 36, 51, 53, 54, 55, 56, 58, 160, 190
rotation, 175

S

scalene triangle, 83
semicircle, 112
sequence, 63, 139, 140, 141, 142, 143, 144, 145, 150, 152, 153, 154, 180, 184
set, 33, 63, 71, 76, 143, 151, 152, 171, 175, 191
similar, 101, 104, 107, 203, 204, 209, 215
slope, 41, 47, 170, 171, 175, 176
solution, 9, 18, 27, 29, 30, 31, 32, 33, 34, 50, 52, 74, 78, 79, 115, 116, 119, 120, 172, 187, 188, 189, 217, 219, 227
solution set, 33
square, 11, 12, 23, 32, 54, 62, 63, 64, 66, 67, 68, 69, 95, 98, 100, 105, 107, 129, 156, 160, 161, 162, 165, 166, 167, 179, 185, 186, 187, 190, 202, 210, 212, 215, 217, 232, 236, 237, 239, 247
square root, 23, 107, 190, 247
straight angle, 90

sum, 1, 23, 38, 39, 43, 46, 47, 48, 51, 53, 54, 58, 62, 64, 65, 70, 71, 74, 75, 76, 77, 95, 100, 116, 122, 123, 127, 129, 139, 140, 141, 142, 143, 146, 148, 149, 150, 154, 170, 179, 183, 185, 232, 236
surface area, 244

T

term, 63, 67, 81, 140, 141, 142, 143, 148, 150, 153, 183, 184
transformation, 222
trapezoid, 87, 96, 109, 118, 200, 203, 225, 229
triangle, 38, 43, 83, 85, 86, 87, 88, 92, 93, 94, 95, 96, 97, 98, 99, 100, 101, 103, 104, 108, 109, 110, 111, 114, 116, 118, 119, 121, 124, 125, 129, 130, 140, 170, 172, 198, 199, 202, 205, 206, 209, 210, 211, 212, 213, 214, 215, 216, 218, 219, 220, 221, 222, 224, 225, 226, 227, 228, 229, 230, 232, 236
trisect, 97, 209, 210

V

variable, 178
vertex, 124, 155, 157, 172, 220, 232, 236
vertical angles, 114
volume, 122, 128, 232, 237, 239, 245

X

x-axis, 129, 171, 175, 176

Y

y-axis, 175

Z

zero, 11, 12, 23, 27, 47, 48, 50, 51, 68, 72, 76, 77, 79, 138, 139, 160, 178, 191, 193

Made in the USA
Lexington, KY
01 April 2013